Lonely Planet

D0520108

LONDON

TOP SIGHTS, AUTHENTIC EXPERIENCES

Emilie Filou, Damian Harper,
Peter Dragicevich, Steve Fallon

Contents

This Year in London

BIKEWORLDTRAVEL / SHUTTERSTOCK ©

London

Another year, another cracker: there are festivals and events galore, big-ticket exhibitions and small pleasures to enjoy. The Elizabeth Line, a new train line that opens in stages this year, also makes London a little easier to visit.

Clockwise from above: Notting Hill Carnival; The Proms; Wimbledon Lawn Tennis Championships; Fireworks over Big Ben on New Year's Eve

JOHN PHILLIPS / STRINGER / GETTY IMAGES ©

★ Top Festivals & Events

Van Gogh & Britain exhibition, March–August (p9)

Wimbledon Championships, July (p12)

The Proms, July–September (p12)

Notting Hill Carnival, August (p13)

New Year's Celebrations, December (p17)

LEFT: BIKEWORLDTRAVEL / SHUTTERSTOCK © RIGHT: BOB THOMAS / GETTY IMAGES ©

This Year in London

January

London is in the throes of winter, with short days: light appears at 8am and is all but gone by 4pm.

☆ London International Mime Festival   Jan

Held over the month of January, this festival (www.mimelondon.com) is a must for lovers of originality, playfulness, physical talent and the unexpected.

🏛 London Art Fair   16-20 Jan

More than 100 major galleries participate in this contemporary-art fair (www.londonart fair.co.uk; pictured above), now one of the largest in Europe, with thematic exhibitions, special events and the best emerging artists.

☆ A Night at the Opera   Jan

The nights are long and cold so what better way to cosy up than inside the stunning Royal Opera House to revel in world-class opera or ballet? (Plus, it's a really good opportunity to dress up.)

⊙ Ride the Elizabeth Line   Jan

Some 15 years in the making, this new train line, which will open in stages throughout the year, zooms east to west across the city, connecting places such as Heathrow Airport, Paddington, Oxford St, the City and Stratford. A boon for locals and visitors alike.

2019

MS JANE CAMPBELL / SHUTTERSTOCK ©

02

February

February is usually chilly and wet (sometimes even snow-encrusted). Schools break off for a week in mid-February.

☘ Chinese New Year   5 Feb
To usher in the year of the pig, Chinatown fizzes, crackles and pops in this colourful street festival (pictured above), which includes a Golden Dragon parade, feasting and partying.

☘ St Valentine's Day   14 Feb
Whether you're single or part of a loved-up couple, you'll be able to choose from themed and alternative parties, special movie nights and dedicated menus. Book ahead as it's a popular night.

☆ BAFTAs   mid-Feb
The British Academy of Film and Television Arts (BAFTA; www.bafta.org) rolls out the red carpet mid-February to hand out its annual cinema awards. It's the British Oscars, if you will. Expect plenty of celebrity glamour.

♟ Pint by the Fire   Feb
What better way to thaw after sightseeing in the cold than with a drink by the fire? Amazingly, London still has plenty of pubs with working fireplaces so make the most of them.

⊙ Painted Hall Reopens   Feb
After two years of meticulous renovation, the 'UK's Sistine Chapel' is reopening to the public. Be one of the first to experience the newly restored, vibrant paintings of the stunning baroque Old Royal Naval College, Greenwich.

Plan Your Trip

This Year in London

PRES PANAYOTOV / SHUTTERSTOCK ©

03

March

March sees spring in the air, with trees beginning to flower and daffodils emerging across parks and gardens. London is getting in the mood to head outdoors again.

🌸 Pancake Races   5 Mar
On Shrove Tuesday, you can catch pancake races and associated silliness at various venues around town (Spitalfields Market, in particular).

🌸 St Patrick's Day Parade & Festival   17 Mar
Top festival for the Irish in London, with a colourful parade through central London and other festivities in and around Trafalgar Sq.

☆ Flare   late Mar
This LGBTIQ film festival, organised by the British Film Institute (www.bfi.org.uk/flare), runs a packed program of film screenings, along with club nights, talks and events.

☆ Head of the River Race   30 Mar
Some 400 crews take part in this colourful annual boat race (pictured above), held over a 7km course on the Thames, from Mortlake to Putney.

2019

MS JANE CAMPBELL / SHUTTERSTOCK ©

April

London is in bloom, with warmer days and a light-hearted vibe. British Summer Time starts late March, moving clocks forward an hour, so it's now light until 7pm.

☆ Oxford & Cambridge Boat Race
early Apr

Crowds line the banks of the Thames for the country's two most famous universities going oar-to-oar from Putney to Mortlake (www.theboatraces.org).

☆ London Marathon
mid-Apr

Some 35,000 runners – most running for charity – pound through London in one of the world's biggest road races (www.virginmoneylondonmarathon.com), heading from Blackheath to the Mall.

🌸 Easter
21 Apr

With Good Friday and Easter Monday both being public holidays, Easter is the longest bank holiday in the UK. Chocolate, which you'll find in many shapes and flavours, is a traditional Easter treat, as are hot-cross buns, a spiced, sticky-glazed fruit bun.

⊙ Van Gogh & Britain at the Tate
27 Mar-11 Aug

Tate Britain (p52) is putting together the largest exhibition of the Dutch painter's work in over a decade. The show will examine Van Gogh's relationship with Britain – the ideas that influenced him and the artists he inspired in turn.

VINCENT VAN GOGH / GETTY IMAGES ©

☆ Udderbelly Festival
Apr-Jul

Housed in a temporary venue in the shape of a purple upside-down cow on the South Bank, this festival of comedy, circus and general family fun (www.udderbelly.co.uk) has become a spring favourite.

Plan Your Trip
This Year in London

May

A delightful time to be in London: days are warming up and Londoners begin to start lounging around in parks, popping on their sunglasses and enjoying two bank-holiday weekends (the first and the last in May).

☆ Shakespeare's Globe Theatre   late Apr–Oct
Watch the work of the world's most famous playwright in a faithful reproduction of a 17th-century theatre (p191). The theatre (pictured above) is outdoors and most of the audience is standing.

⊙ Museums at Night   mid-May
For one weekend in May, numerous museums across London open after-hours (http://museumsatnight.org.uk), with candlelit tours, spooky atmospheres, sleepovers and special events such as talks and concerts.

⊙ Chelsea Flower Show   22-26 May
The world's most renowned horticultural event (www.rhs.org.uk/chelsea) attracts London's green-fingered and flower-mad gardeners. Expect talks, presentations and spectacular displays from the cream of the gardening world.

☆ Regent's Park Open Air Theatre   May-Sep
A popular and very atmospheric summertime fixture in London, this 1250-seat outdoor auditorium (www.openairtheatre. com) plays host to four productions a year: famous plays (Shakespeare often features), new works, musicals and usually one production aimed at families.

OVERSNAP / GETTY IMAGES ©

06

June

The peak season begins with long, warm days (it's light until 10pm) and the arrival of alfresco events.

⊙ Open Garden Squares Weekend 8-9 Jun
Over one weekend, more than 200 gardens in London that are usually inaccessible to the public fling open their gates for exploration (www.opensquares.org).

⚜ Trooping the Colour mid-Jun
The Queen's official birthday (www.trooping-the-colour.co.uk; pictured above) is celebrated with much flag-waving, parades, pageantry and noisy flyovers. The royal family usually attends in force.

☆ Meltdown mid-Jun
The Southbank Centre hands over the curatorial reins to a legend of contemporary music (eg Morrissey, Patti Smith or Guy Garvey) to pull together a full program of

concerts, talks and films (www.southbankcentre.co.uk).

⊙ Royal Academy Summer Exhibition mid-Jun–mid-Aug
This exhibition at the Royal Academy of Arts (p49) showcases works submitted by artists from all over Britain, distilled to a thousand or so pieces.

🍷 Drinking in Beer Gardens Jun
Numerous pubs in London have amazing outdoor spaces, generally referred to as 'beer gardens'. Some are more garden-like than others; regardless, drinking alfresco is a firm favourite of Londoners on sunny afternoons and balmy evenings.

This Year in London

BIKEWORLDTRAVEL / SHUTTERSTOCK ©

July

07

This is the time to munch on strawberries, drink in beer gardens and join in the numerous outdoor activities, including big music festivals and Wimbledon.

🎊 Pride London   early Jul
The gay community paints the town pink in this annual extravaganza (www.pridein london.org), featuring a smorgasbord of experiences, from talks to live events, and culminating in a huge parade (pictured above) across London.

☆ Wireless   early Jul
One of London's top music festivals, with an emphasis on dance and R & B, Wireless (www.wirelessfestival.co.uk) takes place in Finsbury Park in northeast London. It is extremely popular, so book in advance.

☆ The Proms   mid-Jul–Sep
The Proms offers two months of outstanding classical concerts (www.bbc.co.uk/proms) at various prestigious venues, centred on the Royal Albert Hall.

☆ Wimbledon Championships 1-14 Jul
For two weeks a year, the quiet South London village of Wimbledon falls under a sporting spotlight as the world's best tennis players gather to battle for the championships (p203).

PEEPO / GETTY IMAGES ©

☆ Lovebox   mid-Jul
This two-day music extravaganza (www.loveboxfestival.com) in Victoria Park, East London, was created by dance duo Groove Armada. Its raison d'être is dance music, but there are plenty of other genres too, including indie, pop and hip hop.

2019

CARL COURT / STAFF / GETTY IMAGES ©

08

August

School's out for summer, families are holidaying and the hugely popular annual Caribbean carnival dances into Notting Hill. The last weekend brings a bank holiday.

🏊 Outdoor Swimming   Aug
London may not strike you as the place to go for an alfresco swim, but you can enjoy a dip in the Serpentine in Hyde Park or in the ponds of Hampstead Heath (water quality is tested daily).

☆ Summer Screen at Somerset   early Aug
For a fortnight every summer, Somerset House (www.somersethouse.org.uk) turns its stunning courtyard into an open-air cinema screening an eclectic mix of film premieres, cult classics and popular requests.

🍷 Great British Beer Festival   mid-Aug
Organised by the Campaign for Real Ale, this boozy festival (www.gbbf.org.uk; pictured above) cheerfully cracks open casks of ale from the UK and abroad at Olympia exhibition centre.

🎊 Notting Hill Carnival   24-26 Aug
Europe's biggest – and London's most vibrant – outdoor carnival is a celebration of Caribbean London, featuring music, dancing and costumes over the summer bank-holiday weekend.

MS JANE CAMBELL / SHUTTERSTOCK ©

Plan Your Trip
This Year in London

September

The end of summer and start of autumn is a lovely time to be in town, with comedy festivals and a chance to look at London properties normally shut to the public.

✿ The Mayor's Thames Festival — Sep

Celebrating the River Thames, this cosmopolitan festival (www.totallythames.org) brings fairs, street theatre, music, food stalls, fireworks and river races, culminating in the superb Night Procession.

☆ Greenwich Comedy Festival — mid-Sep

This weeklong laugh fest – London's largest comedy festival – brings big names and emerging acts to the National Maritime Museum.

⊙ Open House London — mid-Sep

For a weekend in mid-September the public is invited in to see more than 700 heritage buildings throughout the capital that are normally off limits (www.openhouselondon.org.uk).

✦ Great Gorilla Run — late Sep

It looks bananas, but this gorilla-costume charity run (www.greatgorillarun.org; pictured above) along an 8km route from the City to Bankside and back again is all in aid of gorilla conservation.

TIMOTHY MBUGUA / EYEEM / GETTY IMAGES ©

October

The weather is getting colder, but London's parklands are splashed with gorgeous autumnal colours. Clocks go back to winter time the last weekend of the month.

🎿 Autumn Walks   Oct

London's parks look truly glorious on a sunny day when the trees have turned a riot of yellows and reds. Hyde Park and Greenwich Park are beautiful at this time of year and offer great views of London's landmarks.

☆ London Film Festival   mid-Oct

The city's premier film event (www.bfi.org.uk/lff) attracts big overseas names and show more than 100 British and international films before their cinema release. Masterclasses are given by world-famous directors.

☆ Dance Umbrella Festival   mid-Oct

London's annual festival of contemporary dance (www.danceumbrella.co.uk) features two weeks of performances by British and international dance companies at venues across London.

🗋 Affordable Art Fair   mid-Oct

For four days in March and October, Battersea Park turns into a giant art fair (www.affordableartfair.com), where more than 100 galleries offer works of art from just £100. Plenty of talks and workshops too.

This Year in London

November

London nights are getting longer. It's the last of the parks' autumn colours – enjoy them on a walk and relax by an open fire in a pub afterwards.

🎇 Guy Fawkes Night (Bonfire Night)   5 Nov

Bonfire Night commemorates Guy Fawkes' foiled attempt to blow up Parliament in 1605. Bonfires and fireworks light up the night. Primrose Hill, Highbury Fields, Alexandra Palace, Clapham Common and Blackheath have some of the best fireworks displays.

🎇 Lord Mayor's Show   mid-Nov

In accordance with the Magna Carta of 1215, the newly elected Lord Mayor of the City of London travels in a state coach (pictured above) from Mansion House to the Royal Courts of Justice to take an oath of allegiance to the Crown – nowadays with floats, bands and fireworks (www.lord mayorsshow.london).

☆ London Jazz Festival   late Nov

Musicians from around the world swing into town for 10 days of jazz (www.efglondon jazzfestival.org.uk). World influences are well represented, as are more conventional styles.

🎇 Lighting of the Christmas Tree & Lights   late Nov

A celebrity is called up to switch on all the festive lights that line Oxford, Regent and Bond St, and a towering Norwegian spruce is set up in Trafalgar Sq.

CEDRIC WEBER / SHUTTERSTOCK ©

December

12

A festive mood reigns as Christmas approaches and shops are decorated. Days are increasingly shorter. Christmas Day is the quietest day of the year, with all shops and museums closed and the tube network shut.

🎿 Ice Skating   Dec
From mid-November until January, open-air ice rinks pop up across the city, including one in the exquisite courtyard of Somerset House (p63; pictured above) and another one in the grounds of the Natural History Museum (p105).

🎁 Christmas Shopping   Dec
London has everything you could possibly want and more. Hamleys (p164), with its five storeys of toys, will mesmerise children. Harrods (p161) will wow you with its extravagant window display and over-the-top decorations (and prices!). The festive atmosphere should put a spring in your step.

❄ New Year's Celebrations   31 Dec
On 31 December the famous countdown to midnight is met with terrific fireworks from the London Eye and celebrated by massive crowds. There are parties in every pub and bar in town.

MELIS / SHUTTERSTOCK ©

🎁 Boxing Day   26 Dec
Boxing Day used to be the opening day of the winter sales, and one of the busiest days of the year for shops. Pre-Christmas sales have somewhat dampened the rush but it remains a lively day.

Plan Your Trip
Need to Know

Daily Costs

Budget:
Less than £85

○ Dorm bed: £10–32

○ Market-stall lunch: £5; supermarket sandwich: £3.50–4.50

○ Many museums: free

○ Standby theatre tickets: £5–25

○ Santander Cycles daily rental fee: £2

Midrange:
£85–185

○ Double room in a mid-range hotel: £100–200

○ Two-course dinner with a glass of wine: £35

○ Theatre ticket: £15–60

Top End:
More than £185

○ Four-star/boutique hotel room: over £200

○ Three-course dinner in a top restaurant with wine: £60–90

○ Black-cab trip: £30

○ Top theatre ticket: £65

Advance Planning

Three months before Book weekend performances of top shows; make dinner reservations for renowned restaurants with celebrity chefs; snatch up tickets for must-see temporary exhibitions; book accommodation at boutique properties.

One month before Check listings for fringe theatre, live music and festivals on entertainment sites such as Time Out, and book tickets.

A few days before Check the weather on the Met Office website (www.metoffice.gov.uk).

Useful Websites

Lonely Planet (www.lonelyplanet.com/london) Bookings, traveller forum and more.

Time Out London (www.timeout.com/london) Up-to-date and comprehensive listings.

Londonist (www.londonist.com) A website about London and everything that happens in it.

Transport for London (www.tfl.gov.uk) Essential tool for staying mobile in the capital.

Arriving in London

Heathrow Airport Trains, London Underground (tube) and buses to central London from just after 5am to before midnight (night buses run later and 24-hour tube runs Friday and Saturday) £5.70 to £21.50; taxi £48 to £90.

Currency

Pound sterling (£)

Language

English

Visas

Not required for US, Canadian, Australian, New Zealand or South African visitors for stays of up to six months. EU nationals can stay indefinitely (Brexit may change that).

Money

ATMs are widespread. Major credit cards are accepted everywhere. The best place to change money is in post-office branches, which do not charge a commission.

Mobile Phones

Buy local SIM cards for European and Australian phones, or a pay-as-you-go phone. Set other phones to international roaming.

Time

London is on GMT; during British Summer Time (BST; late March to late October), London clocks are one hour ahead of GMT.

Tourist Information

Visit London (www.visitlondon.com)

For more, see the **Survival Guide** (p228)

When to Go

Summer is peak season: days are long and festivals are afoot, but expect crowds. Spring and autumn are cooler, but delightful. Winter is cold, but quieter.

London

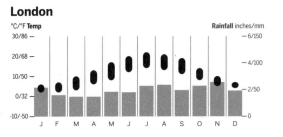

Gatwick Airport Trains to central London from 4.30am to 1.35am £10 to £20; hourly buses to central London around the clock from £5; taxi £100.

Stansted Airport Trains to central London from 5.30am to 1.30am £23.40; round-the-clock buses to central London from £12; taxi from £130.

Luton Airport Trains to central London from 7am to 10pm from £14; round-the-clock buses to central London £10; taxi £110.

London City Airport DLR trains to central London from 5.30am to 12.30am Monday to Saturday, 7am to 11.15pm Sunday from £2.80; taxi around £35.

St Pancras International Train Station In central London (for Eurostar train arrivals from Europe) and connected by many Underground lines to other parts of the city.

Digital London

There are scores of cool apps for travellers. Here are some of our favourite free ones, from inspirational to downright practical. Many museums and attractions also have their own.

Streetmuseum Historical images (photographs, paintings, drawings etc) superimposed on modern-day locations.

Street Art Tours London Hand-picked graffiti and other street-art locations.

Soho Stories Social history of London's most bohemian neighbourhood, told through poems and extracts from novels and newspapers.

CityMapper The best app to work out how to get from A to B.

Hailo Summons the nearest black cab right to the curb.

Uber A taxi, private car or rideshare at competitive prices.

London Bus Live Real-time route finder and bus arrivals for a stop of your choice.

Santander Cycles Find a bike, a route and a place to return it.

Sleeping

Hanging your hat (and anything else you care to remove) in London can be painfully expensive, and you'll almost always need to book your room well in advance. Decent, central hostels are easy enough to find and also offer reasonably priced double rooms. Bed and breakfasts are a dependable and inexpensive, if rather simple, option. Hotels range from cheap, no-frills chains through boutique choices to luxury five-star historic hotels.

Plan Your Trip
Top Days in London

The West End & the South Bank

Plunge into the heart of the West End for some of London's top sights. This itinerary also spans the River Thames to the South Bank, taking in Westminster Abbey, Buckingham Palace, Trafalgar Sq, the Houses of Parliament and the London Eye.

Day 01

❶ Westminster Abbey (p36)

Begin at Westminster Abbey to steep yourself in British history back to 1066.

➡ Westminster Abbey to Buckingham Palace

🚶 Cross the road to Storey's Gate and walk west along Birdcage Walk.

❷ Buckingham Palace (p46)

Peer through the gates, go on a tour of the interior (summer only) or catch the Changing of the Guard at 11.30am.

➡ Buckingham Palace to Cafe Murano

🚶 Stroll through St James's Park and across the Mall to St James's St.

❸ Lunch at Cafe Murano (p149)

In the heart of St James's, this busy restaurant cooks superb northern Italian fare.

➡ Cafe Murano to Trafalgar Sq

🚶 Walk along Jermyn St and down Haymarket to Trafalgar Sq.

ALEXKOZLOV / GETTY IMAGES ©

❹ Trafalgar Square (p56)

Visit London's epicentre (all distances are measured from here), and explore the National Gallery (p55).

➲ Trafalgar Sq to Houses of Parliament

🚶 Walk down Whitehall.

❺ Houses of Parliament (p50)

Dominating the east side of Parliament Sq is the Palace of Westminster, with one of London's ultimate sights, Big Ben.

➲ Houses of Parliament to London Eye

🚶 Cross Westminster Bridge.

❻ London Eye (p94)

Hop on a 'flight' on the London Eye. Pre-book tickets online or grab a fast-track ticket to shorten wait times.

➲ London Eye to Scootercaffe

🚶 Walk down to Waterloo station, cross the Leake St graffiti tunnel under the tracks and turn right on Lower Marsh.

❼ Drinks at Scootercaffe (p179)

Tucked behind Waterloo station, this atmospheric bar is perfect for winding down after traipsing across the city.

From left: Westminster Abbey (p36); Trafalgar Square (p56)

Plan Your Trip
Top Days in London

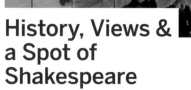

CLAUDIO DIVIZIA / SHUTTERSTOCK ©

History, Views & a Spot of Shakespeare

Get set for more of London's top sights – once again on either side of the Thames. Visit the British Museum in Bloomsbury, climb the dome of St Paul's Cathedral, explore the Tower of London and soak up some Shakespeare.

❶ British Museum (p42)

Begin with a visit to the British Museum and ensure you tick off the highlights, including the Rosetta Stone, the Egyptian mummies and the Parthenon Marbles.

➲ British Museum to St Paul's Cathedral

⊖ Take the Central Line from Holborn to St Paul's.

❷ St Paul's Cathedral (p86)

Don't miss climbing the dome for its astounding views of London, and save some time for the fascinating crypt. Break for lunch at Miyama (p145).

➲ St Paul's Cathedral to Tower of London

🚌 Hop on bus 15 from the cathedral to the Tower of London.

Day
02

ALEXEY FEDORENKO / SHUTTERSTOCK ©

❸ Tower of London (p64)

The millennium of history contained within the Tower of London, including the Crown Jewels, Traitors' Gate, the White Tower and its armour collection, and the all-important resident ravens, deserves at least a couple of hours to fully explore.

➲ Tower of London to Tower Bridge

🚶 Walk along Tower Bridge Approach from the Tower of London to Tower Bridge.

❹ Tower Bridge (p80)

Cross the Thames via elegant Tower Bridge. Check the website for bridge lift times if you want to see it open and close.

➲ Tower Bridge to Oblix at the Shard

🚶 Stroll west along the river to the Shard; the entrance is on St Thomas St.

❺ Drinks at Oblix (p179)

Round off the day with drinks, food, live music and fabulous views of London from the 32nd floor of the Shard, London's most spectacular skyscraper.

➲ Oblix at the Shard to Shakespeare's Globe

🚶 Walk through Borough Market and then follow the Thames west to Shakespeare's Globe.

❻ A Play at Shakespeare's Globe (p85)

Watch one of Shakespeare's famous plays in a theatre as it would have been in Shakespeare's day: outdoors in summer months in the Globe, or by candlelight in the Playhouse.

From left: Millennium Bridge (p91) and St Paul's Cathedral (p86); Tower of London (p64), with Tower Bridge (p80) in the background.

Plan Your Trip

Top Days in London

PI03 / SHUTTERSTOCK ©

Kensington Museums, Knightsbridge Shopping & the West End

Passing through some of London's most attractive and well-heeled neighbourhoods, this route takes in some of the city's best museums and a world-famous department store before delivering you to the bright lights of the West End.

Day

03

❶ Victoria & Albert Museum (p100)

Start your day in South Kensington. Cross off some of the Victoria & Albert's 146 galleries. Or opt for the huge Natural History Museum (p105) or the interactive Science Museum (p107) if you're of a more scientific bent.

➲ Victoria & Albert Museum to Kensington Gardens & Hyde Park

🚶 Walk north along Exhibition Rd and West Carriage Dr.

❷ Lunch at Magazine (p144)

Lunch on lovely modern European food in the other-wordly undulating building designed by the late prize-winning architect Zaha Hadid. Afternoon tea is another great option.

➲ Magazine to Kensington Gardens & Hyde Park

🚶 Magazine is at the heart of Hyde Park and Kensington Gardens.

❸ Kensington Gardens & Hyde Park (p96)

Explore Kensington Gardens (p99) and Hyde Park (p97). Make sure you take a look at the Albert Memorial (p99), take a peek inside Kensington Palace (p98) and stroll along the Serpentine.

⭘ Kensington Gardens & Hyde Park to Harrods

🚶 Stroll through Hyde Park to Knightsbridge, on its southern edge.

❹ Harrods (p161)

A visit to Harrods is both fun and fascinating, even if you don't plan to buy anything. The food court is a great place for edible souvenirs.

⭘ Harrods to Piccadilly Circus

🚇 Walk to Knightsbridge station, then take the Piccadilly Line three stops to Piccadilly Circus.

❺ Piccadilly Circus (p108)

Jump off the tube at this busy roundabout to have a look at the famous statue (Eros' brother) and enjoy a night out in Soho.

⭘ Piccadilly Circus to Yauatcha

🚶 Walk up Shaftesbury Ave, turn left onto Rupert St, which becomes Berwick St, then left into Broadwick St.

❻ Dinner at Yauatcha (p129)

For the most sophisticated and exquisite dim sum, Yauatcha is unrivalled. The selection of tea is second to none. Bookings are essential.

⭘ Yauatcha to Swift

🚶 Turn right on Broadwick St, then right on Wardour St, then left on Old Compton St to Swift.

❼ Drinks at Swift (p183)

Ease further into the evening with drinks at this sophisticated cocktail bar.

From left: Victoria & Albert Museum (p100); Harrods (p161)

Plan Your Trip
Top Days in London

Greenwich to Shoreditch

You don't want to neglect sights further afield, and this itinerary makes a big dent in what's on offer. Lovely Greenwich has a whole raft of stately sights, while an evening in trendy Shoreditch is always fun.

❶ Royal Observatory & Greenwich Park (p114)

Start the day in riverside Greenwich and make sure you visit Greenwich Park and the Royal Observatory. Stride over the Meridian and drink in the fabulous views.

➲ Greenwich Park & Royal Observatory to Goddards at Greenwich

🚶 Amble down the hill towards Greenwich, walk down King William Walk to Greenwich Market.

❷ Lunch at Goddards at Greenwich (p150)

This is the place to try the classic London dish of Pie & Mash (with or without eel). Go classic with minced beef or rogue with a chicken (or vegetarian) pie.

➲ Goddards to *Cutty Sark*

🚶 Cross Greenwich Market; the *Cutty Sark* towers over you.

Day

04

GRAPHICAL_BANK / SHUTTERSTOCK ©

❸ Cutty Sark (p117)

Hop on board this splendidly restored great clipper, star of the tea trade in the late 19th century. The exhibits evoke life on board as well as the history of trade between Britain and the East.

○ *Cutty Sark* to Old Spitalfields Market

🚇🚉 Take the DLR from Cutty Sark station to Bow Church and change for the Hammersmith & City Line to Liverpool St station.

❹ Old Spitalfields Market (p71)

Browse the stalls (and shops) of Old Spital-fields Market. The best days for the market are Thursday, Friday and Sunday. The surrounding streets, Brick Lane especially, are very lively and full of history.

○ Old Spitalfields Market to Queen of Hoxton

🏃 Head north up Bishopgate; turn left on Worship St to the intersection with Curtain Rd.

❺ Cocktails at Queen of Hoxton (p174)

Sample the edgy, creative and offbeat Shoreditch atmosphere by dropping in on this ubercool establishment. Partake in activities, or just soak up the atmosphere from the amazing roof terrace.

○ Queen of Hoxton to Hawksmoor

🏃 Head back to Bishopgate; turn right, then left onto Folgate St, then left onto Commercial St.

❻ Steak at Hawksmoor (p139)

Indulge in the very best meat money can buy at this long-standing Shoreditch institution. There are plenty of fabulous wines to accompany your dinner. Booking essential.

From left: Greenwich Park (p115); Old Spitalfields Market (p71)

Plan Your Trip
Hot Spots For...

NIGHT OWLS

⊙ **Tate Modern** Outstanding modern-art gallery open until 10pm on Friday and Saturday. (p82)

♟ **Cargo** Open until the small hours and one of the best clubs in town. (p127)

✕ **Brick Lane Beigel Baker** Whatever the time of day or night, this bagel shop will sort you out. (p71)

☆ **Comedy Store** The Friday and Saturday 11pm shows are as funny as the 8pm ones. (p194)

⊙ **National Portrait Gallery** Open until 9pm on Thursday and Friday, with a bar and special events. (p55; pictured above)

ROMANCE

♟ **Shoreditch Sky Terrace** Cocktails with views of the City skyline and DJ lounge music. (p127)

☆ **Royal Opera House** Dress up and enjoy world-class opera or ballet in this regal venue. (p193)

✕ **City Social** Phenomenal views and incredible food for an unforgettable dinner. (p146)

⊙ **Kew Gardens** Enjoy a day strolling through these exquisite gardens (pictured below) and glorious greenhouses. (p122)

☆ **Summer Screen at Somerset House** Watch a film alfresco in glorious surrounds. (p13)

HISTORY BUFFS

⊙ **Tower of London** From executions to the dazzling Crown Jewels, the Tower has seen it all. (p64)

☞ **Guide London** Hire a Blue Badge guide for a tailor-made historical tour. (p200)

🍷 **Dukes London** Old-school gentleman's club where Ian Fleming enjoyed a drink. (p181)

⊙ **Westminster Abbey** Almost every monarch since 1066 has been crowned, and many buried, here. (p36)

🍷 **Ye Olde Mitre** One of the city's oldest pubs, with no music to spoil the drinking and chatting. (p175)

FOODIES

⊙ **Borough Market** Admire the foodscapes (pictured above) and revel in the free samples. (p76)

✕ **Dinner by Heston Blumenthal** Gastronomic tour de force combines tradition with modern twists. (p144)

🍷 **Wine Pantry** The best place in town to try English wines. (p140)

🔒 **Vintage House** For all your whisky needs, look no further. (p165)

✕ **Chin Chin Labs** Liquid nitrogen ice cream: as weird as it sounds, more wonderful than you'd imagine. (p145)

BARGAIN HUNTERS

🔒 **Sunday Upmarket** Browse for that unique vintage piece. (p158)

⊙ **British Museum** Most museums of this calibre charge admission fees. Tours are free too. (p42)

🍷 **Sky Pod** For the price of a drink, enjoy panoramic views and tropical roof gardens (pictured above). (p145)

🔒 **Burberry Outlet Store** Genuine Burberry, just 30% cheaper. (p159)

☆ **Shakespeare's Globe** Enjoy world-class Shakespeare productions with a £5 standing ticket. (p191)

Plan Your Trip
What's New

Fourth Plinth Gets Geopolitical

In March 2018 artist Michael Rakowitz took over the Fourth Plinth (p59) on Trafalgar Sq with *The Invisible Enemy Should Not Exist*, a re-creation of a sculpture destroyed by the so-called Islamic State. It will be on show until March 2020.

All Aboard Crossrail

The capital's most ambitious transport project (www.crossrail.co.uk) in a generation started operating in 2018 between London Liverpool St and Shenfield in the east, and Paddington and Heathrow in the west. The line will be fully operational in December 2019.

Southbank Facelift

The brutalist wing of the Southbank Centre (p94), which contains the Hayward Gallery and the Queen Elizabeth Hall, was given a two-year 21st-century makeover and reopened in spring 2018.

All-New Kew

The year 2018 was a big one for Kew Gardens (p122) with the reopening of Temperate House, the world's largest Victorian glasshouse, after five years of extensive renovation, and the reopening of the Great Pagoda.

Technicolor Painted Hall

For the past two years, a team of expert conservators have painstakingly cleaned and revived the Painted Hall of the Old Royal Naval College (p116) in Greenwich. Dubbed the UK's Sistine Chapel, it is one of the most important – and now vibrant – baroque interiors in Europe. A grand re-opening is planned for February.

Above: Painted Hall, Old Royal Naval College (p116)

Plan Your Trip
For Free

Sights

It costs nothing to visit the Houses of Parliament (p50) and watch debates. Another institution of public life, the Changing of the Guard (p47), is free to watch. For one weekend in September, Open House London (p69) opens the doors to some 850 buildings for free.

Museums & Galleries

The permanent collections of all state-funded museums and galleries are open to the public free of charge. They include the Victoria & Albert Museum (p100), Tate Modern (p82), Tate Britain (p52), British Museum (p42), National Gallery (p55) and Nation-al Portrait Gallery (p55). The Serpentine Galleries (p97) are also free.

Views

Why pay good money when some of the finest viewpoints in London are free? Head up to Level 10 of Switch House at Tate Modern (p82) or to the summit of Primrose Hill (p120) in Regent's Park.

Concerts

The beautiful St Martin-in-the-Fields (p59) church on Trafalgar Sq hosts free concerts at 1pm on Monday, Tuesday and Friday.

Walking

Walking is possibly the best way to get a sense of the city and its history. The West End is relatively compact and a great place to walk; otherwise, follow the Thames along the South Bank for sight-seeing combined with iconic London views.

Cycling

Bike-share your way around with Santander Cycles (p237). The access fee is £2 for 24 hours; bike hire is then free for the first 30 minutes.

TITSTUDIO / SHUTTERSTOCK ©

Above: Big Ben and the Houses of Parliament (p50)

Plan Your Trip
Family Travel

KIEVVICTOR / SHUTTERSTOCK ©

Need to Know

○ **Babysitters** Find a babysitter or nanny at Greatcare (www.greatcare.co.uk).

○ **Cots** Available in most hotels, but always request them in advance.

○ **Public transport** Under-16s travel free on buses, under-11s travel free on the tube, and under-fives ride free on trains.

Museums

London's museums are particularly child friendly. You'll find storytelling at the **National Gallery** (p55) for children aged three years and over, arts-and-crafts workshops at the **Victoria & Albert Museum** (p100), train-making workshops at the **Transport Museum** (p62), plenty of finger-painting opportunities at the **Tate Modern** (p82) and **Tate Britain** (p52), and performance and handicraft workshops at **Somerset House** (p63). And what's more, they're all free (check websites for details).

Other excellent activities for children include sleepovers at the **British Museum**

(p42), **Science Museum** (p107) and **Natural History Museum** (p105), though you'll need to book months ahead. The last two are definitive children's museums, with interactive displays and play areas.

Other Attractions

Kids love the **London Zoo** (Map p254; www. zsl.org/zsl-london-zoo; Outer Circle, Regent's Park, NW1; adult/child £29.75/22; ⊙10am-6pm Apr-Sep, to 5.30pm Mar & Oct, to 4pm Nov-Feb; 🚼; 🚌274), **London Eye** (p94) and **London Dungeon** (p95). In wintertime, ice rinks glitter at the Natural History Museum and Somerset House. There's also a seasonal rink further afield at **Hampton Court Palace** (p110).

In addition there are the exciting climbs up the dome of **St Paul's Cathedral** (p86) or the **Monument** (p68). You can also pass time watching the performers in Trafalgar Sq, Covent Garden Piazza or along the South Bank. Many arts and cultural festivals aimed at adults also cater for children. London's parks burst with possibilities:

open grass, playgrounds, wildlife, trees and, in the warmer weather, ice-cream trucks.

Most attractions offer family tickets and discounted entry for kids under 15 or 16 years (children under five usually go free).

Eating & Drinking

Most of London's restaurants and cafes are child friendly and offer baby-changing facilities and high chairs. Note that high-end restaurants and small, quiet cafes may be less welcoming, particularly if you have toddlers or small babies.

The one place that isn't traditionally very welcoming for those with children is the pub. By law, minors aren't allowed into the main bar (walking through is fine), but many pubs have areas where children are welcome, usually a garden or outdoor space. Things are more relaxed during the day on Sunday.

Getting Around

When it comes to public transport, buses are better for children than the tube, which is often very crowded and hot in sum-

Best Sights for Children

Natural History Museum (p105)

Changing of the Guard (p47)

Cutty Sark (p117)

Science Museum (p107)

Unicorn Theatre (p192)

mer. As well as being big, red and iconic, buses in London are usually the famous double-decker ones; kids love to sit on the top deck and get great views of the city. Another excellent way to get around is simply to walk.

Hopping on a boat is an additional way to put fun (and sightseeing!) into getting from A to B.

From left: Somerset House (p63); Changing of the Guard, Buckingham Palace (p46)

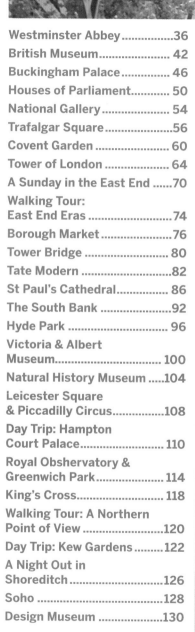

TOP EXPERIENCES

The very best to see and do

Interior of Westminster Abbey

Westminster Abbey

Westminster Abbey is such an important commemoration site that it's hard to overstate its symbolic value or imagine its equivalent anywhere else in the world. With a couple of exceptions, every English sovereign has been crowned here since William the Conqueror in 1066, and most of the monarchs from Henry III (died 1272) to George II (died 1760) are buried here.

Great For...

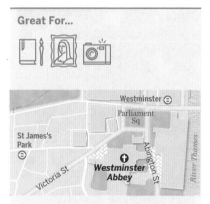

❶ Need to Know

Map p248; ☏020-7222 5152; www.west minster-abbey.org; 20 Dean's Yard, SW1; adult/child £22/9, cloister & gardens free; ⊙9.30am-3.30pm Mon, Tue, Thu & Fri, to 6pm Wed, to 1.30pm Sat; ⊖Westminster

★ **Top Tip**

The abbey gets incredibly busy, even at opening, so come armed with patience.

There is an extraordinary amount to see at the Abbey. The interior is chock-a-block with ornate chapels, elaborate tombs of monarchs and grandiose monuments to sundry luminaries throughout the ages. First and foremost, however, it is a sacred place of worship.

A Regal History

Though a mixture of architectural styles, the Abbey is considered the finest example of Early English Gothic (1190–1300). The original church was built in the 11th century by King (later St) Edward the Confessor, who is buried in the chapel behind the sanctuary and main altar. Henry III (r 1216–72) began work on the new building, but didn't complete it; the French Gothic nave was finished by Richard II in 1388. Henry VII's huge and magnificent Lady Chapel was added in 1519.

The Abbey was initially a monastery for Benedictine monks, and many of the building's features attest to this collegial past (the octagonal Chapter House, the Quire and four cloisters). In 1536 Henry VIII separated the Church of England from the Roman Catholic Church and dissolved the monastery. The king became head of the Church of England and the Abbey acquired its 'royal peculiar' status, meaning it is administered directly by the Crown and exempt from any ecclesiastical jurisdiction.

North Transept, Sanctuary & Quire

Entrance to the Abbey is via the Great North Door. The North Transept is often referred to as Statesmen's Aisle: politicians

Statues of 20th century martyrs, Great West Door

and eminent public figures are commemorated by large marble statues and imposing marble plaques.

At the heart of the Abbey is the beautifully tiled sanctuary (or sacrarium), a stage for coronations, royal weddings and funerals. George Gilbert Scott designed the ornate **high altar** in 1873. In front of the altar is the **Cosmati marble pavement** dating back to 1268. It has intricate designs of small pieces of marble inlaid into plain marble, which predicts the end of the world in AD 19,693! At the entrance to the lovely

QO7 / SHUTTERSTOCK ©

Chapel of St John the Baptist is a sublime Virgin and Child bathed in candlelight.

The Quire, a magnificent structure of gold, blue and red Victorian Gothic by Edward Blore, dates back to the mid-19th century. It sits where the original choir for the monks' worship would have been, but bears no resemblance to the original. Nowadays, the Quire is still used for singing, but its regular occupants are the Westminster Choir: 30 boys and 12 'lay vicars' (men) who sing the daily services.

Chapels & Chairs

The sanctuary is surrounded by chapels. **Henry VII's Lady Chapel**, in the easternmost part of the Abbey, is the most spectacular, with its fan vaulting on the ceiling, colourful banners of the Order of the Bath and dramatic oak stalls. Behind the chapel's altar is the elaborate sarcophagus of Henry VII and his queen, Elizabeth of York.

Beyond the chapel's altar is the **Royal Air Force Chapel**, with a stained-glass window commemorating the force's finest hour, the Battle of Britain (1940), and the 1500 RAF pilots who died. A stone plaque on the floor marks the spot where Oliver Cromwell's body lay for two years (1658) until the Restoration, when it was disinterred, hanged and beheaded. Two bodies, believed to be those of the child princes allegedly murdered in the Tower of London in 1483, were buried here almost two centuries later in 1674.

There are two small chapels either side of Lady Chapel with the tombs of famous monarchs: on the left (north) is where

Elizabeth I and her half-sister **Mary I** (aka Bloody Mary) rest. On the right (south) is the tomb of **Mary Queen of Scots**, beheaded on the orders of her cousin Elizabeth.

The vestibule of the Lady Chapel is the usual place for the rather ordinary-looking **Coronation Chair**, upon which every monarch since the early 14th century has been crowned.

Shrine of St Edward the Confessor

The most sacred spot in the Abbey lies behind the high altar; access is generally restricted to protect the 13th-century flooring. St Edward was the founder of the Abbey and the original building was consecrated a few weeks before his death. His tomb was slightly altered after the original was destroyed during the Reformation, but still contains Edward's remains – the only complete saint's body in Britain. Ninety-minute **verger-led tours** of the Abbey include a visit to the shrine.

Outer Buildings & Gardens

The oldest part of the cloister is the **East Cloister** (or East Walk), dating to the 13th century. Off the cloister are three museums. The octagonal **Chapter House** has one of Europe's best-preserved medieval tile floors and retains traces of religious murals on the walls. It was used as a meeting place by the House of Commons in the second half of the 14th century. To the right of the entrance to Chapter House is what is claimed to be the **oldest door** in Britain – it's been there for 950 years.

The adjacent **Pyx Chamber** is one of the few remaining relics of the original Abbey and holds the Abbey's treasures and liturgical objects. It contains the pyx, a chest with standard gold and silver pieces for testing coinage weights in a ceremony called the Trial of the Pyx.

To reach the 900-year-old **College Garden** (Map p248; ⊘10am-6pm Tue-Thu Apr-Sep, to 4pm Oct-Mar), enter Dean's Yard and the Little Cloisters off Great College St.

South Transept & Nave

The south transept contains **Poets' Corner**, where many of England's finest writers are buried and/or commemorated by monuments or memorials.

In the nave's north aisle is **Scientists' Corner**, where you will find **Sir Isaac Newton's tomb** (note the putto holding a prism to the sky while another feeds material into a smelting oven). Just ahead of it is the north aisle of the Quire, known as **Musicians' Aisle**, where baroque composers Henry Purcell and John Blow are buried, as well as more modern music-makers such as Benjamin Britten and Edward Elgar.

The two towers above the west door are the ones through which you exit. These were designed by Nicholas Hawksmoor and completed in 1745. Just above the door,

Henry VII's Lady Chapel (p39)

perched in 15th-century niches, are the additions to the Abbey unveiled in 1998: 10 stone statues of international 20th-century martyrs who died for their Christian faith. These include American pacifist Dr Martin Luther King, the Polish priest St Maximilian Kolbe, who was murdered by the Nazis at Auschwitz, and Wang Zhiming, publicly executed during the Chinese Cultural Revolution.

New Museum in the Triforium

The **Queen's Diamond Jubilee Galleries**, a new museum and gallery space located in the medieval Triforium, opened in June 2018, replacing the old Westminster Abbey Gallery in the former monks' dormitories. The Triforium looks out over the Abbey, and provides a new perspective.

Its exhibits include the death masks of generations of royalty, wax effigies representing Charles II and William III (who is on a stool to make him as tall as his wife, Mary II), armour and stained glass. Highlights are the graffiti-inscribed Mary Chair (used for the coronation of Mary II) and the Westminster Retable, England's oldest altarpiece, from the 13th century.

☑ **Don't Miss**

Triforium exhibits include wax effigies representing Charles II and William III (who is on a stool to make him as tall as his wife, Mary II).

★ **Top Tip**

The Choir sings the daily services and evensong – at 5pm on weekdays, 3pm on weekends.

MISTERVLAD / SHUTTERSTOCK ©

Great Court

ANNA LEVAN / SHUTTERSTOCK ©

British Museum

Britain's most visited attraction – founded in 1753 when royal physician Hans Sloane sold his 'cabinet of curiosities' – is an exhaustive and exhilarating stampede through 7000 years of human civilisation.

Great For...

☑ **Don't Miss**

The Rosetta Stone, the Mummy of Katebet and the marble Parthenon Sculptures.

The British Museum offers a stupendous selection of tours, many of them free. There are 15 free 30- to 40-minute eyeOpener tours of individual galleries per day. The museum also has free daily gallery talks, a highlights tour (adult/child £12/free, 11.30am and 2pm Friday, Saturday and Sunday) and excellent multimedia iPad tours (adult/child £5/3.50), offering six themed one-hour tours, and a choice of 35-minute children's trails.

Great Court

Covered with a spectacular glass-and-steel roof designed by Norman Foster in 2000, the Great Court is the largest covered public square in Europe. In its centre is the world-famous **Reading Room**, formerly the British Library, which has been frequented by all the big brains of history,

Ramesses the Great statue

❶ Need to Know

Map p254; ☎020-7323 8299; www.british
museum.org; Great Russell St & Montague Pl,
WC1; ⊙10am-5.30pm Sat-Thu, to 8.30pm Fri;
◉Russell Sq or Tottenham Court Rd FREE

✕ Take a Break

Nearby, **Queen's Larder** (Map p254;
☎020-7837 5627; www.queenslarder.co.uk; 1
Queen Sq, WC1; ⊙11.30am-11pm Mon-Fri, noon-
11pm Sat, noon-10.30pm Sun; Russell Sq) is
one of London's most atmospheric pubs.

★ Top Tip

The museum is huge, so pick your inter-
ests and consider the free tours.

from Mahatma Gandhi to Karl Marx. It is currently used for temporary exhibits.

Ancient Egypt, Middle East & Greece

The star of the show here is the Ancient Egypt collection. It comprises sculptures, fine jewellery, papyrus texts, coffins and mummies, including the beautiful and intriguing **Mummy of Katebet** (room 63). The most prized item in the collection (and the most popular postcard in the shop) is the **Rosetta Stone** (room 4), the key to deciphering Egyptian hieroglyphics. In the same gallery is the enormous bust of the pharaoh **Ramesses the Great** (room 4).

Assyrian treasures from ancient Mesopotamia include the 16-tonne **Winged Bulls from Khorsabad** (room 10), the

heaviest object in the museum. Behind it are the exquisite **Lion Hunt Reliefs from Ninevah** (room 10) from the 7th century BC, which influenced Greek sculpture. Such antiquities are all the more significant after the Islamic State's bulldozing of Nimrud in 2015.

A major highlight of the museum is the **Parthenon sculptures** (room 18). The marble frieze is thought to be the Great Panathenaea, a blow-out version of an annual festival in honour of Athena.

Roman & Medieval Britain

Upstairs are finds from Britain and the rest of Europe (rooms 40 to 51). Many items go back to Roman times, when the Empire spread across much of the continent, such as the **Mildenhall Treasure** (room 49), a collection of pieces of 4th-century Roman silverware from Suffolk with both pagan and early-Christian motifs.

Lindow Man (room 50) is the well-preserved remains of a 1st-century man discovered in a bog near Manchester in northern England in 1984 (he has been comically dubbed Pete Marsh). Equally fascinating are artefacts from the **Sutton Hoo Ship-Burial** (room 41), an elaborate Anglo-Saxon burial site from Suffolk dating back to the 7th century.

Perennial favourites are the lovely **Lewis Chessmen** (room 40), 12th-century game pieces carved from walrus tusk and whale teeth that were found on a remote Scottish island in the early 19th century. They served as models for the game of Wizard Chess in the first Harry Potter film.

Enlightenment Galleries

Formerly known as the King's Library, this stunning neoclassical space (room 1) was built between 1823 and 1827 and was the first part of the new museum building as it is seen today. The collection traces how disciplines such as biology, archaeology, linguistics and geography emerged during the Enlightenment of the 18th century.

What's Nearby?
Sir John Soane's Museum   Museum

(Map p245; ☎020-7405 2107; www.soane. org; 12 Lincoln's Inn Fields, WC2; ⊙10am-5pm Wed-Sun; ⊖Holborn) FREE This little museum is one of the most atmospheric and fascinating in London. The building is the beautiful, bewitching home of architect Sir John Soane (1753–1837), which he left

Reading Room (p42)

brimming with surprising personal effects and curiosities, and the museum represents his exquisite and eccentric taste.

Soane, a country bricklayer's son, is most famous for designing the Bank of England.

The heritage-listed house is largely as it was when Soane died and is itself a main part of the attraction. It has a canopy dome that brings light right down to the crypt, a colonnade filled with statuary and a picture gallery where paintings are stowed behind each other on folding wooden panes. This is where Soane's choicest artwork is displayed, including *Riva degli Schiavoni, looking West* by Canaletto, architectural drawings by Christopher Wren and Robert Adam, and the original *Rake's Progress*, William Hogarth's set of satirical cartoons of late 8th-century London lowlife. Among Soane's more unusual acquisitions are an Egyptian hieroglyphic sarcophagus, a mock-up of a monk's cell and slaves' chains.

Charles Dickens Museum
Museum

(Map p254; ☏020-7405 2127; www.dickens museum.com; 48 Doughty St, WC1; adult/child £9/4; ⊙10am-5pm Tue-Sun; ⊖Chancery Lane or Russell Sq) A £3.5-million renovation made this museum, located in a handsome four-storey house that was the great Victorian novelist's sole surviving residence in London, bigger and better than ever. The museum showcases the family drawing room (restored to its original condition), a period kitchen and a dozen rooms containing various memorabilia.

All Saints
Church

(Map p248; ☏020-7636 1788; www.allsaints margaretstreet.org.uk; 7 Margaret St, W1; ⊙7am-7pm; ⊖Oxford Circus) In 1859 architect William Butterfield completed one of the country's most supreme examples of Victorian Gothic Revival architecture, enclosing the 65ft-long nave with extraordinary tiling and sumptuous stained glass.

All Saints was selected by the head of English Heritage in 2014 as one of the top 10 buildings in the UK that have changed the face of the nation, a list that included Westminster Abbey and Christ Church in Oxford.

> ★ **Top Tip**
>
> Check out the outstanding *A History of the World in 100 Objects* radio series (www.bbc.co.uk/podcasts/series/ahow), which retraces two million years of history through 100 objects from the museum's collections.

GTS PRODUCTIONS / SHUTTERSTOCK ©

> ★ **Did You Know?**
>
> Charles Dickens only spent 2½ years in the house that is now the Charles Dickens Museum, but it was here that he wrote many of his most famous works.

LUKASZ PAJOR / SHUTTERSTOCK ©

Buckingham Palace

The palace has been the Royal Family's London lodgings since 1837, when Queen Victoria moved in from Kensington Palace as St James's Palace was deemed too old-fashioned.

Great For...

☑ Don't Miss

Peering through the gates, a tour of the interior (in summer) or the Changing of the Guard.

Commoners can now get a peek of the State Rooms, a mere 19 of the palace's 775 rooms, from late July to September when HRH (Her Royal Highness) takes her holidays in Scotland. The Queen's Gallery and the Royal Mews are open year-round, however.

State Rooms

The tour starts in the **Grand Hall** at the foot of the monumental **Grand Staircase**, commissioned by George IV in 1828. It takes in John Nash's Italianate **Green Drawing Room**, the **State Dining Room** (all red damask and Regency furnishings), the **Blue Drawing Room** (which has a gorgeous fluted ceiling by Nash) and the **White Drawing Room**, where foreign ambassadors are received.

Admission includes entry to a themed special exhibition (eg royal couture during

Sentry from the Queen's Guard

ALEXANDER CHAIKIN / SHUTTERSTOCK ©

Constitution Hill · St James's Park Lake · St James's Park · Buckingham Palace · Birdcage Walk · Buckingham Gate · Petty France · St James's Park

ⓘ Need to Know

Map p248; ☏0303 123 7300; www.royal
collection.org.uk/visit/the-state-rooms-
buckingham-palace; Buckingham Palace Rd,
SW1; adult/child/under 5yr £24/13.50/free;
⊘9.30am-7pm late-July &Aug (last admission
5.15pm), to 6pm Sep (last admission 4.15pm);
Ⓔ Green Park or St James's Park

✕ Take a Break

Enjoy light refreshments in the West
Terrace **Cafe Murano** (p149).

★ Top Tip

Entry to the palace is by timed ticket
which must be booked online. The
self-guided tour takes about two hours.

the Queen's reign, growing up at the
palace etc).

The **Ballroom**, where official receptions
and state banquets are held, was built
between 1853 and 1855 and opened with
a ball a year later to celebrate the end of
the Crimean War. The **Throne Room** is
rather anticlimactic, with his-and-hers pink
chairs initialled 'ER' and 'P', sitting under a
curtained theatre arch.

Picture Gallery & Garden

The most interesting part of the tour is
the 47m-long Picture Gallery, featuring
splendid works by such artists as Van Dyck,
Rembrandt, Canaletto, Poussin, Claude
Lorrain, Rubens, Canova and Vermeer.

Wandering the 18 hectares of gardens
is another highlight – as well as admiring
some of the 350 or so species of flowers
and plants and listening to the many birds,
you'll get beautiful views of the palace and
a peek of its famous lake.

Changing of the Guard

At 11.30am daily from April to July (on
alternate days, weather permitting, for the
rest of the year), the old guard (Foot Guards
of the Household Regiment) comes off
duty to be **replaced** (http://changing-guard.
com) by the new guard on the forecourt of
Buckingham Palace.

Crowds come to watch the carefully
choreographed marching and shouting of
the guards in their bright-red uniforms and
bearskin hats. It lasts about 40 minutes
and is very popular, so arrive early if you
want to get a good spot.

Queen's Gallery

Since the reign of Charles I – a bad king
but one with exquisite taste – the Royal
Family has amassed a priceless collection
of paintings, sculpture, ceramics, furniture

and jewellery. The splendid **Queen's Gallery** (Map p248; www.royalcollection.org.uk/visit/the-queens-gallery-buckingham-palace; South Wing; adult/child £10.30/5.30, incl Royal Mews £19/10; ⏰10am-5.30pm; ⬥St James's Park, Victoria or Green Park) showcases some of the palace's treasures on a rotating basis.

The gallery was originally designed as a conservatory by John Nash. It was converted into a chapel for Queen Victoria in 1843, destroyed in a 1940 air raid and reopened as a gallery in 1962. A £20-million renovation for Elizabeth II's Golden Jubilee in 2002 added three times as much display space.

Royal Mews

Southwest of the palace, the **Royal Mews** (Map p248; www.royalcollection.org.uk/visit/royalmews; adult/child £11/6.40, with Queen's Gallery £19/10; ⏰10am-5pm Apr-Oct, to 4pm Mon-Sat Feb, Mar & Nov; ⬥Victoria) started life as a falconry, but is now a working stable looking after the royals' three-dozen immaculately groomed horses, along with the opulent vehicles – motorised and horse-driven – the monarch uses for transport. The Queen is well known for her passion for horses; she names every horse that resides at the mews. Nash's 1820 stables are stunning.

Highlights for visitors include the enormous and opulent Gold State Coach of 1762, which has been used for every coronation since that of George IV in 1821; the 1911 Glass Coach used for royal weddings (Prince William and Catherine Middleton actually used the 1902 State Landau to make the best of the good weather); and a Rolls-Royce Phantom VI from the royal fleet.

Royal Mews

What's Nearby?

St James's Park
Park

(Map p248; www.royalparks.org.uk/parks/st-jamess-park; The Mall, SW1; ⊙5am-midnight; ⊖St James's Park or Green Park) At just 23 hectares, St James's is one of the smallest but best-groomed of London's royal parks. It has brilliant views of the London Eye, Westminster, St James's Palace, Carlton Tce and the Horse Guards Parade; the sight of Buckingham Palace from the footbridge spanning the central lake is photo-perfect and the best you'll find.

The lake brims with ducks, geese, swans and other waterfowl, and the rocks on its southern side serve as a rest stop for a half-dozen pelicans (fed at 2.30pm daily).

Royal Academy of Arts
Gallery

(Map p248; ☎020-7300 8000; www.royal academy.org.uk; Burlington House, Piccadilly, W1; adult/child from £13.50/free, exhibition prices vary; ⊙10am-6pm Sat-Thu, to 10pm Fri; ⊖Green Park) Britain's oldest society devoted to fine arts was founded in 1768, moving to Burlington House exactly a century later. The collection contains drawings, paintings, architectural designs, photographs and sculptures by past and present Academicians such as Joshua Reynolds, John Constable, Thomas Gainsborough, JMW Turner, David Hockney and Norman Foster.

The famous **Summer Exhibition** (www.royalacademy.org.uk; adult/child £14/free; ⊙10am-6pm mid-Jun–mid-Aug), which has showcased contemporary art for sale by unknown as well as established artists for nearly 250 years, is the Academy's biggest annual event.

Horse Guards Parade
Historic Site

(Map p248; http://changing-guard.com/queens-life-guard.html; Horse Guards Parade, off Whitehall, SW1; ⊙11am Mon-Sat, 10am Sun; ⊖Westminster, Charing Cross or Embankment) In a more accessible version of Buckingham Palace's Changing of the Guard (p47), the mounted troops of the Household Cavalry change guard here daily, at the official vehicular entrance to the royal palaces. A slightly less pompous version takes place at 4pm when the unmounted guards are changed. On the Queen's official birthday in June, the Trooping of the Colour is staged here.

MAXIMOANGEL / SHUTTERSTOCK ©

★ **Did You Know?**

At the centre of Royal Family life is the Music Room, where four royal babies – the Prince of Wales (Prince Charles), Princess Royal (Princess Anne), Duke of York (Prince Andrew) and Duke of Cambridge (Prince William) – have been christened with water from the River Jordan.

River Thames and the Houses of Parliament

JAMES SLOAN / EYEEM / GETTY IMAGES ©

Houses of Parliament

Both the House of Commons and the House of Lords sit in the sumptuous Palace of Westminster, a neo-Gothic confection dating from the mid-19th century. A visit here is a journey to the very heart of British democracy.

Great For...

☑ Don't Miss

Westminster Hall's hammer-beam roof and the Palace's Gothic Revival interior.

Officially called the Palace of Westminster, the Houses of Parliament's oldest part is 11th-century Westminster Hall, one of only a few sections that survived a catastrophic fire in 1834. Its roof, added between 1394 and 1401, is the earliest known example of a hammerbeam roof. The rest was built by Charles Barry and Augustus Pugin, taking 20 years from 1840.

Towers

The most famous feature of the Houses of Parliament is the Clock Tower, official-ly named Elizabeth Tower to mark the Queen's Diamond Jubilee in 2012, but commonly known as **Big Ben** (Map p248). Big Ben is actually the 13.5-tonne bell hanging inside and is thought to be named after Benjamin Hall, the Commissioner of Works when the tower was completed in 1858. Ben rang in the New Year from 1924

Richard the Lionheart statue

BILL45 / SHUTTERSTOCK ©

Westminster
Bridge St   Westminster Bridge
Parliament
Sq
Houses of
Parliament
River Thames
St Margaret St

ℹ Need to Know

Map p248; Palace of Westminster; www.parliament.uk; Parliament Sq, SW1; ⊖Westminster
FREE

✕ Take a Break

Jubilee Café (⊙10am-5.30pm Mon-Fri, to 6pm Sat), near the north door of Westminster Hall, has hot drinks and snacks.

★ Top Tip

There is airport-style security to enter the Houses of Parliament.

until 2017, but has ceased ringing until 2021 while renovations are underway.

At the base of the taller **Victoria Tower** at the southern end is the **Sovereign's Entrance**, which is used by the Queen.

Westminster Hall

One of the most stunning elements of the Palace of Westminster, seat of the English monarchy from the 11th to the early 16th centuries, is Westminster Hall. Originally built in 1099, it is the oldest surviving part of the complex; the awesome hammer-beam roof was added around 1400. It has been described as 'the greatest surviving achievement of medieval English carpentry'. The only other part of the original palace to survive a devastating 1834 fire is the **Jewel Tower** (Map p248; ☎020-7222 2219; www.english-heritage.org.uk/visit/places/jewel-tower; Abingdon St, St James's Park, SW1;

adult/child £5/3; ⊙10am-5pm daily Apr-Oct, 10am-4pm Sat & Sun Nov-Mar), built in 1365 and used to store the monarch's valuables.

Westminster Hall was used for coronation banquets in medieval times, and also served as a courthouse until the 19th century. The trials of William Wallace (1305), Thomas More (1535), Guy Fawkes (1606) and Charles I (1649) all took place here. In the 20th century, monarchs and Sir Winston Churchill lay in state here after their deaths.

House of Commons

The **House of Commons** (Map p248; www.parliament.uk/business/commons; ⊙2.30-10pm Mon & Tue, 11.30am-7.30pm Wed, 10.30am-6.30pm Thu, 9.30am-3pm Fri) is where Members of Parliament (MPs) meet to propose and discuss new legislation and to grill the prime minister and other ministers.

The layout of the Commons Chamber is based on St Stephen's Chapel in the original Palace of Westminster. The chamber, designed by Giles Gilbert Scott, replaced the one destroyed by a 1941 bomb.

Although the Commons is a national assembly of 650 MPs, the chamber has seating for only 437. Government members sit to the right of the Speaker and Opposition members to the left.

House of Lords

The **House of Lords** (Map p248; www.parliament.uk/business/lords; 2.30-10pm Mon & Tue, 3-10pm Wed, 11am-7.30pm Thu, 10am-close of session Fri) is visited via the amusingly named Strangers' Gallery. The intricate 'Tudor Gothic' interior led its poor architect, Augustus Pugin (1812–52), to an early death from overwork and nervous strain.

Most of the 780-odd members of the House of Lords are life peers (appointed for their lifetime by the monarch); there is also a small number – 92 at the time of writing – of hereditary peers and a group of 'crossbench' members (numbering 179, not affiliated to the main political parties), and 26 bishops.

Tours

On Saturdays year-round and on most weekdays during Parliamentary recesses, including Easter, summer and Christmas, visitors can join a 90-minute **guided tour** (Map p248; 020-7219 4114; www.parliament.uk/visiting/visiting-and-tours; adult/child £28/12), conducted by qualified Blue Badge Tourist Guides in seven languages, of both chambers, Westminster Hall and other historic buildings.

What's Nearby?

Tate Britain   Gallery
(020-7887 8888; www.tate.org.uk/visit/tate-britain; Millbank, SW1; 10am-6pm, to

Interior of the House of Lords

9.30pm on selected Fri; ⊖Pimlico) **FREE** With a stunning new art deco–inspired staircase, the more elderly and venerable of the two Tate siblings celebrates paintings from 1500 to the present, with works from Blake, Hogarth, Gainsborough, Barbara Hepworth, Whistler, Constable and Turner, as well as vibrant modern and contemporary pieces from Lucian Freud, Francis Bacon, Henry Moore and Tracey Emin. Join free 45-minute **thematic tours** (⊘11am, noon, 2pm & 3pm daily) and 15-minute **Art in Focus talks** (⊘1.15pm Tue, Thu & Sat). Audio guides (£3.50) are also available.

The star of the show is, undoubtedly, the light-infused visions of JMW Turner. After he died in 1851, his estate was settled by a decree declaring that whatever had been found in his studio (300 oil paintings and about 30,000 sketches and drawings) would be bequeathed to the nation. The collection constitutes a grand and sweeping display of his work, including classics like *The Scarlet Sunset* and *Norham Castle, Sunrise*.

Tate Britain hosts the prestigious and often controversial annual Turner Prize for contemporary art (October to early December).

Churchill War Rooms   Museum

(Map p248; www.iwm.org.uk/visits/churchill-war-rooms; Clive Steps, King Charles St, SW1; adult/child £21/10.50; ⊘9.30am-6pm; ⊖Westminster) Winston Churchill coordinated the Allied resistance against Nazi Germany on a Bakelite telephone from this underground military HQ during WWII. The Cabinet War Rooms remain much as they were when the lights were flicked off in 1945, capturing the drama and dogged spirit of the time, while the multimedia **Churchill Museum** affords intriguing insights into the resolute, cigar-smoking wartime leader.

No 10 Downing Street   Historic Building

(Map p248; www.number10.gov.uk; 10 Downing St, SW1; ⊖Westminster) The official office of British leaders since 1732, when George II presented No 10 to Robert Walpole, this has also been the prime minister's London residence since refurbishment in 1902. For such a famous address, it's a small-looking Georgian building on a plain-looking street, hardly warranting comparison with the White House, for example. Yet it is actually three houses joined into one and boasts roughly 100 rooms plus a 2000-sq-metre garden with a lovely L-shaped lawn.

DAVID MURRAY / GETTY IMAGES ©

CLAUDIO DIVIZIA / SHUTTERSTOCK ©

National Gallery

With some 2300 European paintings on display, this is one of the world's richest art collections, with seminal paintings from the mid-13th to the early 20th century, including works by Leonardo da Vinci, Michelangelo, Titian, Van Gogh and Renoir.

Great For...

☑ Don't Miss

Venus & Mars by Botticelli, *Sunflowers* by Van Gogh and *Rokeby Venus* by Velázquez.

The gallery is not based around a royal collection but around three dozen pictures purchased by the government from a Russian-born merchant and banker named John Julius Angerstein in 1824. They paid £57,000 but had no place to hang them; the paintings remained at Angerstein's residence at 100 Pall Mall. In 1838 a government-funded purpose-built gallery building opened on the northern side of Trafalgar Sq. It has been extended several times, but most notably in 1991 with the opening of the Sainsbury Wing.

Sainsbury Wing

On the gallery's western side, the newest wing houses the oldest paintings, dating from 1250 to 1500. Here you will find largely religious paintings commissioned for private devotion, such as the *Wilton Diptych*, as well as more unusual masterpieces, such

❶ Need to Know

Map p248; ☑020-7747 2885; www.national
gallery.org.uk; Trafalgar Sq, WC2; ⊗10am-
6pm Sat-Thu, to 9pm Fri; ⊖Charing Cross
FREE

✕ Take a Break

The **National Dining Rooms** (Map p248;
☑020-7747 2525; www.nationalgallery.org.
uk/visiting/eat-and-drink; 1st fl, Sainsbury
Wing; mains £14.50-21; ⊗10am-5.30pm Sat-
Thu, to 8.30pm Fri) have high-quality British food and splendid afternoon teas.

★ Top Tip

Take a free tour to learn the stories
behind the gallery's most iconic works.

as Botticelli's *Venus & Mars* and Van Eyck's
Arnolfini Portrait. Leonardo Da Vinci's *Virgin
of the Rocks* is a stunning masterpiece.

West Wing & North Wing

Works from the High Renaissance (1500–
1600) embellish the West Wing where
Michelangelo, Titian, Raphael, Correggio,
El Greco and Bronzino hold court; Rubens,
Rembrandt and Caravaggio grace the North
Wing (1600–1700). Notable are two self-por-
traits of Rembrandt (age 34 and 63) and the
beautiful *Rokeby Venus* by Velázquez.

East Wing

Many visitors flock to the East Wing (1700–
1900), which holds works by 18th-century
British artists such as Gainsborough, Constable and Turner, and seminal Impressionist and post-Impressionist masterpieces by
Van Gogh, Renoir and Monet.

Visiting

The comprehensive audio guides (£4) are
highly recommended, as are the free one-
hour taster tours that leave from the information desk in the Sainsbury Wing daily.

What's Nearby?

National Portrait Gallery   Gallery
(Map p248; ☑020-7321 0055; www.npg.org.
uk; St Martin's Pl, WC2; ⊗10am-6pm Sat-Wed,
to 9pm Thu & Fri; ⊖Charing Cross or Leicester
Sq) **FREE** What makes the National Portrait
Gallery so compelling is its familiarity; in
many cases you'll have heard of the subject
(royals, scientists, politicians, celebrities)
or the artist (Andy Warhol, Annie Leibo-
vitz, Lucian Freud). Highlights include
the famous 'Chandos portrait' of William
Shakespeare, the first artwork the gallery
acquired (in 1856) and believed to be the
only likeness made during the playwright's
lifetime, and a touching sketch of novelist
Jane Austen by her sister.

Nelson's Column (p58)

Trafalgar Square

In many ways Trafalgar Sq is the centre of London, where tens of thousands congregate for anything from Christmas celebrations to political protests. The great square was neglected over many years, until a scheme was launched in 2000 to pedestrianise it and transform it into the kind of space John Nash had intended when he designed it in the 19th century.

Great For...

ⓘ Need to Know

Map p248; ⊖Charing Cross

★ **Top Tip**

Check www.london.gov.uk for events happening in the square during your stay, from street artists to open-air screens.

The Square

The square commemorates the 1805 victory of the British navy at the Battle of Trafalgar against the French and Spanish navies during the Napoleonic wars. The main square contains two beautiful fountains, which are dramatically lit at night. At each corner of the square is a plinth, three topped with statues of military leaders and the fourth, in the northeast corner, now an art space called the Fourth Plinth.

Note the much overlooked, if not entirely ignored, 19th-century brass plaques recording the precise length of imperial units – including the yard, the perch, pole, chain and link – set into the stonework and steps below the National Gallery (p55).

Nelson's Column

Standing in the centre of the square since 1843, the 52m-high Dartmoor granite Nelson's Column honours Admiral Lord Horatio Nelson, who led the fleet's heroic victory over Napoleon. The good (sandstone) admiral gazes down Whitehall towards the Houses of Parliament, his column flanked by four enormous bronze statues of lions sculpted by Sir Edwin Landseer and only added in 1867. The battle plaques at the base of the column were cast with seized Spanish and French cannons.

The Fourth Plinth

Three of the four plinths at Trafalgar Sq's corners are occupied by notables: King George IV on horseback, and military men

Exterior of the National Gallery (p55)

General Sir Charles Napier and Major General Sir Henry Havelock. The fourth, originally intended for a statue of William IV, has remained vacant for the past 150 years (although some say it is reserved for an effigy of Queen Elizabeth II, on her death).

In 1999 the Royal Society of Arts created the unimaginatively titled Fourth Plinth Project (www.london.gov.uk/what-we-do/arts-and-culture/art-and-design/fourth-plinth), to use the empty space for works by contemporary artists. They commissioned three works: *Ecce Homo* by Mark Wallinger (1999), a life-size statue of Jesus, which appeared tiny in contrast to the enormous plinth; Bill Woodrow's *Regardless of History* (2000); and Rachel Whiteread's *Monument* (2001), a resin copy of the plinth, turned upside down.

The mayor's office has since taken over what's now called the Fourth Plinth Commission, continuing with the contemporary-art theme. In 2018 the plinth was occupied by *The Invisible Enemy Should Not Exist*, by Michael Rakowitz, a re-creation of a sculpture destroyed by Isis. In 2020, it will be replaced by Heather Phillipson's *THE END*.

Admiralty Arch

To the southwest of Trafalgar Sq stands Admiralty Arch, from where the ceremonial Mall leads to Buckingham Palace. It is a grand Edwardian monument, a triple-arched stone entrance designed by Aston Webb in honour of Queen Victoria in 1910 and earmarked for transformation into a five-star hotel. The large central gate is opened only for royal processions and state visits.

What's Nearby?
St Martin-in-the-Fields   Church

(Map p248; ☑020-7766 1100; www.stmartin-in-the-fields.org; Trafalgar Sq, WC2; ⊙8.30am-1pm & 2-6pm Mon, Tue, Thu & Fri, 8.30am-1pm & 2-5pm Wed, 9.30am-6pm Sat, 3.30-5pm Sun; ⊖Charing Cross) The 'royal parish church' is a delightful fusion of classical and baroque styles. It was completed by James Gibbs in 1726 and serves as a model for many churches in New England. The church is well known for its excellent classical-music concerts, many by candlelight, and its links to the Chinese community (services in English, Mandarin and Cantonese). It usually closes for one hour at 1pm.

☑ Don't Miss

Every year, Norway gives London a huge Christmas tree, which is displayed on Trafalgar Sq, to commemorate Britain's help during WWII.

CLAUDIO DIVIZIA / SHUTTERSTOCK ©

✕ Take a Break

Gordon's Wine Bar (p181) has a wonderful selection of wines, and serves great platters of cheese and cold meats.

Covent Garden

London's first planned square is now mostly the preserve of visitors, who flock here to shop among the quaint old arcades, enjoy the many street artists' performances or visit some of the excellent nearby sights.

Great For...

ⓘ Need to Know

Map p248; ☎020-7836 5221;
⊖Covent Garden

★ **Top Tip**

Covent Garden tube station gets unpleasantly busy at weekends – walk to Leicester Sq instead.

History

Covent Garden was originally pastureland that belonged to a 'convent' associated with Westminster Abbey in the 13th century. The site was converted in the 17th century by architect Inigo Jones, who designed the elegant Italian-style piazza, which was dominated by a fruit and vegetable market. The market remained here until 1974 when it moved to South London.

The Piazza

Covent Garden seems to heave whatever the time of day or night. The arcades are chock-a-block with boutiques, market stalls, cafes, ice-cream parlours and restaurants. They're a magnet for street artists too.

The streets around the piazza are full of top-end boutiques, including famous British designers. Covent Garden is also home to the Royal Opera House and a number of theatres.

Sights
London Transport Museum
Museum

(Map p248; 020-7379 6344; www.ltmuseum. co.uk; Covent Garden Piazza, WC2; adult/child £17.50/free; ⊙10am-6pm) This entertaining and informative museum looks at how London developed as a result of better transport and contains everything from horse-drawn omnibuses and early taxis to underground trains you can drive yourself, plus everything in between. Immersive exhibition Hidden London, exploring the secret

London Transport Museum

history of underground London, opens in 2019. Check out the museum shop for imaginative souvenirs, including historical tube posters, and 'Mind the Gap' socks.

London Film Museum   Museum

(Map p248; ✆020-7836 4913; www.london filmmuseum.com; 45 Wellington St, WC2; adult/child £14.50/9.50; ⌚10am-6pm Sun-Fri, to 7pm Sat; ⊖Covent Garden) Recently moved from County Hall, south of the Thames, this museum's star attraction is its signature Bond In Motion exhibition. Get shaken and stirred at the largest official collection of 007 vehicles, including Bond's submersible Lotus Esprit *(The Spy Who Loved Me)*, the

---

☑ Don't Miss

Clambering over old tramways at the London Transport Museum, and street-artist performances.

GOGA18128 / SHUTTERSTOCK ©

---

iconic Aston Martin DB5, Goldfinger's Rolls Royce Phantom III and Timothy Dalton's Aston Martin V8 *(The Living Daylights)* and several of Daniel Craig's cars from *Spectre*..

Royal Opera House   Tours

(Map p248; ✆020-7304 4000; www.roh.org. uk; Bow St, WC2; adult/child general tours £9.50/7.50, backstage tours £12/8.50; ⌚general tour 4pm daily, backstage tour 10.30am, 12.30pm & 2.30pm Mon-Fri, 10.30am, 11.30am, 12.30pm & 1.30pm Sat; ⊖Covent Garden) On the north-eastern flank of Covent Garden piazza is the gleaming Royal Opera House. The 'Velvet, Gilt & Glamour Tour' is a general 45-minute turn around the auditorium; more distinctive are the 1¼-hour backstage tours taking you through the venue – a much better way to experience the preparation, excitement and histrionics before a performance.

What's Nearby?

Somerset House   Historic Building

(Map p245; ✆020-7845 4600; www.somerset house.org.uk; The Strand, WC2; ⌚galleries 10am-6pm, courtyard 7.30am-11pm, terrace 8am-11pm; ⊖Temple or Covent Garden) Designed by William Chambers in 1775 for royal societies, Somerset House now contains two fabulous galleries. Near the Strand entrance, the **Courtauld Gallery** (Map p245; http://courtauld.ac.uk; adult/child £8/free, temporary exhibitions vary; ⌚10am-6pm) displays a wealth of 14th- to 20th-century art, including masterpieces by Rubens, Botticelli, Cézanne, Degas, Renoir, Seurat, Manet, Monet, Léger and others. Downstairs, the Embankment Galleries are devoted to temporary (mostly photographic) exhibitions; prices and hours vary.

The grand Edmond J Safra Fountain Court hosts open-air live performances and films in summer, and ice skating in winter. The riverside terrace is a popular spot for coffee with a splendid view of the Thames.

✕ Take a Break

Join the tons of noodle diners at Shoryu (p148) and try the *tonkotsu* ramen.

COPYRIGHT ARTEM VOROBIEV / GETTY IMAGES / MOMENT OPEN ©

ENTRY TO THE TRAITORS GATE

Tower of London

With a history as bleak as it is fascinating, the Tower of London is now one of the city's top attractions, thanks in part to the Crown Jewels.

Great For...

☑ Don't Miss

Colourful Yeoman Warders, spectacular Crown Jewels, famous ravens, and armour fit for a king.

Begun during the reign of William the Conqueror (1066–87), the Tower is in fact a castle containing 22 towers.

Tower Green

The buildings to the west and the south of this verdant patch have always accommodated Tower officials. Indeed, the current constable has a flat in Queen's House built in 1540. But what looks at first glance like a peaceful, almost village-like slice of the Tower's inner ward is actually one of its bloodiest.

Scaffold Site & Beauchamp Tower

Those 'lucky' enough to meet their fate here (rather than suffering the embarrassment of execution on Tower Hill, observed by tens of thousands of jeering and cheering onlookers) numbered but a handful

Royal Armoury, White Tower (p66)

ⓘ Need to Know

Map p245; ☎0844 482 7777; www.hrp.
org.uk/tower-of-london; Petty Wales, EC3;
adult/child £24.80/11.50, audio guide £4/3;
🕙9am-4.30pm Tue-Sat, from 10am Sun-Mon;
🚇Tower Hill

✕ Take a Break

Opposite the Tower, **Wine Library** (Map
p245; ☎020-7481 0415; www.winelibrary.
co.uk; 43 Trinity Sq, EC3; buffet £18; 🕙buffet
11.30am-3.30pm) is great for lunch.

★ Top Tip

Book online for cheaper tickets.

and included two of Henry VIII's wives (and alleged adulterers), Anne Boleyn and Catherine Howard; 16-year-old Lady Jane Grey, who fell foul of Henry's daughter Mary I by attempting to have herself crowned queen; and Robert Devereux, Earl of Essex, once a favourite of Elizabeth I.

Just west of the scaffold site is brick-faced Beauchamp Tower, where high-ranking prisoners left behind unhappy inscriptions and other graffiti.

Chapel Royal of St Peter ad Vincula

Just north of the scaffold site is the 16th-century Chapel Royal of St Peter ad Vincula (St Peter in Chains), a rare example of ecclesiastical Tudor architecture. The church can be visited on a Yeoman Warder tour, or during the first and last hour of normal opening times.

Crown Jewels

To the east of the chapel and north of the White Tower is **Waterloo Barracks**, the home of the Crown Jewels, said to be worth up to £20 billion, but in a very real sense priceless. Here, you file past film clips of the jewels and their role through history, and of Queen Elizabeth II's coronation in 1953, before you reach the vault itself.

Once inside you'll be greeted by lavishly bejewelled sceptres, church plate, orbs and, naturally, crowns. A moving walkway takes you past the dozen or so crowns and other coronation regalia, including the platinum crown of the late Queen Mother, Elizabeth, which is set with the 106-carat Koh-i-Noor (Mountain of Light) diamond, and the State Sceptre with Cross topped with the 530-carat First Star of Africa (or Cullinan I) diamond. A bit further on, exhibited on its own, is the centrepiece: the Imperial State Crown, set with 2868 diamonds (including the 317-carat Second Star of Africa, or Cullinan II), sapphires, emeralds, rubies and pearls. It's worn by the Queen at the State Opening of Parliament in May/June.

White Tower

Built in stone as a fortress in 1078, this was the original 'Tower' of London – its name arose after Henry III whitewashed it in the 13th century. Standing just 30m high, it's not exactly a skyscraper by modern standards, but in the Middle Ages it would have dwarfed the wooden huts surrounding the castle walls and intimidated the peasantry.

Most of its interior is given over to a **Royal Armouries** collection of cannon, guns, and suits of mail and armour for men and horses. Among the most remarkable exhibits on the entrance floor are Henry VIII's two suits of armour, one made for him when he was a dashing 24-year-old and the other when he was a bloated 50-year-old

with a waist measuring 129cm. You won't miss the oversize codpiece. Also here is the fabulous **Line of Kings**, a late 17th-century parade of carved wooden horses and heads of historic kings. On the 1st floor, check out the 2m suit of armour once thought to have been made for the giantlike John of Gaunt and, alongside it, a tiny child's suit of armour designed for James I's young son, the future Charles I. Up on the 2nd floor you'll find the block and axe used to execute Simon Fraser at the last public execution on Tower Hill in 1747.

Medieval Palace & the Bloody Tower

The Medieval Palace is composed of three towers: St Thomas's, Wakefield and Langthorn. Inside **St Thomas's Tower** (1279) you can look at what the hall and

Royal bedroom, St Thomas's Tower

bedchamber of Edward I might once have been like. Here, archaeologists have peeled back the layers of newer buildings to find what went before. Opposite St Thomas's Tower is **Wakefield Tower**, built by Edward's father, Henry III, between 1220 and 1240. Its upper floor is entered from St Thomas's Tower and has been even more enticingly furnished with a replica throne and other decor to give an impression of how, as an anteroom in a medieval palace, it might have looked. During the 15th-century

Wars of the Roses between the Houses of York and Lancaster, King Henry VI was murdered as (it is said) he knelt in prayer in this tower. A plaque on the chapel floor commemorates this Lancastrian king. The **Langthorn Tower**, residence of medieval queens, is to the east.

Below St Thomas's Tower along Water Lane is the famous **Traitors' Gate**, the portal through which prisoners transported by boat entered the Tower. Opposite Traitors' Gate is the huge portcullis of the Bloody Tower, taking its nickname from the 'princes in the Tower' – Edward V and his younger brother, Richard – who were held here 'for their own safety' and later murdered to annul their claims to the throne. An exhibition inside looks at the life and times of Elizabethan adventurer Sir Walter Raleigh, who was imprisoned here three times by the capricious Elizabeth I and her successor James I.

East Wall Walk

The huge inner wall of the Tower was added to the fortress in 1220 by Henry III to improve the castle's defences. It is 36m wide and is dotted with towers along its length. The East Wall Walk allows you to climb up and tour its eastern edge, beginning in the 13th-century **Salt Tower**, probably used to store saltpetre for gunpowder. The walk also takes in **Broad Arrow Tower** and **Constable Tower**, each containing small exhibits. It ends at the **Martin Tower**, which houses an exhibition about the original coronation regalia. Here you can see some of the older crowns, with their precious stones removed. It was from this tower that Colonel Thomas Blood attempted to steal the Crown Jewels in 1671 disguised as a clergyman. He was caught but – surprisingly – Charles II gave him a full pardon.

GOGA81328 / SHUTTERSTOCK ©

Yeoman Warders

A true icon of the Tower, the Yeoman Warders have been guarding the fortress since at least the early 16th century. There can be up to 40 – they number 37 at present – and, in order to qualify for the job, they must have served a minimum of 22 years in any branch of the British Armed Forces. They all live within the Tower walls and are known affectionately as 'Beefeaters', a nickname they dislike.

Currently there are two female Yeoman Warders, Moira Cameron, who in 2007 became the first woman to be given the post, and Amanda Clarke, appointed in 2017. While officially they guard the Tower and Crown Jewels at night, their main role is as tour guides. Free tours leave from the bridge near the entrance every 30 minutes; the last tour is an hour before closing.

What's Nearby?

All Hallows by the Tower   Church

(Map p245; ☏020-7481 2928; www.ahbtt.org.uk; Byward St, EC3; ⊙8am-6pm Mon-Fri, 10am-5pm Sat & Sun Apr-Oct, 8am-5pm Mon-Fri, 10am-5pm Sat & Sun Nov-Mar; ⊖Tower Hill) All Hallows (meaning 'All Saints'), which dates to AD 675, survived virtually unscathed by the Great Fire, only to be hit by German bombs in 1940. Come to see the church itself, by all means, but the best bits are in the atmospheric undercroft (crypt), where you'll the discover a pavement of 2nd-century Roman tiles and the walls of the 7th-century Saxon church.

Monument   Tower

(Map p248; ☏020-7403 3761; www.the monument.org.uk; Fish St Hill, EC3; adult/child £5/2.50, incl Tower Bridge Exhibition £12/5.50; ⊙9.30am-5.30pm Apr-Sept, to 5pm Oct-Mar; ⊖Monument) Sir Christopher Wren's 1677 column, known simply as the Monument, is a memorial to the Great Fire of London of 1666, whose impact on London's history cannot be overstated. An immense Doric column made of Portland stone, the Monument is 4.5m wide and 60.6m tall – the exact distance it stands from the bakery in Pudding Lane where the fire is thought to have started.

The Monument is topped with a gilded bronze urn of flames that some think looks like a big gold pincushion. Although Lilliputian by today's standards, the Monument would have been gigantic when built, towering over London.

Climbing up the column's 311 spiral steps rewards you with some of the best 360-degree views over London (due to its central location as much as to its height). And after your descent, you'll also be the proud owner of a certificate that commemorates your achievement.

Leadenhall Market   Market

(Map p245; www.leadenhallmarket.co.uk; Whittington Ave, EC3; ⊙public areas 24hr; ⊖Bank) A visit to this covered mall off Gracechurch

Leadenhall Market

St is a step back in time. There's been a market on this site since the Roman era, but the architecture that survives is all cobblestones and late 19th-century Victorian ironwork. Leadenhall Market appears as Diagon Alley in *Harry Potter and the Philosopher's Stone* and an optician's shop was used for the entrance to the Leaky Cauldron wizarding pub in *Harry Potter and the Goblet of Fire*.

30 St Mary Axe   Notable Building
(Map p245; www.30stmaryaxe.info; 30 St Mary Axe, EC3; ⊖Aldgate) Nicknamed 'the Gherkin' for its unusual shape, 30 St Mary Axe is arguably the City's most distinctive skyscraper, dominating the skyline despite actually being slightly smaller than the neighbouring NatWest Tower. Built in 2003 by award-winning Norman Foster, the

Gherkin's futuristic exterior has become an emblem of modern London – as recognisable as Big Ben and the London Eye.

The building is closed to the public, though in the past it has opened its doors over the **Open House London** (☏020-7383 2131; www.openhouselondon.org.uk) weekend in September.

★ **Local Knowledge**
Common ravens, which once feasted on the corpses of beheaded traitors, have been here for centuries. Nowadays, they feed on raw beef and biscuits.

★ **Did You Know?**
Yeoman Warders are nicknamed Beefeaters. It's thought to be due to the rations of beef – then a luxury food – given to them in the past.

RANDI SOKOLOFF / SHUTTERSTOCK ©

A Sunday in the East End

The East End has a colourful, multicultural history. Waves of migrants (French Protestants, Jewish, Bangladeshi) have left their mark on the area; add in Cockney heritage and 21st-century hipsters for an incredibly vibrant neighbourhood.

Great For...

☑ **Don't Miss**

The area's food offering is as diverse as its population, from curry houses to modern British cuisine.

On Sundays, this whole area feels like one giant, sprawling market. It is brilliant fun, but pretty exhausting, so pace yourself – there are plenty of cafes and restaurants where you can sit down, relax and take in the atmosphere.

Columbia Road Flower Market

Stop to smell the roses amid the bedlam of London's most fragrant market. A wonderful explosion of colour and life, this weekly **market** (Map p253; www.columbiaroad.info; Columbia Rd, E2; ⏰8am-3pm Sun; ☒Hoxton) sells a beautiful array of flowers, pot plants, bulbs, seeds and everything you might need for the garden. It's a lot of fun and the best place to hear proper Cockney barrow-boy banter ('We got flowers cheap enough for ya muvver-in-law's grave' etc).

Old Spitalfields Market

(p158), where young designers sell their creations, along with arts-and-crafts and cracking food stalls.

Old Spitalfields Market

Traders have been hawking their wares here since 1638 and it's still one of London's best markets. Today's covered **market** (Map p253; www.oldspitalfieldsmarket.com; Commercial St, E1; ⏱10am-5pm Mon-Fri & Sun, 10am-6pm Sat; 🚇Liverpool St) was built in the late 19th century, with the more modern development added in 2006. Sundays are the biggest and best days, but Thursdays are good for antiques and Fridays for independent fashion. There are plenty of food stalls too.

At 84 Commercial St is the Ten Bells pub – famous as one of Jack the Ripper's possible pick-up joints – and across the road is the hulking presence of Christ Church. Running between the two, Fournier St is one of Spitalfields' most intact Georgian streetscapes. As you wander along, note the oddball, Harry Potterish numbering (11½ Fournier St) and keep an eye out for famous artsy residents Tracey Emin and Gilbert & George.

Brick Lane's Famous Bagels

A relic of the Jewish East End, **Brick Lane Beigel Bake** (Map p253; 159 Brick Lane, E2; bagels £1-4.10; ⏱24hr; 🚇Shoreditch High St) still makes a brisk trade serving dirt-cheap homemade bagels (filled with salmon, cream cheese and/or salt beef).

Brick Lane Markets

Head south towards **Brick Lane Market** (Map p253; www.visitbricklane.org; Brick Lane, E1; ⏱10am-5pm Sun; 🚇Shoreditch High St), which spills out into the surrounding streets with everything from household goods to bric-a-brac, secondhand clothes, cheap fashion and ethnic food. The best range and quality of products are to be found in the beautiful Old Truman Brewery (p73) markets: Sunday UpMarket (p158) and Backyard Market

Brick Lane Great Mosque

After some wandering, head over to this fascinating **mosque** (Map p253; Brick Lane Jamme Masjid; www.bricklanejammemasjid.co.uk; 59 Brick Lane, E1; 🚇Liverpool St). No building symbolises the different waves of immigration to Spitalfields quite as well as this one. Built in 1743 as the New French Church for the Huguenots, it was a Methodist chapel from 1819 until it was transformed into the Great Synagogue for Jewish refugees from Russia and Central Europe in 1898. In 1976 it changed faiths yet again, becoming the Great Mosque. Look for the sundial, high up on the Fournier St frontage.

Whitechapel Gallery

From Brick Lane Mosque, continue on to **Whitechapel Gallery** (Map p245; 020-7522 7888; www.whitechapelgallery.org; 77-82 Whitechapel High St, E1; 11am-6pm Tue, Wed & Fri-Sun, to 9pm Thu; Aldgate East) FREE. A firm favourite of art students and the avant-garde cognoscenti, this ground-breaking gallery doesn't have a permanent collection, but is devoted to hosting edgy exhibitions of contemporary art (only some of which are ticketed). It first opened the doors of its main art-nouveau building in 1901 and in 2009 it extended into the library next door, doubling its exhibition space to 10 galleries. It made its name by staging exhibitions by both established and emerging artists, including the first UK shows by Pablo Picasso, Jackson Pollock, Mark Rothko and Frida Kahlo.

What's Nearby?

Geffrye Museum   Museum
(Map p253; www.geffrye-museum.org.uk; 136 Kingsland Rd, E2; 10am-5pm Tue-Sun; Hoxton) FREE If you like nosing around other people's homes, you'll love this museum,

Geffrye Museum

entirely devoted to middle-class domestic interiors. Built in 1714 as a home for poor pensioners, these beautiful ivy-clad almshouses have been converted into a series of living rooms, dating from 1630 to the present day. The main building and rear gardens are currently closed for renovation, due to reopen in 2020. Activities in the front garden and tours of the almshouse are reasons to visit.

Dennis Severs' House · Museum

(Map p253; ☏020-7247 4013; www.dennissevers house.co.uk; 18 Folgate St, E1; day/night £10/15;

> ✕ **Take a Break**
>
> In the evening, check out **93 Feet East** (Map p253; www.93feeteast.co.uk; 150 Brick Lane, E1; ⊙6-11pm Thu, to 1am Fri & Sat, 3-10.30pm Sun; ⊝Liverpool St) on Brick Lane for DJs and cocktails.

DRIMAFILM / SHUTTERSTOCK ©

⊙noon-2pm & 5-9pm Mon, 5-9pm Wed & Fri, noon-4pm Sun; ⊝Liverpool St) This extraordinary Georgian house is set up as if its occupants had just walked out the door. There are half-drunk cups of tea, lit candles and, in a perhaps unnecessary attention to detail, a full chamber pot by the bed. More than a museum, it's an opportunity to meditate on the minutiae of everyday Georgian life through silent exploration.

Old Truman Brewery · Historic Building

(Map p253; www.trumanbrewery.com; 91 Brick Lane, E1; ☒Shoreditch High St) Founded here in the 17th century, Truman's Black Eagle Brewery was, by the 1850s, the largest brewery in the world. Spread over a series of brick buildings and yards straddling both sides of Brick Lane, the complex is now completely given over to edgy markets, pop-up fashion stores, vintage-clothes shops, indie record hunters, cafes, bars and live-music venues. Beer may not be brewed here any more, but it certainly is consumed.

After decades of decline, Truman's Brewery finally shut up shop in 1989 – temporarily as it turned out, with the brand subsequently resurrected in 2010 in new premises in Hackney Wick. In the 1990s the abandoned brewery premises found new purpose as a deadly cool hub for boozy Britpoppers and while it may not have quite the same cachet today, it's still plenty popular.

Several of the buildings are heritage listed, including the Director's House at 91 Brick Lane (built in the 1740s); the old Vat House directly opposite, with its hexagonal bell tower (c 1800); and the Engineer's House right next to it (at 150 Brick Lane), dating from the 1830s.

> ★ **Local Knowledge**
>
> There is plenty of graffiti to admire in the area but if you'd like to see a famous Banksy artwork, make a small detour to Cargo (p127).

Walking Tour: East End Eras

This route offers an insight into the old and new of East London. Wander through and soak up the unique character of its neighbourhoods.

Start ⊖ Bethnal Green
Distance 3.6 miles
Duration 2½ hours

3 Just over Regent's Canal lies **Victoria Park**. Take the left path along the lake to the **Dogs of Alcibiades** howling on plinths.

Mare St

Victoria Park Rd

Grove Rd

2 On beautifully preserved **Cyprus Street** you'll get a taste of what Victorian Bethnal Green would have looked like.

Regent's Canal

Cambridge Heath

1 The **Old Ford Rd** area was bombed during WWII, and tower blocks were subsequently erected on the bomb sites.

Old Ford Rd

Cyprus Pl

Cambridge Heath Rd

START
⊖ Bethnal Green

0
0
500 m
0.25 miles

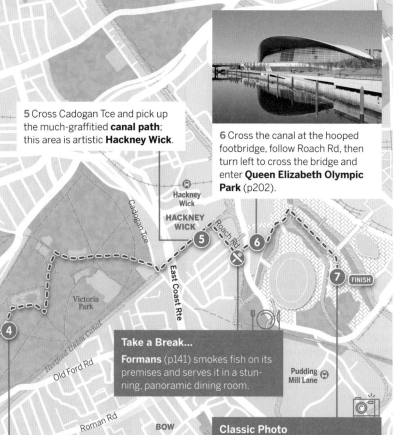

5 Cross Cadogan Tce and pick up the much-graffitied **canal path**; this area is artistic **Hackney Wick**.

6 Cross the canal at the hooped footbridge, follow Roach Rd, then turn left to cross the bridge and enter **Queen Elizabeth Olympic Park** (p202).

Hackney Wick

HACKNEY WICK

Cadogan Tce

Roach Rd

East Coast Rte

5 **6** **7** FINISH

Victoria Park

Hertford Union Canal

Old Ford Rd

4

Pudding Mill Lane

Take a Break...

Formans (p141) smokes fish on its premises and serves it in a stunning, panoramic dining room.

Roman Rd

BOW

Classic Photo

The ArcelorMittal Orbit at Queen Elizabeth Park.

4 Head to the eastern section of the park and see the **Burdett-Coutts Memorial** drinking fountain (1862). Then, pass **East Lake** and exit at the park's eastern tip.

7 Keep the main stadium on your right, cross the River Lea and walk through the playground towards the **ArcelorMittal Orbit**.

Borough Market

Overflowing with food lovers, inveterate gastronomes, wide-eyed visitors and Londoners in search of inspiration for their next dinner party, this fantastic market has become a sight in its own right.

Great For...

ⓘ Need to Know

Map p245; www.boroughmarket.org.uk; 8 Southwark St, SE1; ⏰10am-5pm Wed & Thu, to 6pm Fri, 8am-5pm Sat; ⊖London Bridge

★ **Top Tip**

To miss the worst of the crowds, avoid lunchtimes on Friday and Saturday.

Located here in some form or another since the 13th century, 'London's Larder' has enjoyed an astonishing renaissance in the past 15 years.

The market specialises in high-end fresh products, so you'll find the usual assortment of fruit and vegetable stalls, cheesemongers, butchers, fishmongers, bakeries and delis, as well as gourmet stalls selling spices, nuts, preserves and condiments. Prices tend to be high, but many traders offer free samples, a great perk for visitors and locals alike.

Food window-shopping (and sampling) over, you'll be able to grab lunch from one of the myriad takeaway stalls – anything from sizzling gourmet sausages to chorizo sandwiches and falafel wraps. There also seems to be an unreasonable number of cake stalls – walking out without a treat

will be a challenge! Many of the lunch stalls cluster in Green Market (the area closest to Southwark Cathedral). If you'd rather eat indoors, there are some fantastic cafes and restaurants too.

If you'd like some elbow space to enjoy your takeaway, walk five minutes in either direction along the Thames for river views.

Note that although the full market runs from Wednesday to Saturday, some traders and takeaway stalls do open Mondays and Tuesdays.

What's Nearby?
Southwark Cathedral   Church
(Map p245; ☎020-7367 6700; www.cathedral.
southwark.anglican.org; Montague Cl, SE1;
◎8am-6pm Mon-Fri, 8.30am-6pm Sat & Sun;
◉London Bridge) The earliest surviving
parts of this relatively small cathedral are

Southwark Cathedral

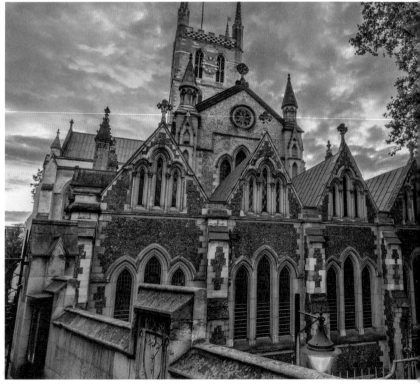

the retrochoir at the eastern end (which contains four chapels and was part of the 13th-century Priory of St Mary Overie), some ancient arcading by the southwest door and an arch that dates to the original Norman church. But most of the cathedral is Victorian. Inside are monuments galore, including a Shakespeare memorial. Catch evensong at 5.30pm on Tuesdays, Thursdays and Fridays, 4pm on Saturdays and 3pm on Sundays.

Shard   Notable Building

(Map p245; www.theviewfromtheshard.com; 32 London Bridge St, SE1; adult/child £30.95/24.95; ☺10am-10pm; ⊜London Bridge) Puncturing

> ### ☑ Don't Miss
> Grazing on free samples at the Borough Market or eating takeaway by the river.

PIOTR PAWEL / SHUTTERSTOCK ©

the skies above London, the dramatic splinter-like form of the Shard has rapidly become an icon of London. The viewing platforms on floors 68, 69 and 72 are open to the public and the views are, as you'd expect from a 244m vantage point, sweeping, but they come at a hefty price – book online at least a day in advance to save £5.

To take in the view for even less, visit one of the building's restaurants or bars; you can pay lower than half the viewing platform ticket price for breakfast or a cocktail and the views are still spectacular.

HMS Belfast   Ship

(Map p245; www.iwm.org.uk/visits/hms-belfast; Queen's Walk, SE1; adult/child £15.45/7.70; ☺10am-5pm; ⊜London Bridge) HMS *Belfast* is a magnet for naval-gazing kids of all ages. This large, light cruiser – launched in 1938 – served in WWII, helping to sink the German battleship *Scharnhorst* and shelling the Normandy coast on D-Day, and later participated in the Korean War. Its 6in guns could bombard a target 14 land miles distant. Displays offer a great insight into what life on board was like, in peace times and during military engagements.

Golden Hinde   Ship

(Map p245; ☏020-7403 0123; www.goldenhinde. co.uk; St Mary Overie Dock, Cathedral St, SE1; self-guided tours adult/child £5/3, events adult/ child £7/5; ☺10am-5pm; ♿; ⊜London Bridge) Stepping aboard this replica of Sir Francis Drake's famous Tudor ship will inspire genuine admiration for the admiral and his rather short (average height: 1.6m) crew, which counted between 40 and 60. It was in a tiny five-deck galleon just like this that Drake and his crew circumnavigated the globe from 1577 to 1580. Visitors can explore the ship by themselves or join a guided tour led by a costumed actor – children love these.

> ### ✕ Take a Break
> Arabica Bar & Kitchen (p148) serves up contemporary Middle Eastern fare.

ANDREW THOMAS / GETTY IMAGES ©

Tower Bridge

One of London's most recognisable sights, Tower Bridge doesn't disappoint in real life. Its neo-Gothic towers and sky-blue suspension struts add extraordinary elegance to what is a supremely functional structure.

Great For...

☑ Don't Miss
The bridge lifting and the view from the top (as well as down through the new glass floor).

History & Mechanics

Tower Bridge was designed by architect Horace Jones, who was also responsible for Smithfield and Leadenhall markets, and completed by engineer John Wolfe Barry. London was a thriving port in 1894 when the bridge was built as a much-needed crossing point in the east. It was equipped with a then-revolutionary steam-driven bascule (counter-balance) mechanism that could raise the roadway to make way for oncoming ships in just three minutes.

The bridge is still operational, although these days it's electrically powered and rises mainly for pleasure craft. It does so around 1000 times a year and as often as 10 times a day in summer; consult the Exhibition website for times to watch it in action.

Tower Bridge and the Shard (p79)

ⓘ Need to Know

Map p245; ⊖Tower Hill or London Bridge

✕ Take a Break

The **Watch House** (Map p245; www.the
watchhouse.com; 199 Bermondsey St, SE1;
mains from £4.95; ⊘7am-6pm Mon-Fri, 8am-
6pm Sat, 9am-5pm Sun; mains from £4.95;
⊖Borough), on the South Bank, sells
fabulous sandwiches and cakes from
local bakers. It does great coffee too.

★ Top Tip

For the best views of the bridge, pop
over to the southern bank of the river.

Tower Bridge Exhibition

A lift leads up from the northern tower
to the **Tower Bridge Exhibition** (Map
p245; ☏020-7403 3761; www.towerbridge.org.
uk; adult/child £9.80/4.20, incl the Monument
£12/5.50; ⊘10am-5.30pm Apr-Sep, 9.30am-
5pm Oct-Mar; ⊖Tower Hill), which explains
the nuts and bolts of it all. If you're not
technically minded, it's still fascinating to
get inside the bridge and look along the
Thames from its two walkways. A lift takes
you to the top of the structure, 42m above
the river, from where you can walk along
the east- and west-facing walkways, lined
with information boards.

The 11m-long glass floor, made of a
dozen see-through panels, is stunning –
acrophobes can take solace in knowing
that each weighs a load-bearing 530kg.
There are a couple of stops on the way

down before you exit and continue on to
the **Victorian Engine Rooms**, which house
the beautifully maintained steam engines
that powered the bridge lifts, as well as
some excellent interactive exhibits and a
couple of short films.

What's Nearby?
City Hall   Notable Building

(Map p245; www.london.gov.uk/city-hall; Queen's
Walk, SE1; ⊘8.30am-5.30pm Mon-Fri; ⊖London
Bridge) Home to the Mayor of London, bul-
bous City Hall was designed by Foster and
Partners and opened in 2002. The 45m,
glass-clad building has been compared to
a host of objects – from an onion, to Darth
Vader's helmet, a woodlouse and a 'glass
gonad'. The scoop amphitheatre outside
the building is the venue for a variety of
free entertainment in warmer weather,
from music to theatre.

Visitors can access the reception hall
and, more excitingly, sit in the Chamber if a
debate is taking place.

Tate Modern and the Millennium Bridge (p91)

Tate Modern

This phenomenally successful gallery combines stupendous architecture and a seminal collection of 20th-century modern art. A huge extension, opened in 2016, dramatically increased its display space.

Great For...

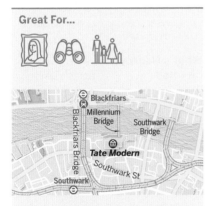

ⓘ Need to Know

Map p245; www.tate.org.uk; Bankside, SE1; ⏱10am-6pm Sun-Thu, to 10pm Fri & Sat; 🚻; 🚇Blackfriars, Southwark or London Bridge
FREE

★ **Top Tip**

Take the **Tate Boat** (www.tate.org.uk/visit/
tate-boat; one-way adult/child £8.30/4.15)
shuttle between Tate Britain (p52) and
Tate Modern.

Boiler House

The original gallery lies in what was once Bankside Power Station. Now called Boiler House, it is an imposing sight: a 200m-long building, made of 4.2 million bricks. Its conversion into an art gallery was a masterstroke of design: the 'Tate Modern effect' is clearly as much about the building and its location as it is about the mostly 20th-century art inside.

Turbine Hall

The first thing to greet you as you pour down the ramp off Holland St (the main entrance) is the astounding 3300-sq-metre Turbine Hall. Originally housing the power station's humongous electricity generators, this vast space has become the commanding venue for large-scale installation art and temporary exhibitions.

Switch House

The Tate Modern extension got its name from the former electrical substation that still occupies the southeast end of the site. It is also constructed of brick, although these are slightly lighter and artistically laid out as a lattice to let light in (and out – the building look stunning after dark).

The interior is rather stark, with raw, unpolished concrete vaguely reminiscent of decrepit brutalist buildings, but the exhibition space is fantastic, giving the collection the room it deserves to breathe and shine.

The Tanks

The three huge subterranean tanks once stored fuel for the power station. These unusual circular spaces are now dedicated to showing live art, performance, installation and film, or 'new art' as the Tate calls it.

Interior of Shakespeare's Globe

Viewing Gallery: Level 10

The views from level 10 are, as you would expect, sweeping. The river views are perhaps not quite as iconic as the full frontal St Paul's view you get from Boiler House, but you get to see Boiler House itself, and a lot more in every direction. The views of the Shard looking east are especially good. And best of all, they are free.

Permanent Collection

Tate Modern's permanent collection is arranged on levels 2 and 4 of Boiler House and levels 0, 2, 3 and 4 of Switch House,

KAMIRA / SHUTTERSTOCK ©

which focuses on art from the 1960s onwards.

More than 60,000 works are on constant rotation. The curators have at their disposal paintings by Georges Braque, Henri Matisse, Piet Mondrian, Andy Warhol, Mark Rothko and Jackson Pollock, as well as pieces by Joseph Beuys, Damien Hirst, Rebecca Horn, Claes Oldenburg and Auguste Rodin.

A great place to begin is the **Start Display** on level 2 of Boiler House: this small, specially curated 'taster' display features some of the best-loved works in the collection and gives useful pointers for how to tackle unfamiliar (and an overwhelming amount of) art.

Special Exhibitions

Special exhibitions are found on levels 3 and 4 of Boiler House and level 2 of Switch House (£12.50 to £18.50, children free). In 2019 don't miss Van Gogh and Britain, a major exhibition exploring Vincent van Gogh's relationship with Britain, where he lived between 1873 and 1876.

What's Nearby?
Shakespeare's
Globe   Historic Building

(Map p245; ☎020-7902 1500; www.shake spearesglobe.com; 21 New Globe Walk, SE1; adult/child £17/10; ⊗9.30am-5pm; 🚻; ⊖Blackfriars or London Bridge) Unlike other venues for Shakespearean plays, the new Globe was designed to resemble the original as closely as possible, which means having the arena open to the fickle London skies, leaving the 700 'groundlings' to stand in London's spectacular downpours. Visits to the Globe include tours of the theatre (half-hourly, generally in the morning from 9.30am, with afternoon tours on Monday too) as well as access to the exhibition space, which has fascinating exhibits about Shakespeare and theatre in the 17th century.

St Paul's Cathedral

St Paul's Cathedral is one of the most majestic buildings in London. Despite the far-higher skyscrapers of the Square Mile, it still manages to gloriously dominate the skyline.

Great For...

ⓘ Need to Know

Map p245; ☎020-7246 8357; www.stpauls.co.uk; St Paul's Churchyard, EC4; adult/child £18/8; ⏱8.30am-4.30pm Mon-Sat; ⊖St Paul's

★ Top Tip

A visit to the church's hallowed ground must be made to fully appreciate its sublime architecture.

There has been a place of Christian worship on this site for over 1400 years. St Paul's Cathedral as we know it is the fifth Christian church to be erected here; it was completed in 1711 and sports the largest church dome in the capital.

Dome

Despite the cathedral's rich history and impressive (and uniform) English baroque interior, many visitors are more interested in climbing the dome for one of the best views of London. The dome actually consists of three parts: a plastered brick inner dome, a nonstructural lead outer dome visible on the skyline and a brick cone between them holding it all together, one inside the other. This unique structure, the first triple dome ever built and second only in size to St Peter's in the Vatican, made the cathedral Christopher Wren's tour de force. It all weighs 59,000 tonnes.

Some 528 stairs take you to the top, but it's a three-stage journey. Through a door on the western side of the southern transept, and some 30m and 257 steps above, you reach the interior walkway around the dome's base. This is the **Whispering Gallery**, so called because if you talk close to the wall it carries your words around to the opposite side, 32m away. Climbing even more steps (another 119) you reach the **Stone Gallery**, an exterior viewing platform 53m above the ground, obscured by pillars and other suicide-preventing measures. The remaining 152 iron steps to the **Golden Gallery** are steeper and narrower than below, but are really worth the effort. From here,

Interior of St Paul's Cathedral

85m above London, you can enjoy superb 360-degree views of the city.

Interior

Just beneath the dome is an **epitaph** written for Wren by his son: *Lector, si monumentum requiris, circumspice* (Reader, if you seek his monument, look around you). In the north aisle you'll find the grandiose **Duke of Wellington Memorial** (1912), which took 54 years to complete – the Iron Duke's horse Copenhagen originally faced the other way, but it was deemed unfitting that a horse's rear end should face the altar.

☑ Don't Miss

Climbing the dome, witnessing the quire ceiling mosaics and visiting the tombs of Admiral Nelson and the Duke of Wellington.

In the north transept chapel is William Holman Hunt's celebrated painting **The Light of the World**, which depicts Christ knocking at a weed-covered door that, symbolically, can only be opened from within. Beyond, in the cathedral's heart, you'll find the spectacular **quire** (or chancel) – its ceilings and arches dazzling with green, blue, red and gold mosaics telling the story of Creation – and the **high altar**. The ornately carved choir stalls by Dutch-British sculptor Grinling Gibbons on either side of the quire are exquisite, as are the ornamental wrought-iron gates, separating the aisles from the altar, by Huguenot Jean Tijou (both men also worked on Hampton Court Palace).

Walk around the altar, with its massive gilded oak **baldacchino** – a kind of canopy with barley-twist columns – to the **American Memorial Chapel**, commemorating the 28,000 Americans based in Britain who lost their lives during WWII. Note the Roll of Honour book turned daily, the state flags in the stained glass and American flora and fauna in the carved wood panelling.

In the south quire aisle, Bill Viola's new and very poignant **video installation** *Martyrs (Earth, Air, Fire, Water)* depicts four figures being overwhelmed by natural forces. A bit further on is an **effigy of John Donne** (1573–1631), metaphysical poet and one-time dean of Old St Paul's that survived the Great Fire.

Crypt

On the eastern side of both the north and south transepts are stairs leading down to the crypt and the **OBE Chapel**, where services are held for members of the Order of the British Empire.

KOTSOVOLOS PANAGIOTIS / SHUTTERSTOCK ©

✕ Take a Break

The **Crypt Cafe** (Map p245; ☎020-7248 1574; www.searcysstpauls.co.uk; Crypt, St Paul's Cathedral, EC4; mains from £8; ☺9am-5pm; ⊖St Paul's) is open for light meals from 9am.

The crypt has memorials to around 300 of the great and the good, including Florence Nightingale, TE Lawrence (of Arabia) and Winston Churchill, while both the Duke of Wellington and Admiral Nelson are actually buried here. On the surrounding walls are plaques in memory of those from the Commonwealth who died in various conflicts during the 20th century, including Gallipoli and the Falklands War.

Wren's tomb is also in the crypt, and many others, notably painters such as Joshua Reynolds, John Everett Millais, JMW Turner and William Holman Hunt, are remembered here too.

The **Oculus**, in the former treasury, projects four short films onto its walls (you'll need the iPad audio tour to hear the sound). If you're not up to climbing the dome, experience it here audiovisually.

Churchyard & Surrounds

Just outside the north transept, there's a simple **monument to the people of London**, honouring the 32,000 civilians killed (and another 50,000 seriously injured) in the city during WWII. Nearby is St Paul's Cross, topped by a gilded statue of the saint – an Edwardian replacement for the original preaching cross that was removed in 1643. Also to the north, at the entrance to Paternoster Sq, is **Temple Bar**, the only surviving gateway to the old City of London. This medieval stone archway once straddled Fleet St at a site marked by a silver dragon, but was removed to Middlesex in 1877. It was placed here in 2004.

Tours

The easiest way to explore the cathedral is by joining a free 1½-hour guided tour, which grants you access to the Geometric Staircase, the Chapel of St Michael and St George, and the quire. These usually take place four times a day (10am, 11am, 1pm and 2pm) Monday to Saturday; head to the desk just past the entrance to check times and book a place. You can also enquire here about the shorter introductory 15- to 20-minute talks.

What's Nearby?
Museum of London   Museum
(Map p245; ☏020-7001 9844; www.museum oflondon.org.uk; 150 London Wall, EC2; ⊙10am-6pm; ⊖Barbican) FREE One of the capital's best museums, this is a fascinating walk through the various incarnations of the city, from Roman Londinium and Anglo-Saxon Ludenwic to 21st-century metropolis, contained in two-dozen galleries. There are a lot of interactive displays with an emphasis on experience rather than learning.

Highlights include a video on the 1348 Black Death, a section of London's old Roman wall, the graffitied walls of a prison cell (1750), a glorious re-creation of a Victorian street, a 1908 taxi cab, a 1928 art deco lift from Selfridges and moving testimonies from ordinary Londoners from WWII.

Millennium Bridge and St Paul's Cathedral (p86)

Free half-hour highlights tours depart daily at 11am, noon, 3pm and 4pm.

Millennium Bridge
Bridge

(Map p245; ⊖St Paul's, Blackfriars) The elegant steel, aluminium and concrete Millennium Bridge staples the south bank of the Thames, in front of Tate Modern, with the north bank, at the steps of Peter's Hill below St Paul's Cathedral. The low-slung frame designed by Sir Norman Foster and Antony Caro looks spectacular, particularly when lit up at night with fibre optics, and the view of St Paul's from the South Bank has become one of London's iconic images.

St Mary-le-Bow
Church

(Map p245; ☎020-7248 5139; www.stmarylebow. co.uk; Cheapside, EC2; ☺7.30am-6pm Mon-Thu, to 4pm Fri; ⊖St Paul's or Bank) One of Wren's great churches, St Mary-le-Bow (1673) is famous as the church with the bells that still dictate who is – and who is not – a true Cockney: it's said that a true Cockney has to have been born within earshot of Bow Bells. The church's delicate steeple showing the four classical orders is one of Wren's finest works.

★ **Local Knowledge**

The cathedral underwent a major clean-up in 2011. To see the difference, check the section of unrestored wall under glass by the Great West Door.

★ **Top Tip**

If you'd rather explore St Paul's on your own, pick up one of the free 1½-hour multimedia tours available at the entrance.

GAGLIARDIIMAGES / SHUTTERSTOCK ©

London Eye (p94)

The South Bank

Ever since the London Eye came up in 2000, the South Bank has become a magnet for visitors and the area is always a buzz of activity. A roll call of riverside sights stretches along the Thames, commencing with the London Eye, running past the cultural enclave of the Southbank Centre and on to the Tate Modern.

Great For...

ⓘ Need to Know

Map p245; ⓇWaterloo, ⊖Southwark

★ **Top Tip**
Book online for the London Eye and
London Dungeon to skip queues.

VALDIS SKUDRE / SHUTTERSTOCK ©

The South Bank has a great vibe. As well as top attractions, there is plenty to take in while enjoying a stroll: views of the north bank of London (including great views of the Houses of Parliament and Big Ben), street artists, office workers on their lunchtime run, and boats toing and froing along the Thames.

South Bank Sights

London Eye   Viewpoint

(Map p245; ☏0871 222 4002; www.londoneye. com; adult/child £27/22; ☺11am-6pm Sep-May, 10am-8.30pm Jun-Aug; ☻Waterloo or Westminster) Standing 135m high in a fairly flat city, the London Eye affords views 25 miles in every direction, weather permitting. Interactive tablets provide great information (in six languages) about landmarks as they

come up in the skyline. Each rotation takes a gracefully slow 30 minutes. At peak times (July, August and school holidays) it may seem like you'll spend more time in the queue than in the capsule, however. Save time and money by buying tickets online.

Southbank Centre   Arts Centre

(Map p245; ☏020-3879 9555; www.southbank centre.co.uk; Belvedere Rd, SE1; ⚟; ☻Waterloo or Embankment) The flagship venue of the Southbank Centre, Europe's largest centre for performing and visual arts, is the **Royal Festival Hall**. Its gently curved facade of glass and Portland stone is more humane than its 1970s Brutalist neighbours. It is one of London's leading music venues and the epicentre of life on this part of the South Bank.

Imperial War Museum

Just north, the austere Queen Elizabeth Hall (p192), which includes the **Purcell Room**, is a Brutalist icon and the second-largest concert venue in the centre, hosting chamber orchestras, quartets, choirs, dance performances and sometimes opera. Underneath its elevated floor is a graffiti-decorated skateboarders' hang-out known as the **undercroft**, due for refurbishment and extension in 2019.

The opinion-dividing 1968 **Hayward Gallery** (Map p245; www.southbankcentre. co.uk; Belvedere Rd, SE1; ⊜Waterloo), another Brutalist beauty, is a leading contemporary-art exhibition space.

EUGENE REGIS / SHUTTERSTOCK ©

London Dungeon   Historic Building

(Map p245; www.thedungeons.com/london; County Hall, Westminster Bridge Rd, SE1; adult/child £30/24; ⊘10am-4pm Mon-Wed & Fri, 11am-4pm Thu, 10am-6pm Sat, 10am-5pm Sun; 🚹; ⊜Waterloo or Westminster) Older kids tend to love the London Dungeon, as the terrifying queues during school holidays and weekends testify. It's all spooky music, ghostly boat rides, macabre hangman's drop-rides, fake blood and actors dressed up as torturers and gory criminals (including Jack the Ripper and Sweeney Todd). Beware the interactive bits.

What's Nearby?

Roupell St   Street

(Map p245; Roupell St, SE1; ⊜Waterloo) Waterloo station isn't exactly scenic, but wander around the backsteets of this transport hub and you'll find some amazing architecture. Roupell St is an astonishingly pretty row of workers' cottages, all dark bricks and coloured doors, dating back to the 1820s. The street is so uniform it looks like a film set.

Imperial War Museum   Museum

(📞020-7416 5000; www.iwm.org.uk; Lambeth Rd, SE1; ⊘10am-6pm; ⊜Lambeth North) FREE Fronted by a pair of intimidating 15in naval guns, this riveting museum is housed in what was the Bethlehem Royal Hospital, also known as Bedlam. Although the museum's focus is on military action involving British or Commonwealth troops largely during the 20th century, it rolls out the carpet to war in the wider sense. The highlight of the collection is the state-of-the-art **First World War Galleries**, opened in 2014 to mark the centenary of the war's outbreak.

The museum is a short tube or bus ride from the South Bank and well worth the effort for anyone interested in WWI or WWII.

BRIAN MINKOFF / SHUTTERSTOCK ©

Hyde Park

One of London's largest royal parks spreads itself over 142 hectares of neat gardens, wild expanses of overgrown grass and glorious trees. As well as being a fantastic green space in the middle of London, it is home to a handful of fascinating sights.

Great For...

☑ **Don't Miss**

The opulence of Apsley House, the Albert Memorial, Royal Albert Hall (p189) and Kensington Palace.

Henry VIII expropriated Hyde Park from the church in 1536, after which it emerged as a hunting ground for kings and aristocrats; later it became a popular venue for duels, executions and horse racing. It was the first royal park to open to the public in the early 17th century, the famous venue of the Great Exhibition in 1851, and during WWII it became a vast potato bed. These days, as well as being an exquisite park, it is an occasional concert and music-festival venue.

Green Spaces

The eastern half of the park is covered with expansive lawns, which become one vast picnic-and-frolic area on sunny days. The western half is more untamed, with plenty of trees and areas of wild grass.

Speakers' Corner

Frequented by Karl Marx, Vladimir Lenin, George Orwell and William Morris,

The Serpentine lake and Hyde Park

ⓘ Need to Know

Map p250; www.royalparks.org.uk/parks/
hyde-park; ⊙5am-midnight; ⊖Marble Arch,
Hyde Park Corner or Queensway

Take Break

Magazine (p144) has a contemporary
take on afternoon tea.

★ Top Tip

Hyde Park is an ideal picnic stop between sights.

Speakers' Corner (Map p250; Park Lane;
⊖Marble Arch) in the northeastern corner
of Hyde Park is traditionally the spot for
oratorical acrobatics and soapbox ranting.

It's the only place in Britain where dem-
onstrators can assemble without police
permission, a concession granted in 1872
after serious riots 17 years before when
150,000 people gathered to demonstrate
against the Sunday Trading Bill before Parliament, only to be unexpectedly ambushed
by police concealed within Marble Arch.

The Serpentine & Galleries

Hyde Park is separated from Kensington
Gardens by the L-shaped **Serpentine** (Map
p250; ✆020-7262 1330; ⊖Knightsbridge or
South Kensington), a small lake.

Straddling the Serpentine lake, the Serpentine Galleries may look like quaint historical buildings, but they are one of London's
most important contemporary-art galleries.
Damien Hirst, Andreas Gursky, Louise Bour-
geois, Gabriel Orozco, Tomoko Takahashi
and Jeff Koons have all exhibited here.

The original exhibition space, **Serpentine Gallery** (Map p250; ✆020-7402
6075; www.serpentinegalleries.org; Kensington
Gardens, W2; ⊙10am-6pm Tue-Sun; ⊖Lancas-
ter Gate or Knightsbridge) **FREE**, is the 1930s
former tea pavillion located in Kensington
Gardens. In 2013 the **Serpentine Sackler
Gallery** (Map p250; ✆020-7402 6075; www.
serpentinegalleries.org; West Carriage Dr, W2;
⊙10am-6pm Tue-Sun; ⊖Lancaster Gate) **FREE**
opened within the Magazine, a former
gunpowder depot across the Serpentine
Bridge in Hyde Park. Built in 1805, it has
been augmented with a daring, undulating
extension designed by Pritzker Prize–win-
ning architect Zaha Hadid.

Apsley House

This stunning house, containing exhibits
about the Duke of Wellington, who defeated
Napoleon Bonaparte at Waterloo, was once
the first building to appear when entering
London from the west and was therefore known as 'No 1 London'. Wellington
memorabilia, including the duke's death

mask, fills the basement gallery, while an astonishing collection of china and silver, and paintings by Velasquez, Rubens, Van Dyck, Brueghel, Murillo and Goya awaits in the 1st-floor Waterloo Gallery.

Diana, Princess of Wales Memorial Fountain

This **memorial fountain** (Map p250; off West Carriage Dr; ⊙10am-8pm Apr-Aug, to 7pm Sep, to 6pm Mar & Oct, to 4pm Nov-Feb; ⊖Knightsbridge or Lancaster Gate) is dedicated to the late Princess of Wales. Designed by Kathryn Gustafson as a 'moat without a castle', the circular double stream is composed of 545 pieces of Cornish granite, its waters drawn from a chalk aquifer more than 100m below ground. Unusually, visitors are actively encouraged to splash about, to the delight of children.

Gun Salutes

Royal Gun Salutes are fired in Hyde Park on 10 June for the Duke of Edinburgh's birthday and on 14 November for the Prince of Wales' birthday. The salutes are fired at midday and include 41 rounds (21 is standard, but being a royal park, Hyde Park gets a bonus 20 rounds).

What's Nearby?

Kensington Palace   Palace

(Map p250; www.hrp.org.uk/kensington-palace; Kensington Gardens, W8; adult/child (when booked online) £15.50/free; ⊙10am-4pm Nov-Feb, to 6pm Mar-Oct; ⊖High St Kensington) Built in 1605, the palace became the favourite royal residence under William and Mary of Orange in 1689, and remained so until George III became king and relocated to Buckingham Palace. Today, it is still a

Kensington Gardens

royal residence, home to the Duke and Duchess of Cambridge (Prince William and Catherine) and their children. The Duke and Duchess of Sussex (Prince Harry and Meghan) live in Nottingham Cottage in the Kensington Palace grounds, and Princess Eugenie of York and Jack Brooksbank live next door in Ivy Cottage

A large part of the palace is open to the public, however, including the King's and Queen's State Apartments. The **King's State Apartments** are the most lavish, starting with the **Grand Staircase**, a dizzying feast of trompe l'oeil. The beautiful

> ### ☑ Don't Miss
> Each year an architect who has never built in the UK is commissioned to build a 'Summer Pavilion' (June to October) for the Serpentine Galleries.

CHRIS JENNER / SHUTTERSTOCK ©

Cupola Room, once the venue of choice for music and dance, is arranged with gilded statues and a gorgeous painted ceiling. The **Drawing Room** is beyond, where the king and courtiers would entertain themselves with cards.

Visitors can also access **Victoria's apartments** where Queen Victoria (1819–1901) was born and lived until she became Queen. An informative narrative about her life is told through a few personal effects, extracts from her journals and plenty of visual props.

Kensington Gardens   Park
(Map p250; ☑0300 061 2000; www.royalparks.org.uk/parks/kensington-gardens; ⊙6am-dusk; ⊖Queensway or Lancaster Gate) Immediately west of Hyde Park and across the Serpentine lake, these picturesque 275-acre gardens are technically part of Kensington Palace. The park is a gorgeous collection of manicured lawns, tree-shaded avenues and basins. The largest is the **Round Pond**, close to the palace. Also worth a look are the lovely fountains in the **Italian Gardens** (Map p250; Kensington Gardens; ⊖Lancaster Gate), believed to be a gift from Albert to Queen Victoria.

Albert Memorial   Monument
(Map p250; ☑tours 020-8969 0104; Kensington Gardens; tours adult/concession £9/8; ⊙tours 2pm & 3pm 1st Sun of month Mar-Dec; ⊖Knightsbridge or Gloucester Rd) This splendid Victorian confection on the southern edge of Kensington Gardens is as ostentatious as the subject. Queen Victoria's German husband Albert (1819–61), was purportedly humble. Albert explicitly insisted he did not want a monument; ignoring the good prince's wishes, the Lord Mayor instructed George Gilbert Scott to build the 53m-high, gaudy Gothic memorial in 1872.

> ### ★ Top Tip
> Deckchairs are available for hire (one/four hours £1.60/4.60) throughout the park from March to October.

Victoria & Albert Museum

The Museum of Manufactures, as the V&A was known when it opened in 1852, was part of Prince Albert's legacy to the nation in the aftermath of the successful Great Exhibition of 1851. Its aims were the 'improvement of public taste in design' and 'applications of fine art to objects of utility'. It's done a fine job so far.

Great For...

ℹ Need to Know

Map p250; V&A; ☎020-7942 2000; www.vam.ac.uk; Cromwell Rd, SW7; ⊙10am-5.45pm Sat-Thu, to 10pm Fri; ⊖South Kensington `FREE`

★ **Top Tip**

The V&A's temporary exhibitions are reliably fantastic, so factor some time to check them out.

Collection

Through 146 galleries, the museum houses the world's greatest collection of decorative arts, from ancient Chinese ceramics to modernist architectural drawings, Korean bronze and Japanese swords, cartoons by Raphael, gowns from the Elizabethan era, ancient jewellery, a Sony Walkman – and much, much more.

Entrance

Entering under the stunning blue-and-yellow blown-glass chandelier by Dale Chihuly, you can grab a museum map (£1 donation requested) at the information desk. (If the 'Grand Entrance' on Cromwell Rd is too busy, there's another around the corner on Exhibition Rd, or you can enter from the tunnel in the basement, if arriving by tube.)

Tours

Several free one-hour guided tours leave the main reception area every day. Times are prominently displayed; alternatively, check the website for details.

Level 1

The street level is mostly devoted to art and design from India, China, Japan, Korea and Southeast Asia, as well as European art. One of the museum's highlights is the **Cast Courts** in rooms 46a and 46b, containing staggering plaster casts collected in the Victorian era, such as Michelangelo's *David*, acquired in 1858.

The **T.T. Tsui Gallery** (rooms 44 and 47e) displays lovely pieces, including a beautifully lithe wooden statue of Guanyin seated in *lalitasana* pose from AD 1200; also check

Ceramics Gallery

out a leaf from the *Twenty Views of the Yuanmingyuan Summer Palace* (1781–86), revealing the Haiyantang and the 12 animal heads of the fountain (now ruins) in Beijing. Within the subdued lighting of the **Japan Gallery** (room 45) stands a fearsome suit of armour in the Domaru style. More than 400 objects are within the **Islamic Middle East Gallery** (room 42), including ceramics, textiles, carpets, glass and woodwork from the 8th century up to the years before WWI. The exhibition's highlight is the gorgeous mid-16th-century **Ardabil Carpet**.

The landscaped **John Madejski Garden** is a lovely shaded inner courtyard. Cross it to reach the original **Refreshment Rooms**

ANTON_IVANOV / SHUTTERSTOCK ©

(Morris, Gamble and Poynter Rooms), dating from the 1860s and redesigned by McInnes Usher McKnight Architects (MUMA), who also renovated the **Medieval and Renaissance galleries** (1350–1600) to the right of the Grand Entrance.

Levels 2 & 4

The **British Galleries**, featuring every aspect of British design from 1500 to 1900, are divided between levels 2 (1500–1760) and 4 (1760–1900). Level 4 also boasts the **Architecture Gallery** (rooms 127 to 128a), which vividly describes architectural styles via models and videos, and the spectacular, brightly illuminated **Contemporary Glass Gallery** (room 129).

Level 3

The **Jewellery Gallery** (rooms 91 to 93) is outstanding; the mezzanine level – accessed via the glass-and-perspex spiral staircase – glitters with jewel-encrusted swords, watches and gold boxes. The **Photographs Gallery** (room 100) is one of the nation's best, with access to over 500,000 images collected since the mid-19th century. **Design Since 1946** (room 76) celebrates design classics, from a 1985 Sony credit-card radio to a 1992 Nike 'Air Max' shoe, Peter Ghyczy's Garden Egg Chair from 1968 and the now-ubiquitous selfie stick.

Level 6

Among the pieces in the **Ceramics Gallery** (rooms 136 to 146) – the world's largest – are standout items from the Middle East and Asia. The **Dr Susan Weber Gallery** (rooms 133 to 135) celebrates furniture design over the past six centuries.

PIG.J / SHUTTERSTOCK ©

Natural History Museum

This colossal building (a reason in itself to visit) is infused with the Victorian spirit of collecting, cataloguing and interpreting the natural world. Seasonal events and excellent temporary exhibitions make it one of the London's best, especially for families.

Great For...

☑ **Don't Miss**

The animatronic *Tyrannosaurus rex*, planet-earth displays, Darwin Centre and Gothic architecture.

Hintze Hall

This grand central hall resembles a cathedral nave – quite fitting for a time when the natural sciences were challenging the biblical tenets of Christian orthodoxy. Naturalist and first superintendent of the museum Richard Owen celebrated the building as a 'cathedral to nature'.

Since summer 2017, the hall has been dominated by the skeleton of a blue whale, displayed in a diving position for dramatic effect. It replaced the diplodocus skeleton cast, which had been the hall's main resident since the 1960s. The hall also features new displays giving a taster of what the museum holds in store.

Blue Zone

Undoubtedly the museum's star attraction, the **Dinosaurs Gallery** takes you on an impressive overhead walkway, past a

Hintze Hall

ⓘ Need to Know

Map p250; www.nhm.ac.uk; Cromwell Rd, SW7; ⏰10am-5.50pm; ⊖South Kensington FREE

✕ Take a Break

The Queen's Arms (p177) beckons with a cosy interior and a right royal selection of ales and ciders on tap.

★ Top Tip

Families can borrow an 'explorer backpack' or buy a themed discover trail (£1).

dromaeosaurus (a small and agile meat eater) before reaching a roaring animatronic T-rex and then winding its way through skeletons, fossils, casts and fascinating displays about how dinosaurs lived and died.

Another highlight of this zone is the **Mammals & Blue Whale Gallery**, with its life-size blue-whale model and extensive displays on cetaceans.

Green Zone

While children love the Blue Zone, adults may prefer the Green Zone, especially the **Treasures in Cadogan Gallery**, on the 1st floor, which houses the museum's most prized possessions, each with a unique history. Exhibits include a chunk of moon rock, an emperor-penguin egg collected by Captain Scott's expedition and a 1st edition of Charles Darwin's *On the Origin of Species*.

Equally rare and exceptional are the gems and rocks held in the **Vault**, including a Martian meteorite and the largest emerald ever found.

Take a moment to marvel at the trunk section of a 1300-year-old **giant sequoia tree** on the 2nd floor: its size is mind-boggling.

Back on the ground floor, the **Creepy Crawlies Gallery** is fantastic, delving into every aspect of insect life and whether they are our friends or foes (both!).

Red Zone

This zone explores the ever-changing nature of our planet and the forces shaping it. In the Volcanoes & Earthquakes Gallery, the **earthquake simulator**, which re-creates the 1995 Kobe earthquake in a grocery store (of which you can see footage) is a favourite, as is the **From the Beginning Gallery**, which retraces earth's history.

In **Earth's Treasury**, you can find out more about our planet's mineral riches and how they are being used in our everyday lives, from jewellery to construction and electronics.

Access to most of the galleries in the Red Zone is via **Earth Hall** and a very tall escalator that disappears into a large earth-metal sculpture. The most intact **stegosaurus fossil skeleton** ever found is displayed at the base.

Orange Zone

The **Darwin Centre** is the beating heart of the museum: this is where the museum's millions of specimens are kept and where its scientists work. The top two floors of the amazing '**cocoon**' building are dedicated to explaining the kind of research the museum does (and how) – windows allow you to see the researchers at work.

If you'd like to find out more, pop into the **Attenborough studio** (named after famous naturalist and broadcaster David Attenborough) for one of the daily talks with the museum's scientists. The studio also shows films throughout the day.

Exhibitions

The museum hosts regular exhibitions (admission fees apply), some of them on a recurrent basis. **Wildlife Photographer of the Year** (Map p250; www.nhm.ac.uk; adult/child £13.50/8, family £28-38; ⊘Oct-Sep), with its show-stopping images, recently celebrated its 50th year, and **Sensational Butterflies**, a tunnel tent on the East Lawn that swarms with what must originally have been called 'flutter-bys', has become a firm summer favourite.

Gardens

A slice of English countryside in SW7, the beautiful **Wildlife Garden** next to the West Lawn encompasses a range of British

Science Museum

lowland habitats, including a meadow with farm gates and a bee tree where a colony of honey bees fills the air.

The museum is transforming its outdoor spaces, tripling the Wildlife Garden in size, creating a piazza in the eastern grounds and adding a geological and palaeontological timeline walk.

From Halloween to January, the Sensational Butterflies lawn is transformed into a glittering and highly popular **ice-skating rink**, complete with a hot drinks stall. Our advice: book your slot well ahead, browse the museum and skate later.

★ Top Tip

As well as the obligatory dinosaur figurines and animal soft toys, the museum's shop has a fantastic collection of children's books.

TUPUNGATO / SHUTTERSTOCK ©

What's Nearby?

Science Museum   Museum
(Map p250; ☎020-7942 4000; www.science museum.org.uk; Exhibition Rd, SW7; ⊙10am-6pm; ⊖South Kensington) FREE With seven floors of interactive and educational exhibits, this scientifically spellbinding museum will mesmerise adults and children alike, covering everything from early technology to space travel. A perennial favourite is **Exploring Space**, a gallery featuring genuine rockets and satellites and a full-size replica of *Eagle*, the lander that took Neil Armstrong and Buzz Aldrin to the moon in 1969. The **Making the Modern World Gallery** next door is a visual feast of locomotives, planes, cars and other revolutionary inventions.

The fantastic **Information Age Gallery** on level 2 showcases how information and communication technologies – from the telegraph to smartphones – have transformed our lives since the 19th century. Standout displays include wireless sent by a sinking *Titanic,* the first BBC radio broadcast and a Soviet BESM 1965 supercomputer.

The 3rd-floor **Flight Gallery** (free tours 1pm most days) is a favourite, with its gliders, hot-air balloons and aircraft, including the *Gipsy Moth,* which Amy Johnson flew to Australia in 1930. There's also a **Red Arrows 3D flight simulation theatre** (adult/child £6/5) and **Fly 360-degree flight simulator capsules** (£12 per capsule). **Launchpad** is stuffed with (free) hands-on gadgets exploring physics and the properties of liquids.

If you've kids under the age of five, pop down to the basement and the **Garden**, where there's a fun-filled play zone, including a water-play area, besieged by tots in orange waterproof smocks.

★ Did You Know?

The entire Natural History Museum and its gardens cover a huge 5.7 hectares; the museum contains 80 million specimens from across the natural world.

LUKASZ PAJOR / SHUTTERSTOCK ©

Leicester Square & Piccadilly Circus

This duo's buzz makes up for what they lack in cultural cachet. It's all flashing signs and crowds, yet no London visit would be complete without passing through these iconic places.

Great For...

☑ Don't Miss

Celebrity-spotting at film premieres on Leicester Sq.

Piccadilly Circus

John Nash had originally designed Regent St and Piccadilly in the 1820s to be the two most elegant streets in town but, curbed by city planners, couldn't realise his dream to the full. He may be disappointed, but suitably astonished, with Piccadilly Circus today: a traffic maelstrom, deluged with visitors and flanked by flashing advertisement panels.

At the centre of the circus stands the famous aluminium statue of Anteros (twin brother of Eros), dedicated to the philanthropist and child-labour abolitionist Lord Shaftesbury. Through the years, the figure has been mistaken for Eros, the God of Love, and the misnomer has stuck (you'll even see signs for 'Eros' from the Underground).

Piccadilly Circus

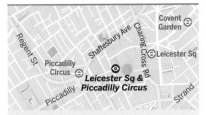

🛈 Need to Know

Map p248; ⊖Leicester Sq

✕ Take a Break

For delicious Levantine food with atti-tude, head to Palomar (p149).

★ Top Tip

Tkts Leicester Sq (www.tkts.co.uk/leicester-square; The Lodge, Leicester Sq, WC2; ⊙10am-7pm Mon-Sat, 11am-4.30pm Sun; ⊖Leicester Sq) has bargain tickets to West End performances.

What's Nearby?
Chinatown   Area

(Map p248; www.chinatownlondon.org; ⊖Leicester Sq) Immediately north of Leicester Sq – but a world away in atmosphere – are Lisle and Gerrard Sts, a focal point for London's growing Chinese community. Although not as big as Chinatowns in many other cities – it's just two streets really – this is a lively quarter with oriental gates, Chinese street signs, red lanterns, restaurants, great Asian supermarkets and shops. The quality of food varies enormously, but there's a good choice of places for dim sum and other cuisine from across China.

To see it at its effervescent best, visit at Chinese New Year in late January/early February. Twenty years ago you would only hear Cantonese but these days you'll hear Mandarin and other dialects, from places as far afield as Fujian, Sichuan and Shanghai. London's original Chinatown was further east at Limehouse but moved here after heavy bombardments in WWII.

Leicester Square

Although Leicester Sq was very fashionable in the 19th century, more recent decades won it associations with pickpocketing, out-rageous cinema-ticket prices and the nick-name 'Fester Sq' during the 1979 Winter of Discontent strikes, when it was filled with refuse. As part of the Diamond Jubilee and 2012 Olympics celebrations, the square was given an extensive £15.5-million make-over to turn it once again into a lively plaza. Today a sleek, open-plan design replaces the once-dingy little park.

It retains its many cinemas and night-clubs, and as a glamorous premiere venue it still attracts celebrities and their spotters.

Pickpocketing used to be rife around Leicester Sq; things have improved but do keep a very close eye on your belongings.

Sunken Garden, Hampton Court Palace

Day Trip: Hampton Court Palace

London's most spectacular Tudor palace, this 16th-century icon concocts an imposing sense of history, from the huge kitchens and grand living quarters to the spectacular gardens, complete with a 300-year-old maze. Tag along with a themed tour led by a costumed historian or grab one of the audio tours to delve into Hampton Court and its residents' tumultuous history.

Great For...

❶ Need to Know

www.hrp.org.uk/hamptoncourtpalace; Hampton Court Palace, KT8; adult/child/family £19/10/34; ⏱10am-4.30pm Nov-Mar, to 6pm Apr-Oct; 🚢Hampton Court Palace, 🚉Hampton Court

★ **Top Tip**

Ask one of the red-tunic-garbed warders for anecdotes and information.

Hampton Court Palace was built by Cardinal Thomas Wolsey in 1515, but was coaxed from him by Henry VIII just before Wolsey (as chancellor) fell from favour. In the 17th century Sir Christopher Wren was commissioned to build an extension on what was one of the most sophisticated European palaces. The result is a beautiful blend of Tudor and 'restrained baroque' architecture.

Entering the Palace

Passing through the magnificent main gate, you arrive in the **Base Court** and beyond that **Clock Court**, named for its 16th-century astronomical clock. The panelled rooms and arched doorways in the **Young Henry VIII's Story** upstairs from Base Court are a rewarding introduction: note the Tudor graffiti on the fireplace.

Henry VIII's Apartments

The stairs inside Anne Boleyn's Gateway lead up to Henry VIII's Apartments, including the stunning **Great Hall**. The **Horn Room**, hung with impressive antlers, leads to the **Great Watching Chamber**, where guards controlled access to the king. Henry VIII's dazzling gemstone-encrusted **crown** has been re-created – the original was melted down by Oliver Cromwell – and sits in the **Royal Pew** (open 10am to 4pm Monday to Saturday and 12.30pm to 1.30pm Sunday), which overlooks the beautiful **Chapel Royal** (still a place of worship after 450 years).

Tudor Kitchens & Great Wine Cellar

Also dating from Henry's day are the delightful Tudor kitchens, once used to rustle up meals for a royal household of some

Great Hall

1200 people. Don't miss the Great Wine Cellar, which handled the 300 barrels each of ale and wine consumed here annually in the mid-16th century.

Cumberland Art Gallery

The restored Cumberland Suite off Clock Court (designed in the 1730s by William Kent, for the Duke of Cumberland) is the venue for viewing a staggering collection of artworks from the Royal Collection, including Rembrandt's *Self-portrait in a Flat Cap* (1642) and Sir Anthony van Dyck's *Charles I on Horseback* (c 1635–6).

☑ Don't Miss

The Great Hall, the Chapel Royal, William III's apartments, the gardens and maze, and Henry VIII's crown.

THE PICTURE STUDIO / SHUTTERSTOCK ©

William III's & Mary II's Apartments

A tour of William III's Apartments, completed by Wren in 1702, takes you up the grand **King's Staircase**. Highlights include the **King's Presence Chamber**, dominated by a throne backed with scarlet hangings. Don't miss the sumptuous **King's Great Bedchamber** (its bed topped with ostrich plumes) and the **King's Closet** (where His Majesty's toilet has a velvet seat). Restored in 2014, the unique **Chocolate Kitchens** were built for William and Mary in around 1689.

William's wife Mary II had her own apartments, accessible via the fabulous **Queen's Staircase** (decorated by William Kent).

Georgian Private Apartments

The Georgian Rooms were used by George II and Queen Caroline on the court's last visit to the palace in 1737. Do not miss the fabulous Tudor **Wolsey Closet** with its early 16th-century ceiling and painted panels, commissioned by Henry VIII.

Garden & Maze

Beyond the palace are the stunning gardens; keep an eye out for the **Real Tennis Court**, dating from the 1620s. The **Kitchen Garden** is a magnificent re-creation of the original one designed for William and Mary.

Don't leave Hampton Court without getting lost in the 800m-long **maze** (adult/child/family £4.20/2.60/12.30; ☺10am-5.15pm Apr-Oct, to 3.45pm Nov-Mar), accessible to those not entering the palace.

★ Top Tip

From April to September, **Westminster Passenger Services Association** (☏020-7930 2062; www.wpsa.co.uk; Westminster Pier, Victoria Embankment, SW1; Kew adult/child one-way £13/6.50, return £20/10, Hampton Court one-way £17/8.50, return £25/12.50; ☺10am-4pm Apr-Oct; ☻Westminster) runs a boat service here from Westminster.

LUKASZ PAJOR / SHUTTERSTOCK ©

Royal Observatory & Greenwich Park

The Royal Observatory, atop a hill within leafy, regal Greenwich Park, is where the study of the sea, the stars and time converge. The prime meridian charts its line through the grounds, dividing the globe into eastern and western hemispheres.

Great For...

☑ Don't Miss

Straddling hemispheres and time zones as you stand astride the actual meridian line in the Meridian Courtyard.

Royal Observatory

Unlike most attractions in Greenwich, the Royal Observatory contains free-access areas (Weller Astronomy Galleries, Great Equatorial Telescope) and ones you pay for (Meridian Line, Flamsteed House).

Flamsteed House & Meridian Courtyard

Charles II ordered construction of the Christopher Wren–designed Flamsteed House, the original observatory building, on the foundations of Greenwich Castle in 1675 after closing the observatory at the Tower of London. Today it contains the magnificent **Octagon Room** and the rather simple apartment where the Astronomer Royal, John Flamsteed, and his family lived. Here you'll also find the brilliant new **Time Galleries**, explaining how the longitude

Flamsteed House

BASPHOTO / SHUTTERSTOCK ©

❶ Need to Know

Map p256; www.rmg.co.uk; Greenwich Park, Blackheath Ave, SE10; adult/child £10/6.50, incl Cutty Sark £20/11.50; ⏰10am-5pm Sep-Jun, to 6pm Jul & Aug; ⓇDLR Cutty Sark, DLR Greenwich or Greenwich

✕ Take a Break

Enjoy a drink with river views on the side at the **Cutty Sark Tavern** (Map p256; ☎020-8858 3146; www.cuttysarkse10. co.uk; 4-6 Ballast Quay, SE10; ⏰11.30am-11pm Mon-Sat, noon-10.30pm Sun; 🕾; ⓇDLR Cutty Sark).

★ Top Tip

Get here before 1pm during the week to see the red Time Ball drop.

problem – how to accurately determine a ship's east-west location – was solved through astronomical means and the invention of the marine chronometer.

In the Meridian Courtyard, where the globe is decisively sliced into east and west, visitors can delightfully straddle both hemispheres, with one foot on either side of the meridian line. Every day the red **Time Ball** at the top of the Royal Observatory drops at 1pm, as it has done ever since 1833.

Astronomy Centre & Planetarium

The southern half of the observatory contains the highly informative (and free) **Weller Astronomy Galleries**, where you can touch the oldest object you will ever encounter: part of the Gibeon meteorite, a mere 4.5 billion years old. Other engaging exhibits include an orrery (a mechanical

model of the solar system, minus the as-yet-undiscovered Uranus and Neptune) from 1780, astronomical documentaries, a first edition of Newton's *Principia Mathematica* and the opportunity to view the Milky Way in multiple wavelengths. To take stargazing further, pick up a Skyhawk telescope from the shop.

The state-of-the-art **Peter Harrison Planetarium** (Map p256; ☎020-8312 6608; www.rmg.co.uk/whats-on/planetarium-shows; Greenwich Park, SE10; adult/child £8/5.50; ⓇGreenwich or DLR Cutty Sark) – London's only planetarium – can cast entire heavens onto the inside of its roof. It runs at least five informative shows a day. Bookings advised.

Greenwich Park

The **park** (Map p256; ☎0300 061 2380; www.royalparks.org.uk; King George St, SE10; ⏰6am-around sunset; ⓇDLR Cutty Sark, Greenwich or Maze Hill) is one of London's loveliest green expanses, with a rose garden, picturesque walks, Anglo-Saxon tumuli and astonishing views from the crown of the hill near the Royal Observatory towards Canary Wharf, the financial district across the Thames.

Covering 74 hectares, this is the oldest enclosed royal park and is partly the work of André Le Nôtre, the landscape architect who designed the palace gardens of Versailles.

Ranger's House (Wernher Collection)

This elegant Georgian **villa** (Map p256; 020-8294 2548; www.english-heritage.org.uk; Greenwich Park, Chesterfield Walk, SE10; adult/child £9/5.40; guided tours 11.30am & 2pm Sun-Wed late Mar-Sep; Greenwich or DLR Cutty Sark), built in 1723, once housed the park's ranger and now contains a collection of

700 works of fine and applied art (medieval and Renaissance paintings, porcelain, silverware, tapestries) amassed by Julius Wernher (1850–1912), a German-born railway-engineer's son who struck it rich in the diamond fields of South Africa in the 19th century.

What's Nearby?

Old Royal Naval College   Historic Building

(Map p256; www.ornc.org; 2 Cutty Sark Gardens, SE10; 10am-5pm, grounds 8am-11pm; DLR Cutty Sark) FREE Designed by Christopher Wren, the Old Royal Naval College is a magnificent example of monumental classical architecture. Parts are now used by the University of Greenwich and Trinity College of Music, but you can still visit the **chapel** and the extraordinary **Painted Hall** (only

View of London from Geenwich Park

viewable via guided tour until 2019 while it undergoes conservation work), which took artist Sir James Thornhill 19 years to complete. Hour-long, yeomen-led tours (£6) of the complex leave at noon daily, taking in areas not otherwise open to the public.

Cutty Sark
Museum

(Map p256; ☏020-8312 6608; www.rmg.co.uk/cuttysark; King William Walk, SE10; adult/child £13.50/7; ☺10am-5pm Sep-Jun, to 6pm Jul & Aug; ▨DLR Cutty Sark) This Greenwich landmark, the last of the great clipper ships to sail between China and England in the 19th century, was closed for six years for an extensive £25-million renovation, largely

JILLIAN CAIN PHOTOGRAPHY / SHUTTERSTOCK ©

precipitated by a disastrous fire in 2007. The exhibition in the ship's hold tells its story as a tea clipper at the end of the 19th century (and then wool and mixed cargo).

Launched in 1869 in Scotland, *Cutty Sark* made eight voyages to China in the 1870s, sailing out with a mixed cargo and coming back with a bounty of tea. As you make your way up, there are films, interactive maps and plenty of illustrations and props to convey what life on board was like. Sleepovers for kids are available.

National Maritime Museum
Museum

(Map p256; ☏020-8312 6565; www.rmg.co.uk/national-maritime-museum; Romney Rd, SE10; ☺10am-5pm; ▨DLR Cutty Sark) **FREE** Narrating the long and eventful history of seafaring Britain, the museum's exhibits are arranged thematically. Highlights include *Miss Britain III* (the first boat to top 100mph on open water) from 1933; the 19m-long golden state barge built in 1732 for Frederick, Prince of Wales; the huge ship's propeller, and the colourful figureheads installed on the ground floor. Families will love these, as well as the ship simulator and the children's gallery on the 2nd floor.

Adults are likely to prefer the fantastic (and slightly more serene) galleries such as **Voyagers: Britons and the Sea** on the ground floor, or the award-winning **Nelson, Navy, Nation 1688–1815**, which focuses on the history of the Royal Navy during the conflict-ridden 17th century. It provides an excellent look at the legendary national hero; the coat in which Nelson was fatally wounded during the Battle of Trafalgar takes pride of place.

GABRIELLE GELSI / SHUTTERSTOCK ©

King's Cross

Formerly a dilapidated red-light district, King's Cross used to be a place better avoided. Fast-forward a couple of decades, though, and the area has metamorphosed, now boasting cool hang-outs and luxury hotels.

Great For...

☑ Don't Miss

The Sir John Ritblatt Gallery at the British Library, Gasholder Park and the fountain on Granary Square.

Granary Square   Square

(Map p254; www.kingscross.co.uk; Stable St, N1)
Next to a sharp bend in the Regent's Canal north of King's Cross Station, Granary Sq is at the heart of a major redevelopment of a 27-hectare expanse once full of abandoned freight warehouses. Its most striking feature is a fountain made of 1080 individually lit water jets, which pulse and dance in sequence. On hot spring and summer days, it becomes a busy urban beach.

British Library   Library

(Map p254; www.bl.uk; 96 Euston Rd, NW1; ⏱galleries 9.30am-6pm Mon & Wed-Fri, to 8pm Tue, to 5pm Sat, 11am-5pm Sun) **FREE**
Consisting of low-slung red-brick terraces and fronted by a large plaza featuring an oversize statue of Sir Isaac Newton, Colin St John Wilson's British Library building is a love-it-or-hate-it affair (Prince Charles

Interior of the British Library

once likened it to a secret-police academy). Completed in 1998, it's home to some of the greatest treasures of the written word, including the Codex Sinaiticus (the first complete text of the New Testament), Leonardo da Vinci's notebooks and a copy of the Magna Carta (1215).

The most precious manuscripts are held in the **Sir John Ritblatt Gallery**, including the stunningly illustrated Jain sacred texts, explorer Captain Scott's final diary and Shakespeare's First Folio (1623). Music fans will love the Beatles' handwritten lyrics and original scores by Bach, Handel, Mozart and Beethoven.

St Pancras Station & Hotel   Historic Building

(Map p254; ☑020-8241 6921; www.stpancras london.com; Euston Rd, NW1) Looking at the jaw-dropping Gothic splendour of St

Pancras, it's hard to believe that the 1873 Midland Grand Hotel languished empty for years and even faced demolition in the 1960s. Now home to a five-star hotel, luxury apartments and the Eurostar terminal, the complex has been returned to its former glory. Tours take you up the glorious grand staircase (the real star of the Spice Girls' 'Wannabe' video) and along the exquisitely decorated corridors into one of the 37 remaining original Victorian rooms. They then head into the station proper, where sky-blue iron girders arc over what was, at the time, the largest unsupported space ever built.

Gasholder Park   Park

(Map p254) Part of the area's impressive redevelopment, this urban green space right by Regent's Canal is a masterpiece of regeneration. The cast-iron structure used to be the frame of Gasholder No 8, the area's largest gas storage cylinder (originally located across the canal). Carefully renovated, and with the addition of a central lawn, beautiful benches and a mirrored canopy, it has metamorphosed into a gorgeous pocket park.

Walking Tour: A Northern Point of View

This walk takes in North London's most interesting locales, including celebrity-infested Primrose Hill and chaotic Camden Town, home to loud guitar bands and the last of London's punks.

Start ⊖Chalk Farm
Distance 2.5 miles
Duration 2 hours

Classic Photo
London's skyline from atop Primrose Hill

2 In **Primrose Hill**, walk to the top of the park, where you'll find a classic view of central London's skyline.

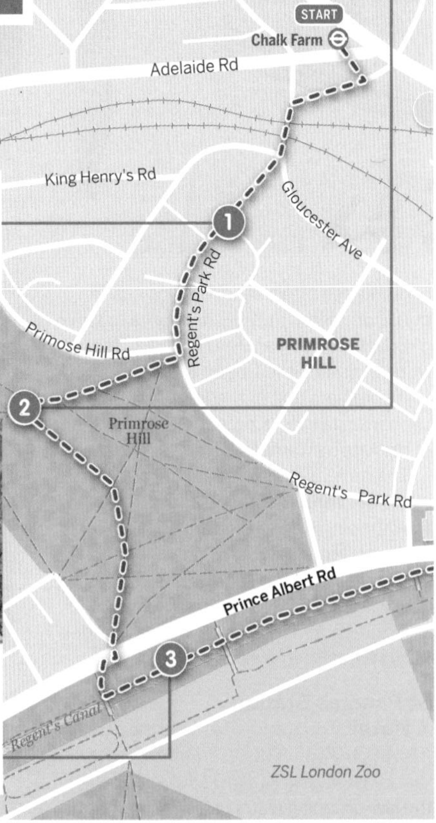
START
Chalk Farm
Adelaide Rd
King Henry's Rd
Gloucester Ave
Regent's Park Rd
Primrose Hill Rd
PRIMROSE HILL
Primrose Hill
Regent's Park Rd
Prince Albert Rd
Regent's Canal
ZSL London Zoo

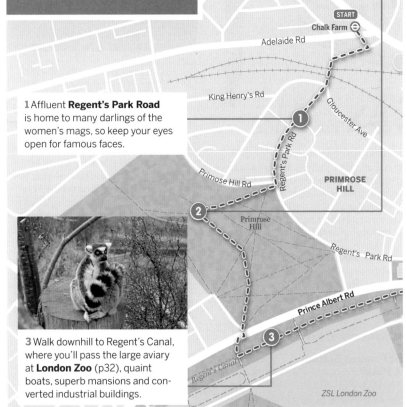

1 Affluent **Regent's Park Road** is home to many darlings of the women's mags, so keep your eyes open for famous faces.

3 Walk downhill to Regent's Canal, where you'll pass the large aviary at **London Zoo** (p32), quaint boats, superb mansions and converted industrial buildings.

0 —————————— 400 m
0 —————————— 0.2 miles

4 At **Camden Lock** turn left into buzzing **Lock Market** (p163), with its original fashion, ethnic art and food stalls.

5 Exit onto **Camden High Street** and turn right onto bar-lined **Inverness Street**, which hosts its own little market.

Chalk Farm Rd

Camden Lock Pl

Camden High St

CAMDEN TOWN

Regent's Canal

Jamestown Rd

Princess Rd

Gloucester Ave

Gloucester Cres

Inverness St

Oval Rd

6 At **Gloucester Crescent** turn left and walk past the glorious Georgian town houses.

Parkway

Take a Break
Food collective **KERB** (p145) offers an A to Z of world cuisine.

Delancey St

FINISH

Regent's Park

Albany St

7 Head towards Delancey St and make a beeline for the **Edinboro Castle** (p182), where this walk ends with a well-deserved drink!

2 JAN-OTTO / GETTY IMAGES © 3 MARCELA NOVOTNA / SHUTTERSTOCK © 4 CEDRIC WEBER / SHUTTERSTOCK ©

Palm House (p124)

Day Trip: Kew Gardens

The gardens at Kew are one of the finest products of British botanical imagination and really should not be missed. Don't worry if you don't know your quiver tree from your alang-alang, a visit to Kew is a journey of discovery for all.

Great For...

Kew Gardens

Syon Park

Mortlake Rd

River Thames

Kew Rd

Kew Gardens

Fulham Cemetery

ℹ Need to Know

www.kew.org; Kew Rd, TW9; adult/child £17/5; ⊙10am-4.15pm Sep-Mar, closes later Apr-Aug; ⊖Kew Bridge

★ **Top Tip**

Kew is a big place so if you're pressed for time, or getting tired, take the **Kew Explorer** (☏020-8332 5648; www.kew.org/kew-gardens/whats-on/kew-explorer-land-train; adult/child £5/2), a hop-on/hop-off road train that takes in the main sights.

In 1759 botanists began rummaging around the world for specimens to plant in the 3-hectare Royal Botanic Gardens at Kew. They never stopped collecting, and the gardens, which have bloomed to 121 hectares, provide the most comprehensive botanical collection on earth (including the world's largest collection of orchids). A Unesco World Heritage Site, the gardens can easily devour a day's exploration.

As well as being a public garden, Kew is a pre-eminent research centre, maintaining its reputation as the most exhaustive botanical collection in the world.

Conservatories

Assuming you travel by tube and enter via Victoria Gate, you'll come almost immediately to the enormous and elaborate 700-glass-paned **Palm House**, a domed hothouse of metal and curved sheets of glass dating from 1848, enveloping a splendid display of exotic tropical greenery; an aerial walkway offers a parrot's-eye view of the lush vegetation. Just northwest of the Palm House stands the tiny and irresistibly steamy **Waterlily House** (☉Mar-Dec), sheltering the gigantic *Victoria cruziana* waterlily, whose vast pads can support the weight of a small adult.

In the southeast of Kew Gardens, **Temperate House** (built in 1860) is the world's largest surviving Victorian glasshouse, covering 4880 sq metres. It reopened in 2018 after five years of vital restoration work.

The angular **Princess of Wales Conservatory** houses plants in 10 different climatic zones – everything from a desert to a mangrove swamp. Look out for stone plants, which resemble pebbles (to deter

Exterior of the Palm House

grazing animals), carnivorous plants, gigantic waterlilies, cacti and a collection of tropical orchids.

Great Pagoda

Kew's 49.5m-tall eight-sided Great Pagoda (1762), designed by William Chambers (the architect of Somerset House), is one of the gardens' architectural icons. During WWII, the pagoda withstood the blast from a stick of Luftwaffe bombs exploding nearby, and was also secretly employed by the Ministry of Defence to test bomb trajectories (which involved cutting holes in each floor).

At the time of writing, the pagoda was closed for restoration, but it is set to reopen to the public in mid-2018. Restoration includes the reinstatement of 80 winged dragons that were part of the original design but disappeared shortly after the tower's inauguration.

Kew Palace

Built in 1631 and the smallest of the royal palaces, adorable red-brick **Kew Palace** (www.hrp.org.uk/kewpalace; ⊙10.30am-5.30pm Apr-Sep), in the northwest of the gardens, is a former royal residence once known as Dutch House. It was the favourite home of George III and his family; his wife, Queen Charlotte, died here in 1818 (you can see the very chair in which she expired). Don't miss the restored **Royal Kitchens** next door.

Arboretum

Covering two thirds of the gardens, the **Arboretum** refers to the more than 14,000 trees at Kew, which are often gathered together according to genera. You can find everything from eucalyptus trees to giant redwoods and Japanese pagoda trees.

Treetop Walkway

In the Arboretum, this fascinating walkway first takes you underground and then 18m up in the air into the tree canopy (a big hit with kids).

Other Highlights

Several long vistas, **Cedar Vista**, **Syon Vista** and **Pagoda Vista**, are channelled by trees from vantage points within Kew Gardens. The idyllic, thatched **Queen Charlotte's Cottage** (⊙11am-4pm Sat & Sun Apr-Sep) in the southwest of the gardens was popular with 'mad' George III and his wife; the carpets of bluebells around here are a drawcard in spring. The **Marianne North Gallery** displays the botanical paintings of Marianne North, an indomitable traveller who roamed the continents from 1871 to 1885, painting plants along the way.

MARK CHILVERS / LONELY PLANET ©

✕ Take a Break

The aptly named Glasshouse (p145) restaurant, with its Michelin star, is the perfect conclusion to a day exploring the gardens.

DIVERSE IMAGES / GETTY IMAGES ©

A Night Out in Shoreditch

Shoreditch has been at the vanguard of cool and edgy bars and clubs for a decade. If you're after good times, there is no better place to come to.

Great For...

☑ Don't Miss

Banksy's famous security guard and poodle graffiti in Cargo's courtyard (visible from the street).

Pre-dinner Drinks

Start your evening at **Kick** (Map p253; www.cafekick.co.uk; 127 Shoreditch High St, E1; ⊙noon-11pm Sun-Thu, to 1am Fri & Sat; 🛜; 🚉Shoreditch High St), where you'll be able to make the best of the generous happy hour (till 7pm daily) and enjoy a couple of games of table football on the side.

For something more cerebral, head to the **Book Club** (Map p253; 📞020-7684 8618; www.wearetbc.com; 100-106 Leonard St, EC2A; ⊙9am-midnight Mon-Wed, to 2am Thu & Fri, 10am-2am Sat, to midnight Sun; 🛜; ⊖Old St), where you could be drawn into anything from a life-drawing lesson to a perfume workshop.

Dinner

Having worked up an appetite, head over to **Sông Quê** (Map p253; www.songque.co.uk; 134 Kingsland Rd, E2; mains £7.20-9.50; ⊙noon-

❶ Need to Know

Map p253; ⊖Old St, ⓡHoxton or
Shoreditch High St

✖ Take a Break

The 24-hour Brick Lane Beigel Bake
(p71) is a godsend for refueling at any
time of the day or night.

★ Top Tip

Not a night owl? No problem, the area
is abuzz with eclectic markets (p70) on
Sundays.

3pm & 5.30-11pm Mon-Fri, noon-11pm Sat, to
10.30pm Sun; ⓡHoxton), one of the best and
longest-standing Vietnamese restaurants
on the 'pho mile' (the area is home to a
large Vietnamese community). The food is
filling and cheap – just what you need for
the night ahead.

Noodles not your thing? As well as host-
ing fabulous live music six nights a week,
Old Street Records (Map p253; ☑020-3006
5911; www.oldstreetrecords.com; 350-354 Old St,
EC1; ⊗5pm-midnight Mon-Wed, to 2am Thu-Sat;
⊖Old St) makes mean pizzas.

Cocktail O'Clock

With a belly full of noodles (or pizza), it's
time for after-dinner cocktails. On spring
and summer nights, head to the glorious
Shoreditch Sky Terrace (Map p253; ☑020-
3310 5555; www.shoreditch.courthouse-hotel.

com; 335-337 Old St, EC1; ⊗4pm-midnight
May-Oct; 🛜; ⊖Old St) for alfresco drinking
and DJs. The rest of the year, the fabulous
Calloch Callay (Map p253; ☑020-7739 4781;
www.calloohcallaybar.com; 65 Rivington St, EC2A;
⊗6pm-1am Mon-Sat; ⊖Old St) won't leave you
wanting, with cocktails as exquisite as the
dimly lit interior. Allow £10 to £12 per drink.

Clubbing

With the night in full swing, you'll have
to fight your way through the throngs of
punters at **Cargo** (Map p253; www.cargo-
london.com; 83 Rivington St, EC2A; ⊗noon-
1am Mon-Thu, to 3am Fri & Sat, to midnight
Sun; ⓡShoreditch High St), one of London's
temples of clubbing, just a short walk away.
The programming is extremely varied; if
the evening's theme isn't to your liking, try
the equally good **XOYO** (Map p253; www.xoyo.
co.uk; 32-37 Cowper St, EC2A; ⊗10pm-3am Mon,
Tue & Thu, 9.30pm-4am Fri & Sat; ⊖Old St).

Whichever one you choose, expect
queuing, and bring some ID. Buy tickets
online (up to the day before) – it's usually
cheaper, and may save queuing.

Soho Square

CHAMELEONSEYE / SHUTTERSTOCK ©

Soho

London's original bohemian quarter may have lost some of its edge to East London over the past 20 years, but it remains a vibrant neighbourhood with classic establishments and a proud gay community.

Great For...

☑ **Don't Miss**

The Christmas lights in the area are spectacular, especially in Regent and Carnaby Sts.

In a district that was once pastureland, the name Soho is thought to have evolved from a hunting cry. While the centre of London nightlife has shifted east, and Soho has recently seen landmark clubs and music venues shut down, the neighbourhood definitely comes into its own in the evenings and remains a proud gay district. During the day you'll be charmed by the area's bohemian side and its sheer vitality.

At Soho's northern end, leafy **Soho Square** is the area's back garden. It was laid out in 1681 and originally called King's Square; a statue of Charles II stands in its northern half. In the centre is a tiny half-timbered mock-Tudor cottage built as a gardener's shed in the 1870s. The space below it was used as an underground bomb shelter during WWII.

South of the square is **Dean Street**, lined with bars and restaurants. No 28 was the

Christmas on Carnaby Street

DUTOURDUMONDE PHOTOGRAPHY / SHUTTERSTOCK ©

ⓘ Need to Know

Map p248; ⊖Oxford Circus, Tottenham Court Rd, Piccadilly Circus or Leicester Sq

✕ Take a Break

Yauatcha (Map p248; ☎020-7494 8888; www.yauatcha.com; 15 Broadwick St, W1; ⊙noon-10pm Sun-Thu, to 10.30pm Fri & Sat; dishes £5-30 ⊖Oxford Circus or Piccadilly Circus) in Soho does the best dim sum in town, hence the Michelin star.

★ Top Tip

Shops in the West End open until 9pm on Thursdays (they usually close at 7pm or 8pm).

home of Karl Marx and his family from 1851 to 1856; they lived here in extreme poverty as Marx researched and wrote *Das Kapital* in the British Museum's Reading Room.

Old Compton Street is the epicentre of Soho's gay village. It's a street loved by all, gay or other, for its great bars, risqué shops and general good vibes.

Seducer and heart-breaker Casanova and opium-addicted writer Thomas de Quincey lived on nearby **Greek Street**, while the parallel **Frith Street** housed Mozart at No 20 for a year from 1764.

You'll find plenty of lovely boutiques in Soho but, with its long rock'n'roll tradition, it is particularly well-known for its thriving **independent music stores**.

What's Nearby?

At the shopping nerve centre of the West End are the elegantly curving Regent Street and the dead-straight east–west artery Oxford Street.

Regent Street

The handsome border that divides the trainer-clad clubbers of Soho from the Gucci-heeled hedge-fund managers of Mayfair, Regent St was designed by John Nash as a ceremonial route linking Carlton House, the Prince Regent's long-demolished town residence, with the 'wilds' of Regent's Park. Nash had to downsize his plan and build the thoroughfare on a curve, but Regent St is today a well-subscribed shopping street lined with some lovely listed buildings. Its anchor tenant is undoubtedly Hamleys, London's premier toy and game store.

Oxford Street

Oxford Street is all about chains, from Marks & Spencer to H&M, Top Shop to Gap, with large branches of department stores, the most famous of which is Selfridges. The small lanes heading south to Mayfair are full of designer boutiques.

Atrium, Design Museum

EUGENE REGIS / SHUTTERSTOCK ©

Design Museum

Since 2016 this slick museum has been in a stunning location by Holland Park. It's a crucial pit stop for anyone with an eye for modern and contemporary aesthetics.

Great For...

☑ **Don't Miss**
The Designer Maker User gallery and the museum's architecture.

Collections & Exhibitions

Dedicated to popularising the importance and influence of design in everyday life, the Design Museum has a revolving program of special exhibitions.

Most exhibitions are ticketed (from £10), as are talks in the auditorium (from £5), but the extensive 2nd-floor **Designer Maker User gallery** is free. Exploring the iconography of design classics, the gallery contains almost 1000 objects that trace the history of modern design, from 1980s Apple computers to water bottles, typewriters, floppy discs and a huge advert for the timeless VW Beetle.

Iconic Building

Until 2016, the museum was housed in a former 1930s banana warehouse that had been given a 1930s modernist makeover

Kyoto Garden, Holland Park

TBRADFORD / GETTY IMAGES ©

ℹ Need to Know

Map p250; ☎020-7940 8790; www.design
museum.org; 224-238 Kensington High St,
W8; ⊗10am-6pm, to 8pm 1st Fri of month;
◎High St Kensington FREE

✕ Take a Break

For a delicious take on Greek cuisine,
head to **Mazi** (Map p250; ☎020-7229
3794; www.mazi.co.uk; 12-14 Hillgate St,
W8; mains £10-24; ⊗noon-3pm Tue-Sun,
6.30-10.30pm Mon-Sat, 6.30-10pm Sun; 🛜;
◎Notting Hill Gate).

★ Top Tip

Choose a sunny day to visit and wander
around Holland Park afterwards.

by museum founder Terence Conrad.
The building, located by the Thames in
Bermondsey, was a design success but
it became too small for the museum's
growing collection. For its new home, the
museum chose another design jewel: the
former Commonwealth Institute building,
a listed 1960s beauty, which was given a
21st-century, £83-million facelift for the
occasion.

What's Nearby?

Holland Park   Park

(Map p250; Ilchester Pl; ⊗7.30am-dusk; ◎High
St Kensington or Holland Park) This handsome
park is divided into dense woodland in
the north, spacious and inviting lawns
by Holland House, sports fields for the
beautiful game and other exertions in the
south, and some lovely gardens, including

the restful Kyoto Garden. The park's many
splendid peacocks are a gorgeous sight
and an adventure playground keeps kids
occupied. Holland House – largely bombed
to smithereens by the Luftwaffe in 1940 –
is the venue of **Opera Holland Park** (Map
p250; ☎0300 999 1000; www.operahollandpark.
com; tickets £18-77) in summer.

Portobello Road
Market   Clothing, Antiques

(Map p250; www.portobellomarket.org; Portobello
Rd, W10; ⊗8am-6.30pm Mon-Wed, Fri & Sat, to
1pm Thu; ◎Notting Hill Gate or Ladbroke Grove)
Lovely on a warm summer's day, Portobello
Road Market is an iconic London attraction
with an eclectic mix of street food, fruit and
veg, antiques, curios, collectables, vibrant
fashion and trinkets. Although the shops
along Portobello Rd open daily and the fruit
and veg stalls (from Elgin Cres to Talbot Rd)
only close on Sunday, the busiest day by far
is Saturday, when antique dealers set up
shop (from Chepstow Villas to Elgin Cres).

DINING OUT

Top-notch restaurants, gastropubs, afternoon tea and more

Dining Out

Once the butt of many a culinary joke, London has transformed itself over the last few decades and today is a global dining destination. World-famous chefs can be found at the helm of several top-tier restaurants, but it is the sheer diversity on offer that is head-spinning: from Afghan to Vietnamese, London delivers an A to Z of world cuisine.

There are restaurants to suit every budget – and every occasion. Dinner in a fabulous restaurant is part and parcel of a great trip to London, but make sure you also sample the cheap-and-cheerful fare on offer in market stalls and sit down in one of the capital's tip-top cafes.

In This Section

Price Ranges & Tipping

The following price ranges refer to a main course.

£ less than £12

££ £12–25

£££ more than £25

Most restaurants automatically tack a 'discretionary' service charge (usually 12.5%) onto the bill. If you feel the service wasn't adequate, you can tip separately (or not at all).

North London
Myriad options, with
hidden delights (p144)

**Clerkenwell, Shoreditch
& Spitalfields**
Famous, creative restaurants
and great bargains (p138)

West London
Eclectic, from vegetarian
to Eastern European
(p151)

East London
Curry houses,
traditional caffs,
cool restaurants
(p140)

The City
Geared towards
the business
lunch (p145)

The West End
Great for Asian,
European and
fusion (p148)

Kensington & Hyde Park
Chic, cosmopolitan
and often pricey
(p143)

The South Bank
Chains on the river,
culinary gems 'inland'
(p146)

River Thames

Useful Websites

Time Out London (www.timeout.
com/london) Has the most up-to-date
listings of restaurants as well as information on harder-to-track eateries and
food trucks.

Open Table (www.opentable.co.uk)
Bookings for numerous restaurants,
as well as meal deals with excellent
discounts.

Wine Pages (www.wine-pages.com)
Keeps a useful directory of BYO
restaurants.

Must-Try Dishes

Sunday roast Your choice of meat
(lamb, beef etc) smothered in gravy and
served with ballooning Yorkshire pudding, roast potatoes and a smorgasbord
of vegetables.

Afternoon tea An indulgent treat consisting of finger sandwiches, a selection
of pastries, scones with clotted cream
and jam, and, of course, tea. It's usually
served after 3pm (skip lunch and don't
plan much in the way of dinner!).

The Best

Experience London's top restaurants and cafes

Gastropubs

Anchor & Hope (p147) Flying the gastropub flag on the South Bank for over a decade.

Empress (p141) Choice East End spot with an excellent Modern British menu.

Asian Cuisine

Talli Joe (p148) A great place to sample some more unusual regional specialities.

Hoppers (p148) The most fabulous introduction to Sri Lankan food ever.

Gunpowder (p139) Punchy Indian cuisine in pocket-sized restaurant.

British Cuisine

Dinner by Heston Blumenthal (p144) Seriously good-looking Knightsbridge choice putting fresh spins on British culinary history.

Rabbit (p143) Hop to King's Rd for seasonal British cuisine.

Hook Camden Town (p144) What sort of British list would it be without fish and chips?

Restaurants with Views

City Social (p146) Wow-factor views from the City to the Shard and beyond.

Skylon (p147; pictured above) The same views in reverse, from the South Bank to the City.

Portrait (p149) Classic views over Nelson's Column and down Whitehall to Big Ben.

Sky Pod (p145) Full-frontal views of the Shard, with sky gardens to boot.

Cafes

Tomtom Coffee House (p143) No one takes their coffee more seriously than these guys.

Nude Espresso (p138) Kings of the single-origin coffee.

Pimlico Fresh (p143) Exquisite coffee, divine breakfasts, lovely lunches; the full package.

Markets

Boiler House (p139) Buzzing array of stalls off Brick Lane.

Real Food Market (p145) Gourmet stalls, with food ideal for picnic or takeaway.

Maltby Street Market (p147) Fabulous drinks stalls (and food).

Ice Cream

Ruby Violet (p144) Next-level flavours.

Chin Chin Labs (p145) Liquid-nitrogen ice cream: weird and utterly wonderful.

☆ Lonely Planet's Top Choices

Padella (p147) Super little bistro serving freshly made pasta at bargain prices.

Towpath (p140) Gorgeous cafe on one of London's typical towpaths.

Arabica Bar & Kitchen (p148) High-end Middle Eastern fusion cuisine at its best.

Shoryu (p116) Amazing noodle bar showcasing London's fabulous range of world cuisine.

✪ Clerkenwell, Shoreditch & Spitalfields

Polpo   Italian £

(Map p253; ☎020-7250 0034; www.polpo.co.uk; 3 Cowcross St, EC1M; dishes £4-12; ⊙11.30am-11pm Mon-Thu & Sat, to midnight Fri, to 4pm Sun; ⊖Farringdon) Occupying a sunny spot on semi-pedestrianised Cowcross St, this sweet little place serves rustic Venetian-style meatballs, *pizzette* (small pizzas) grilled meat and fish dishes. Portions are larger than your average tapas but a tad smaller than a regular main – the perfect excuse to sample more than one of the exquisite dishes. Exceptional value for money.

Nude Espresso   Cafe £

(Map p253; www.nudeespresso.com; 26 Hanbury St, E1; dishes £6.50-12; ⊙7.30am-5.30pm Mon-Fri, 9.30am-5pm Sat & Sun; ⊖Liverpool St) A simply styled, cosy cafe serving top-notch coffee (roasted across the street). Along with the standard blend, it has rotating single-origin coffees and filter as well as espresso-based brews. The sweet treats are delicious, as are the cooked breakfasts, brunch items and light lunches.

Boiler House   Market £

(Map p253; www.boilerhouse-foodhall.co.uk; Old Truman Brewery, 152 Brick Lane, E1; dishes £3-8; ⊙11am-6pm Sat, 10am-5pm Sun; ☝; ⊖Liverpool St) More than 30 food stalls selling anything from Argentinian to Vietnamese pitch up in the brewery's impressive old boiler room at the weekend. There is also a bar, and you can sit at the communal tables to tuck in. Come spring and summer, there are dozens more tables in the backyard.

Gate   Vegetarian ££

(Map p253; ☎020-7278 5483; www.thegaterestaurants.com; 370 St John St, EC1V; mains £11-15; ⊙noon-10pm; ☝☝; ⊖Angel) The Gate can probably take a lot of credit for elevating vegetarian cuisine from uninspiring side dishes to starring in its own culinary right. Blending influences from India, the Middle East and Jewish traditions, the food is a riot of flavours. The elegant dining room is in tune with its Islington surrounds: white walls and dark wooden tables and chairs.

Nude Espresso

Foxlow   Steak ££

(Map p253; www.foxlow.co.uk; 69-73 St John St,
EC1; mains £12-24; ⊙noon-3pm & 5.30-10.30pm
Mon-Sat, 10am-3.30pm Sun; ☎🖊🚶; ⊖Far-
ringdon) 🖊 This lovely brasserie builds on
the extensive experience of its founders
(of Hawksmoor fame), who always put
the quality of their ingredients centre
stage. You can therefore expect succulent
dry-aged steaks from Ginger Pig beef,
slow-cooked ribs, fried chicken and terrific
Sunday roasts. The atmosphere is cosy,
inviting and relaxed, and staff are chummy.
Vegetarians and vegans are well catered for.

Gunpowder   Indian ££

(Map p253; www.gunpowderlondon.com; 11 White's
Row, E1; ⊙noon-3pm & 5.30-10.30pm Mon-Sat;
🖊; ⊖Liverpool St) As you walk into this tiny
Indian place, it's the smell that hits you: a
delicious blend of spices and incense. The
punchy food, inspired by family recipes and
home cooking, lives up to this expectation:
plates are small and designed for sharing,
and the flavours of each dish are divine.

Moro   Spanish, Moroccan ££

(Map p253; ☎020-7833 8336; www.moro.co.uk;
34-36 Exmouth Market, EC1R; mains £16.50-24;
⊙noon-2.30pm & 6-10.30pm Mon-Sat, 12.30-
2.45pm Sun; ⊖Farringdon) The Moorish cuisine
on offer at this Exmouth Market institution
straddles the Straits of Gibraltar, with influences from Spain, Portugal and North Africa
– and a bit of Britain added to the mix. If the
tables are full, you can often perch at the bar
for some tapas, wine and dessert.

Poppie's   Fish & Chips ££

(Map p253; www.poppiesfishandchips.co.uk; 6-8
Hanbury St, E1; mains £12.20-16.90; ⊙11am-
11pm; ⊖Liverpool St) This glorious re-creation
of a 1950s East End chippy comes complete with waitstaff in pinnies and hairnets,
and Blitz memorabilia. As well as the usual
fishy suspects, it does old-time London
staples – jellied eels and mushy peas – plus
kid-pleasing, sweet-tooth desserts (sticky
toffee pudding or apple pie with ice cream),
and there's a wine list.

Takeaway is a lot cheaper (£6.50 to
£8.50).

🍴◎🍴 British Cuisine in a Nutshell

England might have given the world
baked beans on toast, mushy peas and
chip butties (fried potatoes between
slices of buttered white bread), but
that's hardly the whole story.

Modern British food has become a
cuisine in its own right, championing
traditional (and sometimes underrated)
ingredients such as root vegetables,
smoked fish, shellfish, game, salt-marsh
lamb, sausages and offal. Dishes can be
anything from game served with root
vegetables such as Jerusalem artichoke
to seared scallop with samphire (a green
vegetable similar to baby asparagus) or
roast pork belly on rosemary mash.

England does a mean dessert, and
establishments serving British cuisine
revel in these indulgent treats. Favourites include bread-and-butter pudding,
sticky toffee pudding (steamed pudding
with dates, topped with a caramel
sauce), the alarmingly named spotted
dick (steamed suet pudding with cur-
rants and raisins), Eton mess (meringue,
cream and strawberries mixed into
a gooey mess), and seasonal musts
such as Christmas pudding (a steamed
pudding with dried fruit and brandy) and
fruity crumbles (rhubarb, apple etc).

Christmas cake
ANNA_PUSTYNNIKOVA / SHUTTERSTOCK ©

Hawksmoor   Steak £££

(Map p253; ☎020-7426 4850; www.thehawks
moor.com; 157 Commercial St, E1; mains £20-50;
⊙noon-2.30pm & 5-10.30pm Mon-Sat, noon-9pm
Sun; ☎; ⊖Liverpool St) You could easily miss

English Wine

Locally produced sparkling wine has garnered much international attention and it is now served at state banquets in Buckingham Palace and in 1st class on British Airways. Even the Champagne house Taittinger has gotten in on the act, acquiring a vineyard in Kent in 2015. Producers to look out for include Wiston Estate, Furleigh Estate, Theale Vineyard, Ridgeview, Bolney Wine Estate and Hambledon. **Wine Pantry** (Map p245; ☑020-3751 9410; www.ewsco.co.uk; 8 Devonshire Row, EC2;) has the best selection in London.

Bolney Wine Estate
GLYN KIRK / STRINGER / GETTY IMAGES ©

discreetly signed Hawksmoor, but confirmed carnivores will find it worth seeking out. The dark wood, bare bricks and velvet curtains make for a handsome setting in which to gorge yourself on the best of British beef. The Sunday roasts (£20) are legendary.

⊗ East London

Towpath
Cafe £

(Map p253; ☑020-7254 7606; rear 42-44 De Beauvoir Cres, N1; mains £7-9.50; ⊙9am-5pm Tue-Wed, to 9.30pm Thu-Sun; ⊜Haggerston) Occupying four small units on the Regent's Canal towpath, this simple cafe is a super place to sit in the sun and watch the ducks and narrowboats glide by. The coffee and food are excellent too, with delicious cookies and brownies on the counter and cooked dishes chalked up on the blackboard daily.

F Cooke
British £

(Map p255; ☑020-7254 6458; 9 Broadway Market, E8; mains £2.70-4; ⊙10am-7pm Mon-Sat; ⊜London Fields) If you want a glimpse of pregentrification Broadway Market, head to F Cooke pie-and-mash shop. This family business has been going strong since 1900, and the shop has its original signage and tiles, along with plenty of family photographs around the walls and sawdust on the floor. It still serves warm jellied eels too!

Berber & Q
North African ££

(Map p253; ☑020-7923 0829; www.berberandq. com; 338 Acton Mews, E8; mains £12-17; ⊙6-11pm Tue-Fri, 11am-3pm & 6-11pm Sat & Sun; ⊜Haggerston) A mouth-watering barbecue smell greets you as you enter under the railway arches into this very cool Berber-style grill house. Smoked-aubergine dip comes loaded with garlic, sumac and juicy bursts of pomegranate, and is served with charred pita. Lamb *shawarma* is meltingly tender, while piquant treats include harissa hot wings, *merguez* (beef sausage), green *chermoula* chicken thighs and spiced beef kofta.

Yuu Kitchen
Asian ££

(Map p245; ☑020-7377 0411; www.yuukitchen. com; 29 Commercial St, E1; dishes £4.50-8.50; ⊙5.30pm-late Mon & Tue, noon-2.30pm & 5.30pm-late Wed-Fri, noon-4pm & 5.30pm-late Sat & Sun; ✍; ⊜Aldgate East) Manga images pout on the walls and birdcages dangle from the ceiling at this fun, relaxed eatery. Dishes are either bite-sized or designed to be shared, and while the focus is mainly Asian, some dishes from further along the Pacific Rim pop up too. Hence Hawaiian *poke* (raw fish) sits alongside Vietnamese rolls and showstopping *bao* (Taiwanese steamed buns).

Corner Room
Modern British ££

(Map p255; ☑020-7871 0460; www.townhallhotel. com/food-and-drink; Patriot Sq, E2; mains £13-14, 2-/3-course lunch £19/23; ⊙7-10am & noon-4pm Mon-Fri, 7.30-10.30am & 11am-2.30pm Sat & Sun, noon-2.30pm Sat & Sun, 6-9.45pm Sun-Wed, 6-10.15pm Thu-Sat; ⊜Bethnal Green) Someone put this baby in the corner, but we're certainly not complaining. Tucked away on the

Jellied eels

1st floor of the Town Hall Hotel, this relaxed restaurant serves expertly crafted dishes with complex yet delicate flavours, highlighting the best of British seasonal produce.

Bistrotheque
Modern British ££

(Map p255; ☑020-8983 7900; www.bistro theque.com; 23-27 Wadeson St, E2; mains £17-24, 3-course early dinner £25; ☺6-10.30pm Mon-Fri, 11am-4pm & 6-10.30pm Sat & Sun; ☻Bethnal Green) Aside from being too cool to have a sign, this warehouse conversion ticks all the boxes of a contemporary upmarket London bistro (the name made more sense when there was a club-like cabaret space downstairs). The food and service are excellent.

Brawn
European ££

(Map p253; ☑020-7729 5692; www.brawn.co; 49 Columbia Rd, E2; mains £14-19; ☺noon-3pm Tue-Sat, 6-10.30pm Mon-Thu, to 11pm Fri & Sat, noon-4pm Sun; ☻Hoxton) There's a French feel to this relaxed corner bistro, yet the menu wanders into Italian and Spanish territory as well, and even tackles that British institution, the Sunday lunch (three courses £28). Dishes are seasonally driven and delicious, and there's an interesting selection of European wine on offer.

Empress
Modern British ££

(Map p255; ☑020-8533 5123; www.empresse9. co.uk; 130 Lauriston Rd, E9; mains £13.50-18.50; ☺6-10.15pm Mon, noon-3.30pm & 6-10.15pm Tue-Sat, 10am-9.30pm Sun; ☒277) This upmarket pub conversion belts out delicious Modern British cuisine in very pleasant surroundings. On Mondays there's a £10 main-plus-drink supper deal and on weekends it serves an excellent brunch.

Formans
British ££

(Map p255; ☑020-8525 2365; www.formans. co.uk/restaurant; Stour Rd, E3; mains £15-20, brunch £6-10; ☺7-11pm Thu & Fri, 10am-3pm & 7-11pm Sat, noon-5pm Sun; ☎; ☻Hackney Wick) Curing fish since 1905, riverside Formans boasts prime views over the Olympic stadium and an edgy free gallery overlooking its smokery. The menu includes a delectable choice of smoked salmon (including its signature 'London cure'), plenty

CIRCLE CREATIVE STUDIO / SHUTTERSTOCK ©

Burgers at a food-market stall

of other seafood, a few nonfishy things and delicious sponge puddings. There's a great selection of British wines and spirits too.

Typing Room   Modern British **£££**
(Map p255; ✆020-7871 0461; www.typingroom.com; Town Hall Hotel, Cambridge Heath Rd, E2; 5-course meal £65; ⏱6-10pm Tue & Wed, noon-2.30pm & 6-10.30pm Thu-Sat; ⊖Bethnal Green) The chefs at the Typing Room couldn't get away with Ramsay-esque outbursts as their kitchen is positioned, theatre-like, at the entrance of the elegant but informal dining room. Just as well, as it might distract from the painstakingly prepared and exquisitely plated dishes they turn out. Service is faultless, and there's an interesting wine list.

⊗ Greenwich & South London

Paul Rhodes Bakery   Bakery **£**
(Map p256; 37 King William Walk, SE10; tarts from £1.80; ⏱7am-6pm; ᖇDLR Cutty Sark) This handy corner bakery is a tip-top spot for a snack, baked goodies and a coffee.

There are delights such as courgette, kale, hummus and tomato or chicken, bacon and avocado baguettes, marvellous lemon and citrus tarts, gorgeous chocolate tarts and vanilla cheesecake, served up by smiling staff. It's also open early.

Rivington Grill   British **££**
(Map p256; ✆020-8293 9270; www.rivingtongreenwich.co.uk; 178 Greenwich High Rd, SE10; mains £11.25-18.25; ⏱noon-11pm Mon-Fri, from 10am Sat & Sun; ᖇGreenwich) This younger sister of the trendy bar and grill in Hoxton is every bit as stylish, with seating on two levels overlooking a lovely long bar. The seasonally adjusted menu is totally British, with chicken pie, lamb chops, suckling pig and luxury pies rubbing shoulders with grilled sardines, fish and chips and apple-and-rhubarb crumble. Warm and friendly welcome.

Buenos Aires Cafe   Cafe **££**
(Map p256; ✆020-8858 9172; www.buenosairescafe.co.uk/greenwich-restaurant; 15 Nelson Rd, SE10; 2/3-course lunch £11.95/14.95, mains £6.95-28.95; 📶👶; ᖇDLR Cutty Sark) Take a seat in the sunlight-filled orangery at the

rear of this traditionally styled Argentine cafe for a very relaxing coffee at the heart of Greenwich, or choose the courtyard garden. The front is all wood – conservative, but pleasant too – with the walls covered in Maradona stills. Dishes are superb steaks, pasta and pizza. Ask about tango evenings.

Old Brewery
Modern British ££

(Map p256; ☑020-3437 2222; www.oldbrewery greenwich.com; Pepys Bldg, Old Royal Naval College, SE10; mains £11.50-25; ☺10am-11pm Mon-Sat, to 10.30pm Sun; ☜🍴; ☒DLR Cutty Sark) Acquired by Young's in 2016 and entirely refurbished, this excellent and handsome choice within the grounds of the Old Royal Naval College (p116) is both a ravishing restaurant and a pub, with a heady range of craft beers and cocktails. There's outside seating for sunny days.

⊗ Kensington & Hyde Park

Pimlico Fresh
Cafe £

(☑020-7932 0030; 86 Wilton Rd, SW1; mains from £4.50; ☺7.30am-7.30pm Mon-Fri, 9am-6pm Sat & Sun; ☺Victoria) This friendly two-room cafe will see you right whether you need breakfast (French toast, bowls of porridge laced with honey), lunch (homemade quiches and soups, 'things' on toast) or just a good old latte and cake.

Tomtom Coffee House
Cafe £

(Map p250; ☑020-7730 1771; www.tomtom.co.uk; 114 Ebury St, SW1; ☺8am-5pm Mon-Fri, 9am-6pm Sat & Sun; ☜; ☺Victoria) Tomtom has built its reputation on its amazing coffee: not only are the drinks fabulously presented (forget ferns and hearts in your latte, here it's peacocks fanning their tails), but the selection is dizzying; from the usual espresso-based suspects to filter, and a full choice of beans. You can even spice things up with a bonus tot of cognac or whisky (£3).

Rabbit
Modern British ££

(Map p250; ☑020-3750 0172; www.rabbit-restaurant.com; 172 King's Rd, SW3; mains £6-24, set lunch £13.50; ☺noon-midnight Tue-Sat, 6-11pm Mon, noon-6pm Sun; 🖉; ☺Sloane Sq) Three brothers grew up on a farm. One

‖◎‖ British Cheese

For a nation that's traditionally held its nose in response to strong flavours, it makes the exception for some particularly pungent blue cheeses. Stilton is the most famous, but look out for Stinking Bishop and the blues from Wensleydale, Derby, Dorset and Shropshire. The king of the crumbly hard cheeses is aged cheddar, but Cheshire, Lancashire and Caerphilly all have their own varieties.

Great places to sample British cheese include **Rippon Cheese** (p161) and **Borough Market** (p76).

Cheese stall, Borough Market
WEI HUANG / SHUTTERSTOCK ©

became a farmer, another a butcher, while the third worked in hospitality. So they pooled their skills and came up with Rabbit, a breath of fresh air in upmarket Chelsea. The restaurant rocks the agri-chic (yes) look and the creative, seasonal Modern British cuisine is fabulous.

Tom's Kitchen
Modern European ££

(Map p250; ☑020-7349 0202; www.tomskitchen. co.uk/chelsea; 27 Cale St, SW3; mains £16-28; ☺8am-2.30pm & 6-10.30pm Mon-Fri, 9.30am-3.30pm & 6-10.30pm Sat, to 9.30pm Sun; ☜🖉; ☺South Kensington) 🖉 Recipe for success: mix one part relaxed and smiling staff, and one part light and airy decor to two parts divine food and voila: you have Tom's Kitchen. Classics such as grilled steaks, burgers, slow-cooked pork belly and chicken schnitzel are cooked to perfection, while seasonal choices such as the homemade ricotta or pan-fried scallops are sublime.

🍽 Food Markets

The boom in London's eating scene has extended to its markets, which come in three broad categories: food stalls that are part of a broader market and appeal to visitors keen to soak up the atmosphere, such as **Spitalfields** (p71) and **Camden** (www.camdenmarket.com; Camden High St, NW1; ⊙10am-6pm; ⊝Camden Town, Chalk Farm); specialist food and farmers markets, which sell pricey local and/or organic produce and artisanal products, such as **Borough** (p76); and the many colourful general markets, where the oranges and lemons come from who knows where and the barrow boys and girls speak with perfect Cockney or Caribbean accents such as at **Portobello Road** (p131).

Camden Market food stall
I WEI HUANG / SHUTTERSTOCK ©

Magazine International ££

(Map p250; ☎020-7298 7552; www.magazine-restaurant.co.uk; Serpentine Sackler Gallery, West Carriage Dr, W2; mains £13-24, 2-/3-course lunch menu £17.50/21.50; ⊙9am-6pm Tue-Sat; ☎; ⊝Lancaster Gate, Knightsbridge) Located in the elegant extension of the Serpentine Sackler Gallery (p97), Magazine is no ordinary museum cafe. The food is as contemporary and elegant as the building, and artworks from current exhibitions add yet another dimension. The afternoon tea (£25, with one cocktail) is particularly original: out with cucumber sandwiches, in with gin-cured sea trout, goat's curd and coconut granita.

Orangery Cafe ££

(Map p250; ☎020-3166 6113; www.orangery kensingtonpalace.co.uk; Kensington Palace, Kensington Gardens, W8; mains £12.50-16.50, afternoon tea £27.50; ⊙10am-5pm; ✒; ⊝Queensway, High St Kensington) The Orangery, housed in an 18th-century conservatory on the grounds of Kensington Palace (p98), is lovely for a late breakfast or lunch, but the standout experience here is English afternoon tea. Book ahead to bag a table on the beautiful terrace.

Dinner by Heston Blumenthal Modern British £££

(Map p250; ☎020-7201 3833; www.dinnerby heston.com; Mandarin Oriental Hyde Park, 66 Knightsbridge, SW1; 3-course set lunch £45, mains £30-49; ⊙noon-2pm & 6-10.15pm Mon-Fri, noon-2.30pm & 6-10.30pm Sat & Sun; ☎; ⊝Knightsbridge) Sumptuously presented Dinner is a gastronomic tour de force, taking diners on a journey through British culinary history (with inventive modern inflections). Dishes carry historical dates to convey context, while the restaurant interior is a design triumph, from the glass-walled kitchen and its overhead clock mechanism to the large windows looking onto the park. Book ahead.

❽ North London

Ruby Violet Ice Cream £

(Map p254; www.rubyviolet.co.uk; Midlands Goods Shed, 3 Wharf Rd, N1C; 1/2 scoops £3/5.50; ⊙10am-7pm Sun-Thu, to 10pm Fri & Sat; ⊝King's Cross St Pancras) 🌿 This parlour is taking ice cream to the next level: flavours are wonderfully original (masala chai, Belgian chocolate, raspberry and sweet potato) and toppings and hot sauces are house-made. Plus, there's Pudding Club on Friday and Saturday nights, when you can sink your spoon into a mini baked Alaska or hot chocolate fondant and ice cream.

Hook Camden Town Fish & Chips £

(Map p254; www.hookrestaurants.com; 65 Parkway, NW1; mains £8-12; ⊙noon-3pm & 5-10pm Mon-Thu, noon-10.30pm Fri & Sat, to 9pm Sun;

; ⊖Camden Town) 🍴 In addition to working entirely with sustainable small fisheries and local suppliers, Hook makes all its sauces on-site and wraps its fish in recycled materials, supplying diners with extraordinarily fine-tasting morsels. Totally fresh, the fish arrives in panko breadcrumbs or tempura batter, with seaweed salted chips. Craft beers and fine wines are also on hand.

Chin Chin Labs — Ice Cream £

(Map p254; www.chinchinlabs.com; 49-50 Camden Lock Pl, NW1; ice creams £4-5; ☺noon-7pm; ⊖Camden Town) This is food chemistry at its absolute best. Chefs prepare the ice-cream mixture and freeze it on the spot by adding liquid nitrogen. Flavours change regularly and match the seasons (spiced hot cross bun, passionfruit and coconut, for instance). Sauces and toppings are equally creative. Try the ice-cream sandwich if you can: ice cream wedged inside gorgeous brownies or cookies.

Real Food Market — Market £

(Map p254; www.realfoodfestival.co.uk; King's Cross Sq, N1; dishes £4-8; ☺noon-7pm Wed-Fri; 🍴; ⊖King's Cross St Pancras) This lovely market brings together 24 gourmet food stalls three times a week. You can get anything from lovely cheeses, cured meats, smoked haddock and artisan bread to takeaway dishes and delicious cakes.

KERB Camden Market — Market £

(Map p254; www.kerbfood.com; Camden Lock Market; mains £6-8; ☺noon-5pm; 🍴; ⊖Camden Town) From Argentinian to Vietnamese, the KERB food-market collective is like an A–Z of world cuisines. Each stall looks more mouth-watering than the next, and there should be enough choice to keep even the fussiest of eaters happy. Eat on the big communal tables or find a spot along the canal.

Caravan — International ££

(Map p254; ☎020-7101 7661; www.caravanrestaurants.co.uk; 1 Granary Sq, N1C; mains £7-19; ☺8am-10.30pm Mon-Fri, 10am-10.30pm Sat, 10am-4pm Sun; 🍴🎏; ⊖King's Cross St Pancras) Housed in the lofty Granary Building,

Caravan is a vast industrial-chic destination for tasty fusion bites from around the world. You can opt for several small plates to share tapas-style, or stick to main-sized plates. The outdoor seating area on Granary Sq is especially popular on warm days.

⊗ Richmond, Kew & Hampton Court

Glasshouse — Modern European ££

(☎020-8940 6777; www.glasshouserestaurant.co.uk; 14 Station Pde, TW9; 2-/3-course lunch Mon-Fri £30/35, 1-/2-/3-course dinner £32.50/45/55; ☺noon-2.30pm & 6.30-10.30pm Tue-Sat, 12.30-4pm Sun; 🎏🍴; ⊠Kew Gardens, ⊖Kew Gardens) A day at Kew Gardens finds a perfect conclusion at this Michelin-starred gastronomic highlight. The glass-fronted exterior envelops a delicately lit, low-key interior, where the focus remains on divinely cooked food. Diners are rewarded with a consistently accomplished menu from chef Berwyn Davies that combines English mainstays with modern European innovation.

⊗ The City

Sky Pod — Bar

(Map p245; ☎0333 772 0020; www.skygarden.london; L35, 20 Fenchurch St, EC3; ☺7am-11pm Mon, to midnight Tue, to 1am Wed-Fri, 8am-1am Sat, 8am-11pm Sun; ⊖Monument) You'll need a booking for the **Sky Garden** (☎020-7337 2344; www.skygarden.london; L35-37, 20 Fenchurch St, EC3; ☺10am-6pm Mon-Fri, 11am-9pm Sat & Sun; ⊖Monument) FREE to access this rooftop bar, and if you'd like a guaranteed table to sit at, you're best to book one at the same time. The views are extraordinary, although it does get cold up here in winter. Note, it doesn't accept shorts, sportswear, trainers or flip-flops after 5pm.

Miyama — Japanese ££

(Map p245; ☎020-7489 1937; www.miyama-restaurant.co.uk; 17 Godliman St, EC4; mains £8-26; ☺11.30am-2.30pm & 5.45-9.30pm Mon-Fri;

St Paul's) There's the sense of a well-kept secret about this friendly Japanese restaurant, tucked away in a basement of a nondescript building (enter from Knightrider St). Miyama offers something for everyone, from soba and udon noodles to sushi and bento boxes. Sit at the sushi or teppanyaki bar for culinary drama, or opt for the more discreet main restaurant.

Sauterelle   European £££

(Map p245; 020-7618 2480; www.royal exchange-grandcafe.co.uk; Royal Exchange, Threadneedle St, EC3; mains £26-30; noon-11pm Mon-Fri; Bank) Take a seat on the elegant mezzanine of the **Royal Exchange** (Map p245; 020-7283 8935; www.theroyal exchange.co.uk; Threadneedle St, EC3; Bank) and prepare to be pampered with professional service and a menu of sophisticated British, French and Italian fare. Prices befit the sumptuous surroundings, but the restaurant also offers an excellent-value set menu (two/three courses £20/25), although you may need to ask to be shown it.

City Social   Modern British £££

(Map p245; 020-7877 7703; www.citysocial london.com; L24, 25 Old Broad St, EC2; mains £26-38; noon-3.30pm & 6-11.30pm Mon-Fri, 5-11.30pm Sat; Bank) Should you need to impress someone (even yourself) bring him, her and/or said self to this glamour puss on the 24th floor of Tower 42. Come for the extraordinary views (even from the toilets!), the art deco decor and, especially, Jason Atherton's Michelin-starred meals. Excellent pasta and fish dishes sit alongside the likes of Lancashire rabbit and Romney Marsh lamb.

⊗ The South Bank

Padella   Italian £

(Map p245; www.padella.co; 6 Southwark St, SE1; dishes £4-11.50; noon-3.45pm & 5-10pm Mon-Sat, noon-3.45pm & 5-9pm Sun; London Bridge) Yet another fantastic addition to the foodie enclave of Borough Market (p76), Padella is a small, energetic bistro specialising in handmade pasta dishes, inspired by the owners' extensive culinary adventures

Scotch-eggs stall, Maltby Street Market

ELENACHAYKINA / GETTY IMAGES ©

in Italy. The portions are small, which means that, joy of joys, you can (and should!) have more than one dish. Outstanding.

Four Corners Cafe Cafe £

(Map p245; www.four-corners-cafe.com; 12 Lower Marsh, SE1; ⊙7.30am-6.30pm Mon-Fri, 9am-5pm Sat; ; Waterloo) With its excellent coffee (from Ozone Roasters) and unusually large selection of teas, Four Corners Cafe attracts a loyal following. Occasional visitors will feel at home with the travel theme: from the map-lined coffee counter to the old guidebook collection (some Lonely Planet numbers!). The place has a buzz.

Maltby Street Market Market £

(Map p245; www.maltby.st; Maltby St, SE1; dishes £5-10; ⊙9am-4pm Sat, 11am-4pm Sun; Bermondsey) Started as an alternative to the juggernaut that is Borough Market, Maltby Street Market is becoming a victim of its own success, with brick-and-mortar shops and restaurants replacing the old workshops, and throngs of visitors. That said, it boasts some original – and all top-notch – food stalls selling smoked salmon from East London, African burgers, seafood and lots of pastries.

Baltic Eastern European ££

(Map p245; 020-7928 1111; www.balticrestau rant.co.uk; 74 Blackfriars Rd, SE1; mains £11.50-22, 2-course lunch menu £17.50; ⊙noon-3pm & 5.30-11.15pm Tue-Sat, noon-4.30pm & 5.30-10.30pm Sun, 5.30-11.15pm Mon; ; Southwark) In a bright and airy, high-ceilinged dining room with glass roof and wooden beams, Baltic is travel on a plate: dill and beetroot, dumplings and blini, pickle and smoke, rich stews and braised meat. From Polish to Georgian, the flavours are authentic and the dishes beautifully presented. The wine and vodka lists are equally diverse.

Anchor & Hope Gastropub ££

(Map p245; www.anchorandhopepub.co.uk; 36 The Cut, SE1; mains £12-20; ⊙noon-2.30pm Tue-Sat, 6-10.30pm Mon-Sat, 12.30-3.15pm Sun; Southwark) A stalwart of the South Bank food scene, the Anchor & Hope is a quintessential gastropub: elegant but not formal,

❖ Vegetarians & Vegans

London has been one of the best places for vegetarians to dine out since the 1970s, initially due mostly to its many Indian restaurants, which have always catered for people who don't eat meat for religious reasons. A number of dedicated vegetarian restaurants have since cropped up, offering imaginative, filling and truly delicious meals. Most nonvegetarian places generally offer a couple of veggie dishes, and some top-end places offer full vegetarian degustation menus. Vegans, however, will find it harder outside of Indian or dedicated vegan establishments, although these have been growing in number in recent years.

SIMON MCGILL / GETTY IMAGES ©

and utterly delicious (European fare with a British twist). The menu changes daily but think salt-marsh lamb shoulder cooked for seven hours; wild rabbit with anchovies, almonds and rocket; and *panna cotta* with rhubarb compote.

Skylon Modern European ££

(Map p245; 020-7654 7800; www.skylon-restaurant.co.uk; 3rd fl, Royal Festival Hall, South-bank Centre, Belvedere Rd, SE1; 3-course menu grill/restaurant £25/30; ⊙grill noon-11pm Mon-Sat, to 10.30pm Sun, restaurant noon-2.30pm & 5-10.30pm Mon-Sat, 11.30am-4pm Sun; ; Waterloo) This excellent restaurant inside the Royal Festival Hall (p192) is divided into grill and fine-dining sections by a large **bar** (Royal Festival Hall, Southbank Centre, Belvedere Rd, SE1; ⊙noon-1am Mon-Sat, to 10.30pm Sun;

🍴 Celebrity Chefs

London's food renaissance was partly led by a group of telegenic chefs who built culinary empires around their names, made famous by their TV shows. Gordon Ramsay is the most (in)famous of the lot and his London venues are still standard bearers for top-quality cuisine. Other big names include Jamie Oliver and Heston Blumenthal, whose mad-professor-like experiments with food have earned him rave reviews.

Dinner by Heston Blumenthal (p144)
CHRISPICTURES / SHUTTERSTOCK ©

🛜; 🚇Waterloo). The decor is cutting-edge 1950s: muted colours and period chairs (trendy then, trendier now), while floor-to-ceiling windows bathe you in magnificent views of the Thames and the city. Booking is advised.

Arabica Bar & Kitchen
Middle Eastern £££

(Map p245; 📞020-3011 5151; www.arabica barandkitchen.com; 3 Rochester Walk, Borough Market, SE1; dishes £6-14; 🕐noon-11pm Mon-Fri, 9am-11.30pm Sat, noon-9pm Sun; 🖉; 🚇London Bridge) Pan–Middle Eastern cuisine is a well-rehearsed classic these days, but Arabica Bar & Kitchen has managed to bring something fresh to its table: the decor is contemporary and bright, the food delicate and light, and there's an emphasis on sharing (two to three small dishes per person). The downside of this tapas approach is that the bill adds up quickly.

✖ The West End

Shoryu
Noodles £

(Map p248; www.shoryuramen.com; 9 Regent St, SW1; mains £10-14.50; 🕐11.15am-midnight Mon-Sat, to 10.30pm Sun; 🚇Piccadilly Circus) Compact, well-mannered and central, noodle-parlour Shoryu draws in reams of noodle diners to feast at its wooden counters and small tables. It's busy, friendly and efficient, with helpful and informative staff. Fantastic *tonkotsu* (pork-broth) ramen is the name of the game here, sprinkled with nori (dried, pressed seaweed), spring onion, *nitamago* (soft-boiled eggs) and sesame seeds. No bookings.

Kahve Dünyası
Cafe £

(Map p248; Coffee World; 📞020-7287 9063; http://kahvedunyasi.co.uk; Unit 3, 200 Piccadilly, W1; cakes £3.85-4.95; 🕐7.30am-10pm Mon-Fri, to 10.30pm Sat, to 9.30pm Sun; 🚇Piccadilly) As lovers of all things Turkic, we were (and remain) over the moon that a branch of our favourite Turkish cafe chain has opened in central London, with pistachio-based desserts, real *lokum* (Turkish delight) and mastic ice cream. Oh, and Turkish coffee – the best in the world. Stunning service. Eat-off-the-floor clean.

Hoppers
Sri Lankan £

(Map p248; www.hopperslondon.com; 49 Frith St, W1; dishes £4.50-21; 🕐noon-2.30 & 5.30-10.30pm Mon-Thu, noon-10.30pm Fri & Sat; 🚇Tottenham Court Rd, Leicester Sq) This pint-sized and enormously popular place specialises in hoppers, the Sri Lankan national dish that is a thin pancake of rice flour and coconut milk with spices. Eat them (or dosas) with various types of *kari* (curry) or *kothu,* a dish of chopped roti with spices and meat, shellfish or vegetables. The decor here is Old Ceylon, and the service swift but personable.

Talli Joe
Indian £

(Map p248; 📞020-7836 5400; www.tallijoe. com; 152-156 Shaftesbury Ave, WC2; dishes £4-11.50; 🕐noon-10.30pm Mon-Sat, to 4pm Sun; 🚇Leicester Sq, Tottenham Court Rd) Talli Joe is a colourful and very new breed of Indian restaurants serving 'half plates' (meaning share portions). The menu has been composed by the legendary Joe, who has travelled the length and breadth of India for regional dishes. So expect the unexpected: from Keralan-style fish curry and Bohri chicken from Gujarat, to a Kolkata street snack of five-spiced potatoes.

Palomar   Israeli ££
(Map p248; 020-7439 8777; http://thepalomar. co.uk; 34 Rupert St, W1; mains £9-17; noon-2.30pm & 5.30-11pm Mon-Sat, 12.30-3.30pm & 6-9pm Sun; ; Piccadilly Circus) The buzzing vibe at this good-looking celebration of modern-day Jerusalem cuisine (in all its permutations) is infectious, but the noise in the back dining room might drive you mad. Choose instead the counter seats at the front. The 'Yiddish-style' chopped chicken-liver pâté, the Jerusalem-style polenta and the 'octo-hummus' are all fantastic, but portions are smallish, so it's a good idea to share a few.

Barrafina   Spanish ££
(Map p248; 020-7440 1456; www.barrafina. co.uk; 26-27 Dean St, W1; tapas £6.50-15.80; noon-3pm & 5-11pm Mon-Sat, 1-3.30pm & 5.30-10pm Sun; Tottenham Court Rd) Tapas are always better value in Spain but the quality of this food justifies the layout. Along with *gambas al ajillo* (prawns in garlic; £9), there are more unusual things, such as tuna tartar (£12.50) and grilled quail with alioli (£9.50). Customers sit along the bar so it's not a good choice for groups. No reservations, so prepare to queue.

The Delaunay   Brasserie ££
(Map p245; 020-7499 8558; www.the delaunay.com; 55 Aldwych, WC2; mains £7.50-35; 7am-midnight Mon-Fri, 8am-midnight Sat, 9am-11pm Sun; ; Temple, Covent Garden) This smart brasserie southeast of Covent Garden is a kind of Franco-German hybrid, where schnitzels and wieners sit happily beside *croque-monsieurs* and *choucroute alsacienne* (Alsace-style sauerkraut). Even more relaxed is the adjacent **Counter at**

the Delaunay (Map p245; 020-7499 8558; www.thedelaunay.com/counter; 55 Aldwych, WC2; soups & sandwiches £4.50-10; 7am-8pm Mon-Wed, to 10.30pm Thu & Fri, 10.30am-10.30pm Sat, 11am-5.30pm Sun; Temple, Covent Garden).

Cafe Murano   Italian ££
(Map p248; 020-3371 5559; www.cafemurano. co.uk; 33 St James's St, SW1; mains £18-25, 2-/3-course set meal £19/23; noon-3pm & 5.30-11pm Mon-Sat, 11.30am-4pm Sun; Green Park) The setting may seem somewhat demure at this superb and busy restaurant, but with such a sublime northern Italian menu on offer, it sees no need to be flashy and of-the-moment. You get what you come for, and the lobster linguini, pork belly and cod with mussels and samphire are as close to culinary perfection as you'll get.

Claridge's Foyer & Reading Room   British £££
(Map p250; 020-7107 8886; www.claridges. co.uk; 49-53 Brook St, W1; afternoon tea £60, with champagne £70; afternoon tea 2.45-5.30pm; ; Bond St) Extend that pinkie finger to partake in afternoon tea within the classic art deco foyer and Reading Room of this landmark hotel, where the gentle clink of fine porcelain and champagne glasses could be a defining memory of your trip to London. The setting is gorgeous and dress is elegant, smart casual (ripped jeans and baseball caps won't get served).

Portrait   Modern European £££
(Map p248; 020-7312 2490; www.npg.org.uk/ visit/shop-eat-drink.php; 3rd fl, National Portrait Gallery, St Martin's Pl, WC2; mains £19.50-28, 2-/3-course menu £27.95/31.50; 10-11am, 11.45am-3pm & 3.30-4.30pm daily, 6.30-8.30pm Thu, Fri & Sat; ; Charing Cross) This stunningly located restaurant above the excellent National Portrait Gallery (p55) comes with dramatic views over Trafalgar Sq and Westminster. It's a fine choice for tantalising food and the chance to relax after a morning or afternoon of picture-gazing at the gallery. The breakfast/brunch (10am to 11am) and afternoon tea (3.30pm to 4.30pm) come highly recommended.

London on a Plate

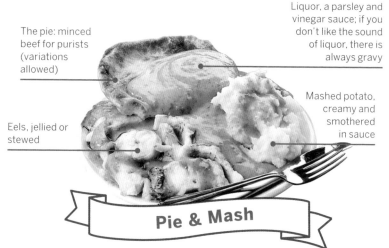

The pie: minced beef for purists (variations allowed)

Liquor, a parsley and vinegar sauce; if you don't like the sound of liquor, there is always gravy

Mashed potato, creamy and smothered in sauce

Eels, jellied or stewed

CKP1001 / SHUTTERSTOCK ©

Pie & Mash

Pie & Mash in London

From the middle of the 19th century until just after WWII, the staple lunch for many Londoners was a spiced-eel pie (eels were once plentiful in the Thames) served with mashed potatoes and liquor. The staple modern-day filling is minced beef (curried meat is also good). Pie-and-mash restaurants are rarely fancy, but they offer something of a time-travel culinary experience.

Fried baby eels
JULTUD / SHUTTERSTOCK ©

☆ Top Spots for Pie & Mash

M Manze (www.manze.co.uk; 87 Tower Bridge Rd, SE1; mains from £2.95; ⊙11am-2pm Mon, 10.30am-2pm Tue-Thu, 10am-2.30pm Fri, to 2.45pm Sat; ⊖Borough)

Goddards at Greenwich (Map p256; ☎020-8305 9612; www.goddardsat greenwich.co.uk; 22 King William Walk, SE10; dishes £3.30-7.30; ⊙10am-7pm Sun-Thu, to 8pm Fri & Sat; ⓇDLR Cutty Sark)

Cockney's Pie and Mash (Map p250; ☎020-8960 9409; 314 Portobello Rd, W10; ⊙11.30am-5.30pm Tue-Thu, to 7pm Fri, to 5.30pm Sat)

Pollen Street Social
Modern European £££

(Map p248; 020-7290 7600; www.pollenstreet
social.com; 8-10 Pollen St, W1; mains £34-38,
3-course lunch £37; noon-2.30pm & 6-10.30pm
Mon-Sat; Oxford Circus) Jason Atherton's
cathedral to haute cuisine would be beyond
reach of many people not on a hefty
expense account, but the excellent-value
set lunch (£32/37 for two/three courses)
makes it fairly accessible to all. A generous
two-hour slot allows ample time to linger
over such delights as lime-cured salmon,
braised West Country ox cheek and your
choice from the dessert bar.

West London

Taquería
Mexican £

(Map p250; 020-7229 4734; www.taqueria.
co.uk; 139-143 Westbourne Grove; tacos £7.20-
10.20; noon-11pm Mon-Thu, to 11.30pm Fri &
Sat, to 10.30pm Sun; Notting Hill Gate)
You won't find fresher or more limp
(they're not supposed to be crispy!) tacos
anywhere in London because these ones
are made on the premises. Starting life
as a stall on Portobello Rd and recently
refurbished, it's a small, casual place with
a great vibe, committed to environmental
mores: the eggs, chicken and pork are
free-range, the meat British, the fish Marine
Stewardship Council–certified, and the
milk and cream organic.

Geales
Seafood ££

(Map p250; 020-7727 7528; www.geales.com;
2 Farmer St, W8; 2-course express lunch £9.95,
mains £9-33.50; noon-3pm Tue-Fri, 5.30-11pm
Mon-Fri, noon-11pm Sat & Sun; Notting Hill
Gate) Frying since 1939 (a bad year for the
European restaurant trade) Geales has
endured with its quiet location on the corner
of Farmer St. The succulent fish in crispy
batter is a fine catch, but the fish pie is also
great. Look out for the good-value express
lunch, available from Tuesday to Friday.

Ledbury
French £££

(Map p250; 020-7792 9090; www.theledbury.
com; 127 Ledbury Rd, W11; 4-course set lunch £75,
4-course dinner £120; noon-2pm Wed-Sun &

Breakfast Buzz

The Brits have always been big on
breakfast – and they even invented
one, the Full English. It's something of
a protein overload but there's nothing
quite like it to mop up the excesses
of a night on the tiles. A typical plate
will include bacon, sausages, baked
beans in tomato sauce, eggs (fried or
scrambled), mushrooms, tomatoes
and toast (maybe with Marmite). You'll
find countless brightly lit, grotty caffs
(cafes) – nicknamed 'greasy spoons' –
serving these monster plates. They're
also a must at gastropubs.

Making a comeback on the breakfast
table is porridge (boiled oats in water or
milk, served hot), sweet or savoury. Top-
end restaurants serving breakfast have
played a big part in glamming up what
was essentially poor folk's food. It's great
with banana and honey, fruit compote or
even plain with some chocolate powder.

Full English breakfast
ETORRES / SHUTTERSTOCK ©

6.30-9.45pm daily; Westbourne Park, Royal
Oak, Notting Hill Gate) With two Michelin stars
and swooningly elegant, Brett Graham's
artful French restaurant attracts well-heeled
diners in jeans with designer jackets. Dishes
such as hand-dived scallops, Chinese water
deer, smoked bone marrow, quince and red
leaves, or Herdwick lamb with salt-baked
turnips, celery cream and wild garlic are
triumphs. London gastronomes have the
Ledbury on speed dial, so reservations well
in advance are crucial.

TREASURE HUNT

Begin your shopping adventure

Treasure Hunt

From charity-shop finds to designer bags, there are thousands of ways to spend your hard-earned cash in London. Many of the big-name shopping attractions, such as Harrods and Hamleys, have become must-sees in their own right. Chances are that with so many temptations, you'll give your wallet a full workout.

Perhaps the biggest draw for visitors is the capital's famed markets. These treasure troves of small designers, unique jewellery pieces, original framed photographs and posters, colourful vintage pieces and bric-a-brac are the antidote to impersonal, carbon-copy shopping centres.

In This Section

Taxes & Refund

○ In stores displaying a 'tax free' sign, visitors from non-EU countries are entitled to claim back the Value Added Tax (VAT) on purchases.

○ The retailer should provide a VAT 407 form, which needs to be completed and presented at Customs when leaving the country, along with the receipt and goods. See www.gov.uk/tax-on-shopping/taxfree-shopping.

North London
It's all about Camden Market (p162)

Clerkenwell, Shoreditch & Spitalfields
Vintage, vintage, vintage, fashion and jewellery (p158)

West London
Famous market, vintage stores and lovely boutiques (p167)

The West End
Shopping galore, from franchises to boutiques (p164)

The City
Good for suits but little else (p163)

East London
Wonderful markets, discounted fashion (p159)

Kensington & Hyde Park
High fashion and glamorous shopping (p161)

The South Bank
Fabulous food and small designer shops (p163)

River Thames

Greenwich & South London
Eclectic markets, up-and-coming fashion (p160)

Opening Hours

○ Shops generally open from 9am or 10am to 6pm or 7pm Monday to Saturday.

○ Most stores in popular strips open on Sunday, typically from noon to 6pm but sometimes 10am to 4pm.

○ West End stores open to 9pm on Thursday; those in Chelsea, Knightsbridge and Kensington open late on Wednesday.

Sales

Winter sales Run from Boxing Day (26 December) to the tail end of January.

Summer sales Usually start the last week of June and run until the the end of July.

The Best...

Experience London's best shopping

Fashion Shops

Selfridges (p165) Everything from streetwear to high fashion under one roof.
Collectif (p158) Spitalfields store taking inspiration from the 1940s and '50s.
Browns (p159) Great for up-and-coming designers.

Bookshops

John Sandoe Books (p161) Gorgeous bookshop full of gems.
Hatchards (p164) London's oldest bookshop, selling the good stuff since 1797.
Gosh! (p165) A compulsory stop for lovers of graphic novels.

Markets

Sunday UpMarket (p158) Load up on delicious food before tackling the designer stalls.
Camden Market (p163) Everything from authentic antiques to tourist tat.
Portobello Road Market (p131) Classic Notting Hill sprawl, perfect for vintage everything.
Broadway Market (p159) Local market known for its food but with plenty more.
Old Spitalfields Market (p71) One of London's best for young fashion designers.

For Music

Rough Trade East (p158) Excellent selection of vinyl and CDs, plus in-store gigs.
Casbah Records (p160) Classic vinyl and memorabilia.
Reckless Records (p165) A superb selection of secondhand CDs and vinyl.

For Vintage

Beyond Retro (p159) London vintage empire with a rock-n-roll heart.

British Red Cross (p162) Chelsea cast-offs of exceptional quality.

Gay's the Word (p167) A literary institution for the LGBTIQ community.

For Jewellery

Tatty Devine (p159; pictured above) Fun, creative perspex jewellery.

E.C.One (p159) Fine, contemporary pieces by designer-makers.

For Souvenirs

Arty Globe (p161) Unusual fish-eye photographs of London.

We Built This City (p165) Great London-themed souvenirs, minus the tackiness.

Jo Loves (p162) Perfumes & candles devised by Jo Malone.

☆Lonely Planet's Top Choices

Sunday UpMarket (p158) Up-and-coming designers, cool tees and terrific food.

Fortnum & Mason (p165) The world's most glamorous grocery store.

Conran Shop (p162) A treasure trove of cool things.

Hatchards (p165) A bookworm's paradise in historical settings.

Greenwich Market (p160)

Clerkenwell, Shoreditch & Spitalfields

Sunday UpMarket
Market

(Map p253; www.sundayupmarket.co.uk; Old Truman Brewery, 91 Brick Lane, E1; ⊙11am-6pm Sat, 10am-5pm Sun; ⓡShoreditch High St) The Sunday Upmarket (which in fact opens Saturdays and Sundays) sprawls within the beautiful red-brick buildings of the Old Truman Brewery (p73). You'll find young designers in the **Backyard Market** (www.backyardmarket.co.uk; 146 Brick Lane, E1; ⊙11am-6pm Sat, 10am-5pm Sun), a drool-inducing array of food stalls in the Boiler House (p138), antiques and bric-a-brac in the **Tea Rooms** (☏020-7770 6028; www.bricklane-tearooms.co.uk; ⊙11am-6pm Sat, 10am-5pm Sun), and a huge range of vintage clothes in the basement Vintage (Up)Market across the street.

Collectif
Fashion & Accessories

(Map p253; www.collectif.co.uk; 58 Commercial St, E1; ⊙10am-6pm; ⊖Liverpool St) If you love the feminine silhouette of the 1940s and the pin-up look of the 1950s, you will swoon over Collectif's vintage-inspired dresses, shirts, coats and accessories.

Rough Trade East
Music

(Map p253; www.roughtrade.com; Old Truman Brewery, 91 Brick Lane, E1; ⊙9am-9pm Mon-Thu, to 8pm Fri, 10am-8pm Sat, 11am-7pm Sun; ⓡShoreditch High St) It's no longer directly associated with the legendary record label (home to The Smiths, The Libertines and The Strokes, among many others), but this huge record shop is still the best for music of an indie, soul, electronica and alternative persuasion.

Magma
Books, Gifts

(Map p253; www.magmabooks.com; 117-119 Clerkenwell Rd, EC1R; ⊙10am-7pm Mon-Sat; ⊖Chancery Lane) This much-loved shop sells coffee-table books, magazines and almost anything on the design cutting edge. It has some lovely children's books.

Blitz London
Vintage

(Map p253; www.blitzlondon.co.uk; 55-59 Hanbury St, E1; ⊙11am-7pm; ⊖Liverpool St) One of the capital's best secondhand

clothes stores, with more than 20,000 hand-selected items of men's and women's clothing, shoes and accessories spanning four decades since the 1960s. You'll find anything from mainstream brands such as Nike to designer labels like Burberry.

Vintage (Up)Market
Vintage

(Map p253; www.vintage-market.co.uk; Old Truman Brewery, F Block, 85 Brick Lane, E1; ⊘11am-6pm Thu-Sat, 10am-6pm Sun; ⊕Liverpool St) This basement market has a fabulous selection of vintage fashion, posters and vinyl, and even the odd piece of furniture. Although it is part of the Sunday Upmarket, it is open from Thursday to Sunday.

Tatty Devine
Jewellery

(Map p253; ☎020-7739 9191; www.tattydevine. com; 236 Brick Lane, E2; ⊘10am-6.30pm Mon-Fri, 11am-6pm Sat, 10am-5pm Sun; ⊞Shoreditch High St) Harriet Vine and Rosie Wolfenden make hip and witty perspex jewellery that's become the favourite of many young Londoners. Their original designs feature all manner of flora- and fauna-inspired necklaces, as well as creations sporting moustaches, dinosaurs and bunting. Name necklaces (made to order; from £27.50) are also a treat.

E.C.One
Jewellery

(Map p253; ☎020-7713 6185; www.econe. co.uk; 41 Exmouth Market, EC1R; ⊘10am-6pm Mon-Sat; ⊕Farringdon) Husband-and-wife team Jos and Alison Skeates sell gorgeous contemporary collections by British and international jewellery designers. Watch the jewellers at work at the rear of the shop.

ⓐ East London

Broadway Market
Market

(Map p255; www.broadwaymarket.co.uk; Broadway Market, E8; ⊘9am-5pm Sat; ▣394) There's been a market down this pretty street since the late 19th century. The focus these days is artisan food, arty knick-knacks, books, records and vintage clothing. Stock up on edible treats then head to **London Fields** (Richmond Rd, E8; ⊞London Fields) for a picnic.

British Designers

London-based designers are well established in the fashion world and a visit to Stella McCartney, Vivienne Westwood, Paul Smith or Burberry is an experience in its own right. Other names to watch out for include Molly Goddard, available at **Browns** (Map p250; ☎020-7629 1416; www.brownsfashion.com; 23-27 South Molton St, W1; ⊘10am-7pm Mon-Wed & Sat, to 8pm Thu & Fri, noon-6pm Sun; ⊕Bond St), Christopher Kane and Mimi Wade, both available at **Selfridges** (p165).

Stella McCartney
DOSFOTOS / GETTY IMAGES ©

Beyond Retro
Vintage

(Map p255; ☎020-7729 9001; www.beyondretro. com; 110-112 Cheshire St, E2; ⊘10am-7pm Mon-Wed, Fri & Sat, to 8pm Thu, 11.30am-6pm Sun; ⊞Shoreditch High St) Huge selection of vintage clothes, including shoes and sunglasses, expertly collected in a lofty warehouse.

Pringle of Scotland Outlet Store
Clothing

(Map p255; ☎020-8533 1158; www.pringle scotland.com; 90 Morning Lane; ⊘10am-6.30pm Mon-Sat, 11am-5pm Sun; ⊞Hackney Central) There are proper bargains to be had at this excellent outlet store that stocks seconds and end-of-line items from the Pringle range. Expect high-quality merino, cashmere and lambswool knitwear for men and women.

Burberry Outlet Store
Clothing

(Map p255; www.burberry.com; 29-31 Chatham Pl, E9; ⊘10am-7pm; ⊞Hackney Central) This outlet shop has excess international stock

Vintage

The realm of vintage apparel has moved from being sought out by those looking for something offbeat and original, to an all-out mainstream shopping habit. Vintage designer garments and odd bits and pieces from the 1920s to the 1980s are all gracing the rails in some surprisingly upmarket boutique vintage shops.

The less self-conscious charity shops – especially those in areas such as Chelsea, Kensington and Islington – are your best bets for real bargains on designer wear (usually, the richer the area, the better the secondhand shops).

Camden Lock Market (p163)
I WEI HUANG / SHUTTERSTOCK ©

from the reborn-as-trendy Brit brand's current and last-season collections. Prices are around 30% lower than those in the main shopping centres – but still properly pricey.

Traid   Clothing
(Map p255; ☑020-7923 1396; www.traid.org.uk; 106-108 Kingsland High St, E8; ☺11am-7pm Mon-Sat, to 5pm Sun; ⊖Dalston Kingsland) Banish every preconception you have about charity shops, for Traid is nothing like the ones you've seen before: big and bright, with not a whiff of mothball. The offerings aren't necessarily vintage but rather quality, contemporary secondhand clothes for a fraction of the usual prices.

Westfield Stratford City   Mall
(http://uk.westfield.com; Westfield Ave, E20; ☺10am-9pm Mon-Fri, 9am-9pm Sat, noon-6pm

Sun; ☎; ⊖Stratford) Right by Queen Elizabeth Olympic Park, this is Britain's third-largest mall – a behemoth containing more than 250 shops, 70 places to eat and drink, a 17-screen cinema, a bowling alley, a 24-hour casino and a Premier Inn hotel.

⑨ Greenwich & South London

Greenwich Market   Market
(Map p256; www.greenwichmarketlondon.com; College Approach, SE10; ☺10.30am-5pm; ☒DLR Cutty Sark) One of the smallest of London's ubiquitous markets, but Greenwich Market holds its own in quality. On Tuesdays, Wednesdays, Fridays and weekends, stallholders tend to be small, independent artists, offering original prints, wholesome beauty products, funky jewellery and accessories, cool fashion pieces and so on. On Tuesdays, Thursdays and Fridays, you'll find vintage, antiques and collectables. Loads of street food too.

Casbah Records   Music
(Map p256; ☑020-8858 1964; www.casbah records.co.uk; 320-322 Creek Rd, SE10; ☺11.30am-6pm Mon, 10.30am-6pm Tue-Fri, 10.30am-6.30pm Sat & Sun; ☒DLR Cutty Sark) This funky meeting ground of classic, vintage and rare vinyl (Bowie, Rolling Stones, soul, rock, blues, jazz, indie etc) – as well as CDs, DVDs and memorabilia – originally traded at Greenwich Market before upgrading to this highly browsable shop.

Arty Globe   Gifts & Souvenirs
(Map p256; ☑020-7998 3144; www.artyglobe.com; 15 Greenwich Market, SE10; ☺11am-6pm; ☒DLR Cutty Sark) The unique fisheye-view drawings of various areas of London (and other cities, including New York, Paris and Berlin) by architect Hartwig Braun are works of art and appear on the shopping bags, place mats, notebooks, coasters, mugs and jigsaws available in this tiny shop. They make excellent gifts.

🅴 Kensington & Hyde Park

John Sandoe Books
Books

(Map p250; ☎020-7589 9473; www.johnsan doe.com; 10 Blacklands Tce, SW3; ⊘9.30am-6.30pm Mon-Sat, 11am-5pm Sun; ⊜Sloane Sq) The perfect antidote to impersonal book superstores, this atmospheric three-storey bookshop in 18th-century premises is a treasure trove of literary gems and hidden surprises. It's been in business for six decades and loyal customers swear by it, while knowledgable booksellers spill forth with well-read pointers and helpful advice.

Harrods
Department Store

(Map p250; ☎020-7730 1234; www.harrods.com; 87-135 Brompton Rd, SW1; ⊘10am-9pm Mon-Sat, 11.30am-6pm Sun; ⊜Knightsbridge) Garish and stylish in equal measure, perennially crowded Harrods is an obligatory stop for visitors, from the cash-strapped to the big spenders. The stock is astonishing, as are many of the price tags. High on kitsch, the 'Egyptian Elevator' resembles something out of an Indiana Jones epic, while the memorial fountain to Dodi and Di (lower ground floor) merely adds surrealism.

Conran Shop
Design

(Map p250; ☎020-7589 7401; www.conranshop. co.uk; Michelin House, 81 Fulham Rd, SW3; ⊘10am-6pm Mon, Tue & Fri, to 7pm Wed & Thu, to 6.30pm Sat, noon-6pm Sun; ⊜South Kensington) The original design store (going strong since 1987), the Conran Shop is a treasure trove of beautiful things, from radios to sunglasses, kitchenware to children's toys and books, bathroom accessories to greeting cards. Browsing bliss. Spare some time to peruse the magnificent art nouveau/ deco Michelin House the shop is housed in.

Rippon Cheese
Food

(☎020-7931 0628; www.ripponcheeselondon. com; 26 Upper Tachbrook St, SW1; ⊘8am-4.30pm Mon-Fri, 8.30am-5pm Sat; ⊜Victoria, Pimlico) A potently inviting pong greets you as you near this cheesemonger with its 500 varieties of mostly English and French cheeses. Ask the knowledgable staff for

Harrods

recommendations (and taste as you go!) and stock up for a picnic in a London park.

Jo Loves   Cosmetics
(Map p250; ☎020-7730 8611; www.joloves.com; 42 Elizabeth St, SW1; ⏰10am-6pm Mon-Wed, Fri & Sat, to 7pm Thu, noon-5pm Sun; ⊖Victoria) Famed British scent-maker Jo Malone opened Jo Loves in 2013 on a street where she once had a Saturday job as a young florist. The shop features the entrepreneur's signature candles, fragrances and bath products in a range of delicate scents: Arabian amber, white rose and lemon leaves, oud and mango. All products come exquisitely wrapped in red boxes with black bows.

Pickett   Gifts & Souvenirs
(Map p250; ☎020-7823 5638; www.pickett. co.uk; cnr Sloane St & Sloane Tce, SW1; ⏰9.30am-6.30pm Mon-Tue, Thu & Fri, 10am-7pm Wed, to 6pm Sat; ⊖Sloane Sq) ✒ Walking into Picketts as an adult is a bit like walking into a sweet shop as a child: the exquisite leather goods are all so colourful and beautiful that you don't really know where to start. Choice items include the perfectly finished

handbags, the exquisite roll-up backgammon sets and the men's grooming sets. All leather goods are made in Britain.

British Red Cross   Vintage
(☎020-7376 7300; 69-71 Old Church St, SW3; ⏰10am-6pm Mon-Sat, noon-5pm Sun; ⊖Sloane Sq) The motto 'One man's rubbish is another man's treasure' couldn't be truer in this part of London, where the 'rubbish' is made up of designer gowns, cashmere jumpers and perhaps a first edition or two. Obviously the price tags are a little higher than in your run-of-the-mill charity shop (£40 rather than £5 for a jumper or jacket), but it's still a bargain for the quality and browsing is half the fun.

❾ North London

Stables Market   Market
(Map p254; www.camdenmarket.com; Chalk Farm Rd, NW1; ⏰10am-6pm; ⊖Chalk Farm) Connected to the Lock Market, the Stables is the best part of the Camden Market complex, with antiques, Asian artefacts, rugs, retro

Stables Market

furniture and clothing. As the name suggests, it used to be an old stables complex, complete with horse hospital, where up to 800 horses (who worked hauling barges on Regent's Canal) were housed.

Camden Lock Market Market
(Map p254; www.camdenmarket.com; 54-56 Camden Lock Pl, NW1; ⊗10am-6pm; ⊜Camden Town) Right next to the canal lock, this is the original Camden Market, with diverse food stalls, ceramics, furniture, oriental rugs, musical instruments and clothes.

Harry Potter Shop at Platform 9¾ Gifts & Souvenirs
(Map p254; www.harrypotterplatform934.com; King's Cross Station, N1; ⊗8am-10pm Mon-Sat, 9am-9pm Sun; ⊜King's Cross St Pancras) With Pottermania refusing to die down, and Diagon Alley impossible to find when your junior witches and wizards are seeking a wand of their own, take the family directly to King's Cross Station. This little wood-panelled store also stocks jumpers sporting the colours of Hogwarts' four houses (Gryffindor having pride of place) and assorted merchandise, including, of course, the books.

⊙ The City

London Silver Vaults Arts & Crafts
(Map p245; ☑020-7242 3844; www.silvervaultslondon.com; 53-63 Chancery Lane, WC2; ⊗9am-5.30pm Mon-Fri, to 1pm Sat; ⊜Chancery Lane) The 30-odd shops that work out of these secure subterranean vaults make up the largest collection of silver under one roof in the world. The different businesses tend to specialise in particular types of silverware, from cutlery sets to picture frames, animal sculptures and lots of jewellery.

⊙ The South Bank

Southbank Centre Shop Homewares
(Map p245; www.southbankcentre.co.uk; Festival Tce, SE1; ⊗10am-9pm Mon-Fri, to 8pm Sat,

Chain Stores

Many bemoan the fact that chains have taken over the main shopping centres, leaving independent shops struggling to balance the books. But chains are cheap, fashionable and always conveniently located, so Londoners (and others) keep going back for more. As well as familiar overseas retailers, such as Gap, H&M, Urban Outfitters and Zara, you'll find plenty of home-grown chains, including luxury womenswear brand Reiss (www.reiss.com) and shoe designer L.K.Bennett (www.lkbennett.com), and global giant Topshop, for whom supermodel Kate Moss has designed a number of limited-edition collections.

Urban Outfitters
MUBUS7 / SHUTTERSTOCK ©

noon-8pm Sun; ⊜Waterloo) This is the place to come for quirky London books, 1950s-inspired homewares, original prints and creative gifts for children. The shop is rather eclectic but you're sure to find unique gifts or souvenirs to take home.

Lovely & British Gifts & Souvenirs
(Map p245; ☑020-7378 6570; www.facebook.com/lovelyandbritish; 132a Bermondsey St, SE1; ⊗10am-6pm Mon-Fri, to 7pm Sat, 11am-5pm Sun; ⊜London Bridge) As the name suggests, this gorgeous Bermondsey boutique prides itself on stocking prints, jewellery and homewares (crockery especially) from British designers. It's an eclectic mix of wares, with very reasonable prices, which make lovely presents or souvenirs.

South Bank Book Market   Market
(Map p245; Riverside Walk, SE1; ☺11am-7pm, shorter hours winter; ⊖Waterloo) The South Bank Book Market sells prints and secondhand books daily under the arches of Waterloo Bridge. You'll find anything here, from fiction to children's books, and comics to classics.

ⓐ The West End

Fortnum & Mason   Department Store
(Map p248; ☏020-7734 8040; www.fortnumand mason.com; 181 Piccadilly, W1; ☺10am-8pm Mon-Sat, 11.30am-6pm Sun; ⊖Piccadilly Circus) With its classic eau-de-Nil (pale green) colour scheme, 'the Queen's grocery store' established in 1707 refuses to yield to modern times. Its staff – men and women – still wear old-fashioned tailcoats and its glamorous food hall is supplied with hampers, cut marmalade, speciality teas, superior fruitcakes and so forth. Fortnum & Mason remains the quintessential London shopping experience.

Hatchards   Books
(Map p248; ☏020-7439 9921; www.hatchards. co.uk; 187 Piccadilly, W1; ☺9.30am-8pm Mon-Sat, noon-6.30pm Sun; ⊖Green Park, Piccadilly Circus) London's oldest bookshop dates back to 1797. Holding three royal warrants, it's a stupendous bookshop now in the Waterstones (a British book retailer) stable, with a solid supply of signed editions and bursting at its smart seams with very browsable stock. There's a strong selection of 1st editions on the ground floor and regularly scheduled literary events.

Hamleys   Toys
(Map p248; ☏0371 704 1977; www.hamleys.com; 188-196 Regent St, W1; ☺10am-9pm Mon-Fri, 9.30am-9pm Sat, noon-6pm Sun; ⊖Oxford Circus) Claiming to be the world's oldest (and some say, the largest) toy store, Hamleys moved to its address on Regent St in 1881. From the basement's Star Wars Collection and ground floor where staff blow bubbles and glide foam boomerangs through the air with practised nonchalance to Lego World and a cafe on the 5th floor, it's a rich layer cake of playthings.

Hamleys' Christmas display window

ELENA ROSTUNOVA / SHUTTERSTOCK ©

We Built
This City
Gifts & Souvenirs

(Map p248; ✆020-3642 9650; www.webuilt-this
city.com; 56-57 Carnaby St, W1; ⊙10am-7pm
Mon-Wed, to 8pm Thu-Sat, 11am-7pm Sun;
⊖Oxford Circus) Taking a commendable
stand against Union Jack hats and black-
cab key rings, We Built This City is a shop
selling London-themed souvenirs that the
recipient might actually want. The products
are artistic and thoughtful, and celebrate
the city's creative side.

Cambridge
Satchel
Company
Fashion & Accessories

(Map p248; ✆020-3077 1100; www.cambridge
satchel.com; 31 James St, WC2; ⊙10am-8pm
Mon-Fri, to 7pm Sat, 11am-6pm Sun; ⊖Covent
Garden) The classic British leather-satchel
concept has morphed into a trendy and
colourful array of backpacks, totes, clutch-
es, work and music bags, minisatchels and
more for men and women.

Vintage House
Drinks

(Map p248; ✆020-7437 2592; www.vintage
house.london; 42 Old Compton St, W1; ⊙9am-
11pm Mon-Fri, 10am-11pm Sat, noon-10pm Sun;
⊖Leicester Sq) A whisky connoisseur's paradise, this shop stocks more than 1400 varieties of single malt Scotch, from smooth
Macallan to peaty Lagavulin. It also offers a
huge array of spirits and liqueurs that you
wouldn't find in your average off-licence.

Gosh!
Books

(Map p248; ✆020-7636 1011; www.goshlondon.
com; 1 Berwick St, W1; ⊙10.30am-7pm; ⊖Picca-
dilly Circus) Make your way here for graphic
novels, manga and children's books, such
as the Tintin and Asterix series. It's also a
great place for gifts for kids and teenagers.

Reckless Records
Music

(Map p248; ✆020-7437 4271; www.reckless.
co.uk; 30 Berwick St, W1; ⊙10am-7pm; ⊖Oxford
Circus, Tottenham Court Rd) This outfit hasn't
really changed in spirit since it first opened
its doors in 1984. It still stocks secondhand
records and CDs, from punk, soul, dance
and independent to mainstream.

James Smith
& Sons
Fashion & Accessories

(Map p248; ✆020-7836 4731; www.james-smith.
co.uk; 53 New Oxford St, WC1; ⊙10am-5.45pm
Mon, Tue, Thu & Fri, 10.30am-5.45pm Wed, 10am-
5.15pm Sat; ⊖Tottenham Court Rd) Nobody
makes and stocks such elegant umbrellas
(not to mention walking sticks and canes)
as this place. It's been fighting the British
weather from the same address since
1857 and, thanks to London's ever-present
downpours, will hopefully do great business
for years to come. Prices start at around
£40 for a pocket umbrella.

Liberty
Department Store

(Map p248; ✆020-7734 1234; www.liberty.
co.uk; Great Marlborough St, W1; ⊙10am-8pm
Mon-Sat, noon-6pm Sun; ⊖Oxford Circus) An
irresistible blend of contemporary styles
in an old-fashioned mock-Tudor atmosphere (1875), Liberty has a huge cosmetics
department and an accessories floor, along
with a breathtaking lingerie section, all at
sky-high prices. A classic London gift or
souvenir is a Liberty fabric print, especially
in the form of a scarf.

Selfridges
Department Store

(Map p250; ✆0800 123 400; www.selfridges.
com; 400 Oxford St, W1; ⊙9.30am-9pm Mon-Sat,
11.30am-6pm Sun; ⊖Bond St) Selfridges loves
innovation – it's famed for its inventive window displays by international artists, gala
shows and, above all, its amazing range of
products. It's the trendiest of London's one-
stop shops, with labels such as Alexander
McQueen, Tom Ford, Missoni, Victoria
Beckham and so on; an unparalleled
food hall; and Europe's largest cosmetics
department.

Stanford's
Books, Maps

(Map p248; ✆020-7836 1321; www.stanfords.
co.uk; 12-14 Long Acre, WC2; ⊙9am-8pm Mon-
Sat, 11.30am-6pm Sun; ⊖Leicester Sq, Covent
Garden) Trading from this address since 1853,
this granddaddy of travel bookshops and
seasoned seller of maps, guides, globes and
literature is a destination in its own right.
Ernest Shackleton, David Livingstone and,

Top London Souvenirs

1 Tea

The British drink par excellence, with plenty of iconic names to choose from. For lovely packaging too, try Fortnum & Mason (p164; pictured above) or Harrods (p161).

2 Vintage Clothes & Shoes

Your London vintage fashion finds will forever be associated with your trip to the city. Start your search at the Sunday UpMarket (p158).

3 British Design

With its cool and understated chic, British design has made a name for itself worldwide. Try the Conran Shop (p161; pictured above).

4 Music

London is brilliant for buying records. Try Rough Trade East (p158) or Reckless Records (p165; pictured above).

5 London Toys

Double-decker buses, Paddington Bears, guards in bearskin hats: London's icons make for great souvenirs. Hamleys (p164) is the place to go.

more recently, Michael Palin and Brad Pitt have all popped in and shopped here.

Gay's the Word   Books

(Map p254; ☎020-7278 7654; www.gaystheword. co.uk; 66 Marchmont St, WC1; ☺10am-6.30pm Mon-Sat, 2-6pm Sun; ☻Russell Sq) This London gay institution has been selling books nobody else stocks since 1979, with a superb range of gay- and lesbian-interest books and magazines plus a real community spirit. Used books available as well.

Agent Provocateur   Clothing

(Map p248; ☎020-7439 0229; www.agentprovo cateur.com; 6 Broadwick St, W1; ☺11am-7pm Mon-Wed, Fri & Sat, 11am-8pm Thu, noon-5pm Sun; ☻Oxford Circus) For women's lingerie designed to be worn and seen, and certainly *not* hidden, pull up to wonderful Agent Provocateur, originally set up by Joseph Corré, son of Vivienne Westwood. Its sexy and saucy corsets, and bras and nighties for all shapes and sizes, exude confident and positive sexuality. Lovely staff too.

Skoob Books   Books

(Map p254; ☎020-7278 8760; www.skoob. com; 66 The Brunswick, off Marchmont St, WC1; ☺10.30am-8pm Mon-Sat, to 6pm Sun; ☻Russell Sq) Skoob (you work out the name) has got to be London's largest secondhand bookshop, with some 55,000 titles spread over 2000 sq ft of floor space (plus more than a million further books in a warehouse outside town). If you can't find it here, it probably doesn't exist.

Molton Brown   Cosmetics

(Map p248; ☎020-7240 8383; www.molton brown.co.uk; 18 Russell St, WC2; ☺10am-7pm Mon-Sat, 11am-6pm Sun; ☻Covent Garden) A fabulously fragrant British natural-beauty range, Molton Brown is *the* choice for boutique-hotel, posh-restaurant and 1st-class-airline bathrooms. Its skincare products offer plenty of pampering for both men and women. In this store you can also pick up home accessories.

⊙ West London

Rough Trade West   Music

(Map p250; ☎020-7229 8541; www.roughtrade. com; 130 Talbot Rd, W11; ☺10am-6.30pm Mon-Sat, 11am-5pm Sun; ☻Ladbroke Grove) With its underground, alternative and vintage rarities, this home of the eponymous punk-music label remains a haven for vinyl junkies.

Rellik   Vintage

(Map p250; ☎020-8962 0089; www.rellik london.co.uk; 8 Golborne Rd; ☺10am-6pm Tue-Sat; ☻Westbourne Park) Incongruously located opposite one of London's most notorious tower blocks (the God-awful-yet-heritage-listed) concrete Trellick Tower – Rellik is a fashionista-favourite retro store. It stocks vintage numbers from the 1920s to the 1980s, and rummaging among the frippery, it's not unusual to find an Yves Saint-Laurent coat, a Chloe suit or an Ossie Clark dress.

Royal Trinity Hospice   Clothing

(Map p250; ☎020-7361 1530; www.royaltrinity hospice.london/kensington; 31-33 Kensington Church St, W8; ☺10am-6pm Mon-Sat, 11am-5pm Sun; ☻High St Kensington) For designer labels and top-end items in female clothing, shoes and bags, it's well worth a browse through this well-supplied charity shop on Kensington Church St. Stock turnover is pretty high, so fresh items are always coming in, and the sister shop alongside has menswear and further odds and ends.

Book & Comic Exchange   Books

(Map p250; ☎020-7598 2233; www.mgeshops. com/book-comic-exchange; 30 & 32 Pembridge Rd; ☺10am-8pm; ☻Notting Hill Gate) Stuffed with surprises, this shop is inundated with early issues of *Superboy, Batman, Justice League, The Flash, The Hulk, Spiderman, The Silver Surfer* and a host of other superhero comics, backed up by sizeable slabs of collectable music magazines and walls densely stuffed with secondhand books, as well as a geeky 'sci-fi corridor' and a scattering of collectible 1st editions.

BAR OPEN

Afternoon pints, all-night clubbing and beyond

Bar Open

You need only glance at William Hogarth's Gin Lane *print from 1751 to realise that Londoners and alcohol have had more than a passing acquaintance. Londoners are enthusiastic drinkers and going to the pub is an integral part of socialising in the capital.*

The metropolis offers a huge variety of venues in which to wet your whistle, from cosy neighbourhood pubs to glitzy all-night clubs, and everything in between. Note that when it comes to clubbing, a little planning will help you keep costs down and skip queues.

In This Section

Opening Hours

Pubs traditionally open at 11am or midday and close at 11pm, with an earlier closing on Sunday. Some bars and pubs open later and remain open until around 2am or 3am on weekends. Clubs generally open at 10pm on the weekend and close between 3am and 7am.

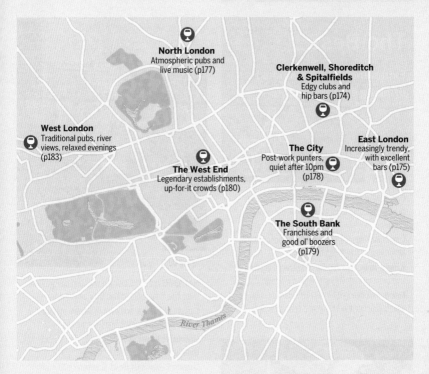

North London
Atmospheric pubs and
live music (p177)

**Clerkenwell, Shoreditch
& Spitalfields**
Edgy clubs and
hip bars (p174)

West London
Traditional pubs, river
views, relaxed evenings
(p183)

The West End
Legendary establishments,
up-for-it crowds (p180)

The City
Post-work punters,
quiet after 10pm
(p178)

East London
Increasingly trendy,
with excellent
bars (p175)

The South Bank
Franchises and
good ol' boozers
(p179)

River Thames

Costs & Tipping

Many clubs are free or cheaper mid-
week. Some places are considerably
cheaper if you arrive earlier in the
night – or book online.

Tipping isn't customary.

Useful Resources

London on the Inside (www.londonon-
theinside.com)

Skiddle (www.skiddle.com) Comprehensive info on clubnights, DJs and
events.

Time Out (www.timeout.com/london)
Has details of bars, pubs and nightlife.

The Best...

Experience London's finest drinking establishments

Pubs

Cat & Mutton (p176) Great East London boozer, mixing history with modern-day hippery.

Lamb & Flag (p181) Pint-sized perennial favourite in the West End.

King's Arms (p179) Cosy stalwart on one of the best-preserved streets in London.

Fox & Anchor (p174) Glorious Victorian establishment with period features aplenty.

Views

Netil360 (p175) Uberhip rooftop bar gazing over the East End to the City skyline.

Oblix (p179) It's not even halfway up the Shard, but the views are legendary.

Galvin at Windows (p183) Fabulous cocktails and views west across Hyde Park.

Queen Elizabeth Roof Garden (p182; pictured above) Alfresco drinks on the Thames.

Cocktail Bars

Dukes London (p181) Bond-worthy martinis in Ian Fleming's favourite St James's bar.

Zetter Townhouse Cocktail Lounge (p174) Luxe, antique-filled lounge tucked away in Clerkenwell.

Little Bird Gin (p179) Pop-up bar serving cocktails in jam jars from small-batch gin-maker.

American Bar (p181) Live piano music and art deco lines at this historic venue.

Beer Gardens

Windsor Castle (p182) Come summer, regulars abandon the Windsor's historic interior for the chilled-out garden.

Earl of Lonsdale (p183) Old-time Notting Hill pub with a large and leafy beer garden.

Edinboro Castle (p184) A festive place to stretch out on a summer evening

Clubs

Fabric (p175) Massive club with a global reputation.
Notting Hill Arts Club (p182) Attracts an eclectic and musically curious crowd.
Heaven (p182) Perennially popular mixed/gay club.

For Date Nights

Cocktail Trading Co (p175) Impress with cocktails & classy settings.
Queen Elizabeth Roof Garden (p179) Alfresco drinks on the South Bank with views of the Thames.

Bars

Bar Pepito (p178) A delightful, pocket-sized Andalucian bar dedicated to sherry.
Gordon's Wine Bar (p183; pictured above) A long-standing institution in darkened vaults.
Queen of Hoxton (p174) A games room, a roof terrace, movie nights, dance lessons and of course, DJs.
Proud Camden (p178) A jack of all trades kind of place, featuring live music, DJs and art exhibitions.

☆Lonely Planet's Top Choices

Cat & Mutton (p177) An atmospheric hip and historic East London pub.
Dukes London (p183) Get your Bond on in Ian Fleming's favourite St James's bar.
Edinboro Castle (p116) A wonderful spot for a pint on a summer evening.
Oblix (p179) Incredible views from one of London's iconic buildings, the Shard.

Clerkenwell, Shoreditch & Spitalfields

Cocktail Trading Co   Cocktail Bar
(Map p253; www.thecocktailtradingco.co.uk; 68 Bethnal Green Rd, E1; ⏱5pm-midnight Mon-Fri, 2pm-midnight Sat, 2-10.30pm Sun; ☒Shoreditch High St) In an area famous for its edgy, don't-give-a-damn attitude, this exquisite cocktail bar stands out for its classiness and cocktail confidence. The drinks are truly unrivalled, from the flavours to the presentation – bottles presented in envelopes, ice cubes as big as a Rubik's cube and so on. The decor is reminiscent of a colonial-era gentlemen's club, just warmer and more welcoming.

Zetter Townhouse Cocktail Lounge   Cocktail Bar
(Map p253; ☎020-7324 4545; www.thezetter townhouse.com; 49-50 St John's Sq, EC1V; ⏱7.30am-12.45am; ☎; ☻Farringdon) Tucked away behind an unassuming door on St John's Sq, this ground-floor bar is decorated with plush armchairs, stuffed animal heads and a legion of lamps. The cocktail list takes its theme from the area's distilling history – recipes of yesteryear plus homemade tinctures and cordials are used to create interesting and unusual tipples. House cocktails are all £11.

Fox & Anchor   Pub
(Map p253; www.foxandanchor.com; 115 Charterhouse St, EC1M; ⏱7am-11pm Mon-Fri, 8.30am-11pm Sat & Sun; ☎; ☻Barbican) Behind the Fox & Anchor's wonderful art nouveau facade is a stunning traditional Victorian pub that has retained its three beautiful snugs at the back of the bar. Fully celebrating its proximity to Smithfield Market, the food is gloriously meaty. Only the most voracious of carnivores should opt for the City Boy Breakfast (£19.50).

Queen of Hoxton   Bar
(Map p253; www.queenofhoxton.com; 1 Curtain Rd, EC2A; ⏱4pm-midnight Mon-Wed, to 2am Thu-Sat; ☎; ☻Liverpool St) This industrial-chic bar has a games room, basement and varied music nights (including dance lessons and ukulele jamming sessions), but the real drawcard is the vast rooftop bar, decked out with

Ye Olde Mitre

flowers, fairy lights and even a wigwam. It has fantastic views across the city.

Ye Olde Mitre
Pub

Map p253; www.yeolldemitreholborn.co.uk; 1 Ely Ct, EC1N; ☺11am-11pm Mon-Fri; 🎧; ⊖Farringdon) A delightfully cosy historic pub with an extensive beer selection, tucked away in a backstreet off Hatton Garden, It was built in 1546 for the servants of Ely Palace. There's no music, so rooms echo only with amiable chit-chat. Queen Elizabeth I danced around the cherry tree by the bar, they say.

Worship St
Whistling Shop
Cocktail Bar

(Map p253; 🖉020-7247 0015; www.whistlingshop.com; 63 Worship St, EC2A; ☺5pm-midnight Mon & Tue, to 1am Wed & Thu, to 2am Fri & Sat; ⊖Old St) While the name is Victorian slang for a place selling illicit booze, this subterranean drinking den's master mixologists explore the experimental limits of cocktail chemistry and aromatic science, as well as concocting the classics. Many ingredients are made with rotary evaporators in the onsite lab. Also runs cocktail masterclasses.

Fabric
Club

(Map p253; 🖉0207 336 8898; www.fabriclondon.com; 77a Charterhouse St, EC1M; cover £5-25; ☺11pm-7am Fri, to 8am Sat, to 5.30am Sun; ⊖Farringdon, Barbican) London's leading club, Fabric's three separate dance floors in a huge converted cold store opposite Smithfield meat market draws impressive queues (buy tickets online). FabricLive (on selected Fridays) rumbles with drum 'n' bass and dubstep, while Fabric (usually on Saturdays but also on selected Fridays) is the club's signature live DJ night. Sunday's WetYourSelf! delivers house, techno and electronica.

Jerusalem Tavern
Pub

(Map p253; www.stpetersbrewery.co.uk; 55 Britton St, EC1M; ☺11am-11pm Mon-Fri; 🎧; ⊖Farringdon) Pick a wood-panelled cubicle at this tiny and highly atmospheric pub housed in a building dating from 1720 and select from the fantastic beverages brewed by St Peter's Brewery in Suffolk. Be warned: it's hugely popular and often very crowded.

🍾🍸 The Pub

The pub (public house) is at the heart of London life and is one of the capital's great social levellers. Virtually every Londoner has a 'local' and looking for your own is a fun part of any visit to the capital.

Pubs in the City and other central areas are mostly after-work drinking dens, busy from 5pm onwards with the postwork crowd during the week. But in more residential areas, pubs come into their own at weekends, when long lunches turn into sloshy afternoons and groups of friends settle in for the night. Many also run popular quizzes on week nights. Other pubs entice punters through the doors with live music or comedy. Some have developed such a reputation for the quality of their food that they've been dubbed gastropubs.

You can order almost any beverage you like in a pub: beer, wine, soft drinks, spirits and sometimes hot drinks too. Some specialise in craft beer, offering drinks from local microbreweries, including real ale, fruit beers, organic ciders and other rarer beverages. Others, particularly the gastropubs, invest in a good wine list.

East London

Netil360
Rooftop Bar

(Map p255; www.netil360.com; 1 Westgate St, E8; ☺noon-8.30pm Wed & Sun, to 10.30pm Thu-Sat Apr-Nov; 🎧; ⊖London Fields) Perched atop Netil House, this uberhip rooftop cafe-bar

👍 Beer

The raison d'être of a pub is first and foremost to serve beer. On draught (drawn from the cask), it is served by the pint (570mL) or half-pint (285mL) and, more occasionally, third-of-a-pint for real-ale tasting.

Pubs generally serve a good selection of lager (highly carbonated and drunk cool or cold) and a smaller selection of real ales or 'bitter' (still or only slightly gassy, drunk at room temperature, with strong flavours). The best-known British lager brand is Carling, though you'll find everything from Fosters to San Miguel.

Among the multitude of ales on offer in London pubs, London Pride, Courage Best, Burton Ale, Adnam's, Theakston (in particular Old Peculiar) and Old Speckled Hen are among the best. Once considered something of an old man's drink, real ale has enjoyed a renaissance among young Londoners, riding tandem with the current fashion for craft beer (small-batch beers from independent brewers). Staff at bars serving good selections of real ales and craft beers are often hugely knowledgable, just like a sommelier in a restaurant, so ask them for recommendations if you're not sure what to order.

Stout, the best known of which is Irish Guinness, is a slightly sweet, dark beer with a distinct flavour that comes from malt that is roasted before fermentation.

offers incredible views over London, with brass telescopes enabling you to get better acquainted with workers in the Gherkin. In between drinks you can knock out a game of croquet on the Astroturf, or perhaps book a hot tub for you and your mates to stew in.

Cat & Mutton   Pub
(Map p255; ☎020-7249 6555; www.catandmut ton.com; 76 Broadway Market, E8; ⊙noon-11pm Mon, to midnight Tue-Thu, to 1am Fri, 10am-1am Sat, noon-11.30pm Sun; ⊖London Fields) At this fabulous Georgian pub, Hackney hipsters sip pints under the watchful eyes of hunting trophies, black-and-white photos of old-time boxers and a portrait of Karl Marx. If it's crammed downstairs, as it often is, head up the spiral staircase to the comfy couches. DJs play on the weekends.

Satan's Whiskers   Cocktail Bar
(Map p255; ☎020-7739 8362; www.facebook. com/satanswhiskers; 343 Cambridge Heath Rd, E2; ⊙5pm-midnight; ⊖Bethnal Green) Unassuming and indeed unappealing till you get inside, this little cocktail bar exorcises first impressions with welcoming staff, an ever-changing drinks menu, crazy taxidermy and good music, making it a memorable stop on a Bethnal Green crawl.

Dove Freehouse   Pub
(Map p255; ☎020-7275 7617; www.dovepubs.com; 24-28 Broadway Market, E8; ⊙noon-11pm Sun-Fri, 11am-11pm Sat; 🛜; ⊖London Fields) Alluring at any time, the Dove has a rambling series of rooms and a wide range of Belgian Trappist, wheat and fruit-flavoured beers. Drinkers spill on to the street in warmer weather, or hunker down in the low-lit back room.

Bethnal Green
Working Men's Club   Club
(Map p255; ☎020-7739 7170; www.workersplay time.net; 42-44 Pollard Row, E2; ⊙pub 6pm-late Wed-Sat, club hours vary; ⊖Bethnal Green) As it says on the tin, this is a true working men's club. Except that this one has opened its doors and let in all kinds of off-the-wall club nights, including trashy burlesque, gay and lesbian shindigs, retro nights, beach parties and bake-offs. Expect sticky carpets, a

Cat & Mutton

shimmery stage set and a space akin to a school-hall disco.

Kensington & Hyde Park

Anglesea Arms   Pub
(Map p250; ☏020-7373 7960; www.anglesea arms.com; 15 Selwood Tce, SW7; ☺11am-11pm Mon-Sat, noon-10.30pm Sun; ☻South Kensington) Seasoned with age and decades of ale-quaffing patrons (including Charles Dickens, who lived on the same road, and DH Lawrence), this old-school pub boasts considerable character and a strong showing of brews, while the terrace out front swarms with punters in warmer months. Arch-criminal Bruce Reynolds masterminded the Great Train Robbery over drinks here.

Queen's Arms   Pub
(Map p250; www.thequeensarmskensington. co.uk; 30 Queen's Gate Mews, SW7; ☺noon-11pm Mon-Sat, to 10.30pm Sun; ☻Gloucester Rd) Just around the corner from the Royal Albert Hall is this blue-grey-painted godsend. Located in an adorable cobbled-mews setting off bustling Queen's Gate, it beckons with a cosy interior and a right-royal selection of ales – including selections from small, local cask brewers – and ciders on tap.

North London

Bar Pepito   Wine Bar
(Map p254; www.camino.uk.com/location/ bar-pepito; 3 Varnishers Yard, The Regent's Quarter, N1; ☺5pm-midnight Mon-Fri, 6pm-midnight Sat; ☻King's Cross St Pancras) This tiny, intimate Andalusian bodega specialises in sherry and tapas. Novices fear not: the staff are on hand to advise. They're also experts at food pairings. To go the whole hog, try a tasting flight of selected sherries and matching snacks.

Proud Camden   Bar
(Map p254; www.proudcamden.com; Stables Market, Chalk Farm Rd, NW1; ☺11am-1.30am Mon-Sat, to midnight Sun; ☻Chalk Farm) Proud occupies a former horse hospital within Stables Market, with private booths in the old stalls, fantastic artworks on the walls and a kooky

garden terrace complete with a hot tub. It's also one of Camden's best music venues, with live bands and DJs most nights (entry free to £15).

Euston Tap   Bar

(Map p254; ☑020-3137 8837; www.eustontap. com; 190 Euston Rd, NW1; ⓒnoon-11pm Mon-Sat, to 10pm Sun; ⊖Euston) This specialist drinking spot inhabits a monumental stone structure on the approach to Euston Station. Craft-beer devotees can choose between 16 cask ales, 25 keg beers and 150 brews by the bottle. Grab a seat on the pavement, take the tight spiral staircase upstairs or take away.

Drink, Shop & Do   Bar

(Map p254; ☑020-7278 4335; www.drinkshopdo. co.uk; 9 Caledonian Rd, N1; ⓒ7.30am-midnight Mon-Thu, 7.30am-2am Fri, 10.30am-2am Sat, to 6pm Sun; 🛜; ⊖King's Cross St Pancras) This kooky little outlet will not be pigeonholed. As its name suggests, it is many things to many people: a bar, a cafe, an activities centre, a disco even. But the idea is that there will always be drinking (be it tea or gin), music and things to do – anything from dancing to building Lego robots.

Craft Beer Co   Craft Beer

(Map p253; www.thecraftbeerco.com; 55 White Lion St, N1; ⓒ4-11pm Mon-Thu, noon-1am Fri & Sat, to 10.30pm Sun; ⊖Angel) Riding the wave of the craft-beer craze, this lovely pub is pushing the envelope by offering its drinkers a daily beer menu with dozens of brews from around the world, whether from kegs, casks, bottles or cans. It has a burger menu

Richmond, Kew & Hampton Court

Tap on the Line   Pub

(☑020-8332 1162; www.tapontheline.co.uk; Station Approach, TW9; 🛜; ⊖Kew Gardens) Right by the platform at Kew Gardens tube station (the only London tube station platform with its very own pub), this lovingly re-stored Victorian yellow-brick boozer makes for a glorious conclusion to a summer's

rambling around Kew. With outside seating in the courtyard at the front, it's also a fine haven for a pub lunch. There's live music on Sundays from 7pm.

The City

Jamaica Wine House   Pub

(Map p245; ☑020-7929 6972; www.jamaicawine house.co.uk; 12 St Michael's Alley, EC3; ⓒ11am-11pm Mon-Fri; ⊖Bank) Not a wine bar at all, the 'Jam Pot' is a historic wood-lined pub that stands on the site of what was London's first coffee house (1652). Reached by a narrow alley, it's slightly tricky to find but well worth seeking out for the age-old ambience of its darkened rooms.

Ye Olde Cheshire Cheese   Pub

(Map p245; ☑020-7353 6170; Wine Office Court, 145 Fleet St, EC4; ⓒ11.30am-11pm Mon-Fri, noon-11pm Sat; ⊖Chancery Lane) Rebuilt in 1667 after the Great Fire, this is one of London's most famous pubs, accessed via a narrow alley off Fleet St. Over its long history, Dr Johnson, Thackeray and Dickens have all supped in its gloriously gloomy surrounds. The vaulted cellars are thought to be remnants of a 13th-century monastery.

City of London Distillery   Cocktail Bar

(Map p245; ☑020-7936 3636; www.cityoflon dondistillery.com; 22 Bride Lane, EC4; ⓒ4-11pm Mon-Sat; ⊖Blackfriars) Hogarth's famous *Gin Lane* print provides a warning before you descend the stairs to one of the few bars in London to distill its own 'mother's ruin' on-site. If you'd like to know more about what goes on in the shiny distilling vats, proudly displayed behind glass windows, book a tour or attend a gin-making class.

Madison   Cocktail Bar

(Map p245; ☑020-3693 5160; www.madison london.net; rooftop, 1 New Change, EC4; ⓒ11am-midnight Mon-Thu, to 1am Fri & Sat, noon to 9pm Sun; ⊖St Paul's) Perched atop One New Change with a drop-dead gorgeous view of St Paul's, Madison offers a large open-air roof terrace with a restaurant on one side and a cocktail bar on the other; we come for the latter. Drinkers must be aged over 21; no trainers or flip-flops admitted, however fashionable. Expect to queue.

The South Bank

Oblix   Bar
(Map p245; www.oblixrestaurant.com; 32nd fl, Shard, 31 St Thomas St, SE1; ⊘noon-11pm; ⊜London Bridge) On the 32nd floor of the Shard (p79), Oblix offers mesmerising vistas of London. You can come for anything from a coffee (£3.50) to a cocktail (from £13.50) and enjoy virtually the same views as the official viewing galleries of the Shard (but at a reduced cost and with the added bonus of a drink). Live music every night from 7pm.

The downside is Oblix's popularity: it can be hard to get in, especially at mealtimes when many of the tables are reserved for diners. Note that reasonably smart attire is expected, so no trainers/sneakers or flip-flops. Children welcome before 6pm.

Scootercaffe   Bar
(Map p245; 132 Lower Marsh, SE1; ⊘8.30am-11pm Mon-Thu, to midnight Fri, 10am-midnight Sat, to 11pm Sun; ☎; ⊜Waterloo) A well-established fixture on the up-and-coming Lower Marsh road, this funky cafe-bar and former scooter-repair shop with a Piatti scooter in the window serves killer hot chocolates, coffee and decadent cocktails. Unusually, you're allowed to bring in takeaway food.

Little Bird Gin   Cocktail Bar
(Map p245; www.littlebirdgin.com; Maltby St, SE1; ⊘5-10pm Thu & Fri, 10am-10pm Sat, 11am-4pm Sun; ⊜London Bridge) This South London–based distillery opens a pop-up bar in a workshop at Maltby Street Market (p147) to ply merry punters with devilishly good cocktails (£5 to £7), served in jam jars or apothecary's glass bottles.

King's Arms   Pub
(Map p245; ☎020-7207 0784; www.thekingsarmslondon.co.uk; 25 Roupell St, SE1; ⊘11am-11pm Mon-Fri, noon-11pm Sat, noon-10.30pm

🍷 Clubbing

When it comes to clubbing, London is up there with the best of them. You'll probably know what you want to experience – it might be big clubs such as Fabric (p175), or sweaty shoebox clubs with the freshest DJ talent – but there's plenty to tempt you to branch out from your usual tastes and try something new. Whether thumping techno, indie rock, Latin, ska, pop, dubstep, grime, minimal electro, R&B or hip hop, there's something going on every night.

There are clubs across town, though it has to be said that the best of them are moving further out of the centre every year, so be prepared to take a hike on a night bus. The East End is the top area for cutting-edge clubs, especially Shoreditch. Dalston and Hackney are popular for makeshift clubs in restaurant basements and former shops – so it's great for night-fun hunters. Camden Town still favours the indie crowd, while King's Cross has a bit of everything. The gay party crowd mainly gravitates south of the river, especially Vauxhall, although they still maintain a toehold in the West End and East End.

Fabric (p175)
PYMCA \ UIG / AGE FOTOSTOCK ©

Sun; ⊜Waterloo) Relaxed and charming, this neighbourhood boozer at the corner of a terraced Waterloo backstreet was a funeral parlour in a previous life. The large traditional bar area, complete with open fire in winter, serves up a good selection of ales and bitters. It gets packed with after-work crowds between 6pm and 8pm.

Rake   Pub

(Map p245; 📞020-7407 0557; www.utobeer. co.uk; 14 Winchester Walk, SE1; ⊙noon-11pm Mon-Fri, 11am-11pm Sat, noon-10pm Sun; ⊖London Bridge) With a fantastic line of beers to slake any thirst, the Rake offers more than 130 labels – many of them international craft brews – at any one time. There are 10 taps, and the selection of craft beers, real ales, lagers and ciders (with one-third-pint measures) changes constantly. It's a teensy place yet always busy; the bamboo-decorated decking outside is especially popular.

Anspach & Hobday   Microbrewery

(Map p245; www.anspachandhobday.com; 118 Druid St, SE1; ⊙5-9.30pm Fri, 10.30am-6.30pm Sat, 12.30-5pm Sun; ⊖London Bridge) It's all about porter at this microbrewery, although lighter ales are also brewed. Beer aficionados will love trying brews from the experimental range; beers come in large 750ml bottles and are rotated regularly. There's a nice outdoor seating area.

Jensen   Distillery

(Map p245; www.jensengin.com; 55 Stanworth St, SE1; ⊙10am-4pm Sat, from 11am Sun; ⊖London Bridge) A micro gin distillery, Jensen Gin produces two main kinds: Bermondsey Dry, a variation of the famous London Dry gin; and Old Tom, a more intense, opaque gin that is unsweetened. The distillery throws open its doors at weekends for tastings, sales (750ml bottles cost £20 to £25) and cocktails (£5.95).

The West End

American Bar   Bar

(Map p250; www.thebeaumont.com/dining/ american-bar; The Beaumont, Brown Hart Gardens, W1; ⊙11.30am-midnight Mon-Sat, to 11pm Sun; 📶; ⊖Bond St) Sip a bourbon or a classic cocktail in the classic 1930s art deco ambience of this stylish bar at the hallmark **Beaumont hotel** (📞020-7499 1001; www.thebeaumont.com; Brown Hart Gardens, W1; d/studio/ste incl breakfast from £495/720/1575; ❄📶; ⊖Bond St). It's central, period and like a gentleman's club, but far from stuffy. Only

From left: London pub; Dukes London; American Bar (Savoy)

a few years old, the American Bar feels like it's been pouring drinks since the days of the flapper and jazz age.

American Bar   Cocktail Bar

(Map p248; ☏020-7836 4343; www.fairmont. com/savoy-london/dining/americanbar; Savoy, The Strand, WC2; ⊗11.30am-midnight Mon-Sat, noon-midnight Sun; ⊖Covent Garden) Home of the Hanky Panky, White Lady and other classic infusions created on-site, the seriously dishy and elegant American Bar is an icon of London, with soft blue and rust art deco lines and live piano music. Cocktails start at £17.50 and peak at a stupefying £5000 (the Original Sazerac, containing Sazerac de Forge cognac from 1857).

Dukes London   Cocktail Bar

(Map p248; ☏020-7491 4840; www.dukeshotel. com/dukes-bar; Dukes Hotel, 35 St James's Pl, SW1; ⊗2-11pm Mon-Sat, 4-10.30pm Sun; ☎; ⊖Green Park) Sip to-die-for martinis like royalty in a gentleman's-club-like ambience at this tucked-away classic bar where white-jacketed masters mix up some awesomely good preparations. Ian Fleming used to frequent the place, perhaps

perfecting his 'shaken, not stirred' James Bond maxim. Smokers can ease into the secluded Cognac and Cigar Garden to light up cigars purchased here.

Lamb & Flag   Pub

(Map p248; ☏020-7497 9504; www.lambandflag coventgarden.co.uk; 33 Rose St, WC2; ⊗11am-11pm Mon-Sat, noon-10.30pm Sun; ⊖Covent Garden) Everybody's favourite pub in central London, pint-sized Lamb & Flag is full of charm and history, and is on the site of a pub that dates from at least 1772. Rain or shine, you'll have to elbow your way to the bar through the merry crowd drinking outside. Inside are brass fittings and creaky wooden floors.

Gordon's Wine Bar   Bar

(Map p248; ☏020-7930 1408; https://gordons winebar.com; 47 Villiers St, WC2; ⊗11am-11pm Mon-Sat, noon-10pm Sun; ⊖Embankment, Charing Cross) Cavernous, candlelit and atmospheric, Gordon's (founded in 1890) is a victim of its own success – it's relentlessly busy and unless you arrive before the office crowd does (around 6pm), forget about landing a table. The French and New World

VIEW PICTURES / AGE FOTOSTOCK ©

London in a Glass

Sunshine, shades and good company to serve

One part Pimms, three parts lemonade

Highball glass (not a pint, this is a classy drink) and ice

Strawberries, orange and fresh mint – the bare minimum

For additional flourish, lemon, lime and cucumber slices

ERAINBOW / SHUTTERSTOCK ©

Pimms & Lemonade

Pimms & Lemonade in London

Pimms, a gin-based fruity spirit, is the quintessential British summer drink: no sunny afternoon in a beer garden would be complete without a glass (or a jug) of it. It is served with lemonade, mint and fresh fruit. Most pubs and bars serve it, although they may only have all the trimmings in summer.

Top Three Places for Pimms

Edinboro Castle (Map p254; www.edin borocastlepub.co.uk; 57 Mornington Tce, NW1; ⊙noon-11pm Mon-Sat, to 10.30pm Sun; 🛜; ⊖Camden Town)

Queen Elizabeth Roof Garden (Map p245; www.southbankcentre.co.uk; Queen Elizabeth Hall, Southbank Centre, Belvedere Rd, SE1; ⊙10am-10pm Apr-Sep; ⊖Waterloo)

Windsor Castle (Map p250; www.thewind sorcastlekensington.co.uk; 114 Campden Hill Rd, W11; ⊙noon-11pm Mon-Sat, to 10.30pm Sun; 🛜; ⊖Notting Hill Gate) wines are heady and reasonably priced; buy by the glass, the beaker (12cL), the schooner (15cL) or the bottle.

Craft Beer Company   Craft Beer

(Map p248; ☎020-7240 0431; www.thecraft beerco.com/covent-garden; 168 High Holborn, WC1; ⏰noon-midnight Sun-Wed, to 1am Thu-Sat; ⊖Tottenham Court Rd) Probably the best place to go in London to enjoy craft beer, this branch of a six-strong chain boasts 15 cask pumps of UK-sourced beers as well as 30 keg lines and 200-plus bottles and cans of beers from around the world. Most pints are under £5.

Lamb   Pub

(Map p254; ☎020-7405 0713; www.thelamblon don.com; 94 Lamb's Conduit St, WC1; ⏰11am-11pm Mon-Wed, to midnight Thu-Sat, noon-10.30pm Sun; ⊖Russell Sq) The Lamb's central mahogany bar with beautiful Victorian 'snob screens' (so-called as they allowed the well-to-do to drink in private) has been a favourite with locals since 1729. Nearly three centuries later, its popularity hasn't waned, so come early to bag a booth and sample its good selection of Young's bitters and genial atmosphere.

Swift   Cocktail Bar

(Map p248; ☎020-7437 7820; www.barswift.com; 12 Old Compton St, W1; ⏰3pm-midnight Mon-Sat, to 10.30pm Sun; ⊖Leicester Sq, Tottenham Court Rd) Our favourite new place for cocktails, Swift (as in the bird) has a black-and-white, candlelit Upstairs Bar designed for those who want a quick tipple before dinner or the theatre, while the Downstairs Bar (open from 5pm), with its sit-down bar and art deco sofas, is a place to hang out. There's live jazz and blues at the weekend.

Heaven   Club, Gay

(Map p248; http://heaven-live.co.uk; Villiers St, WC2; ⏰11pm-5am Mon, to 4am Thu & Fri, 10.30pm-5am Sat; ⊖Embankment, Charing Cross) This perennially popular mixed/gay club under the arches beneath Charing Cross Station is host to excellent live gigs and club nights. Monday's Popcorn (mixed dance party, with an all-welcome door policy) offers one of the best weeknight's clubbing in the capital. The celebrated G-A-Y takes place here on Thursday (G-A-Y Porn Idol), Friday (G-A-Y Camp Attack) and Saturday (plain ol' G-A-Y).

Galvin at Windows   Bar

(Map p250; ☎020-7208 4021; www.galvinat windows.com; 28th fl, London Hilton on Park Lane, 22 Park Lane, W1; ⏰11am-1am Mon-Wed, to 2am Thu & Fri, 3pm-2am Sat, 11am-11pm Sun; 🛜; ⊖Hyde Park Corner) From the 28th floor of the London Hilton on Park Lane, this swish bar gazes on to awesome views, especially come dusk. Cocktail prices reach similar heights (£10 to £18), but the leather seats are inviting and the marble bar is gorgeous. The one-Michelin-star restaurant (same views) offers a giveaway weekday lunch menu (two/three courses £31/37).

West London

Earl of Lonsdale   Pub

(Map p250; 277-281 Portobello Rd, W11; ⏰noon-11pm Mon-Fri, 10am-11pm Sat, noon-10.30pm Sun; ⊖Notting Hill Gate, Ladbroke Grove) A perfect bolthole for those traipsing Portobello Rd and named after the bon vivant founder of the AA (Automobile Association, *not* Alcoholics Anonymous), the Earl is peaceful during the day, with both old biddies and young hipsters inhabiting the reintroduced snugs. There are Samuel Smith's ales, a fantastic back room with sofas plus banquettes, open fires, a magnificent beer garden and cheery staff.

Notting Hill Arts Club   Club

(Map p250; www.nottinghillartsclub.com; 21 Notting Hill Gate, W11; ⏰6pm-late Mon-Fri, 4pm-late Sat & Sun; 🛜; ⊖Notting Hill Gate) London simply wouldn't be what it is without places like NHAC. Cultivating the underground-music scene, this small basement club attracts a musically curious and experimental crowd. Dress code: no suits and ties.

SHOWTIME

From a night out at the theatre
to live-music venues

Showtime

Whatever it is that sets your spirits soaring or your booty shaking, you'll find it in London. The city's been a world leader in theatre ever since a young man from Stratford-upon-Avon set up shop here in the 16th century. And if London started swinging in the 1960s, its live rock and pop scene has barely let up since.

The trick to bagging tickets to high-profile events and performances is to book ahead – or hope there will be standby tickets on the day. And don't worry if you miss out: there are literally hundreds of smaller gigs and performances every night and the joy is to stumble upon them.

In This Section

Tickets & Websites

Book well ahead for live performances and, if you can, buy directly from the venue.

On the day of performance, you can buy discounted tickets for West End productions from Tkts Leicester Square (www.tkts.co.uk/leicester-square).

Regent's Park Open Air Theatre (p191)

The Best...

Theatre

Shakespeare's Globe (p191) Shakespeare, as it would have been 400 years ago.

National Theatre (p192) Contemporary theatre on the South Bank.

Old Vic (p192) A heavy hitter in London's theatrical scene.

Unicorn Theatre (p192) Top-quality theatre for young audiences.

Live Music

Royal Albert Hall (p189) Gorgeous, grand and spacious, yet strangely intimate.

Pizza Express Jazz Club (p193) Top-class jazz in the basement of a chain restaurant.

O2 Arena (p189) A massive venue for the biggest gigs.

Ronnie Scott's (p194) Britain's most famous jazz club.

Royal Opera House (p193) One of the world's great opera venues, with classical ballet too.

✪ Clerkenwell, Shoreditch & Spitalfields

Electric Cinema   Cinema
(Map p253; ☏020-3350 3490; www.electriccine
ma.co.uk; 64-66 Redchurch St, E2; tickets £11-19;
🚇Shoreditch High St) Run by Shoreditch
House, an uberfashionable private mem-
ber's club, this is cinema-going that will impress a date, with space for an intimate 48
on the comfy armchairs. There's a full bar
and restaurant in the complex, and you can
take your purchases in with you. Tickets go
like crazy, so book ahead.

Sadler's Wells   Dance
(Map p253; ☏020-7863 8000; www.sadlers
wells.com; Rosebery Ave, EC1R; ⊖Angel) A
glittering modern venue that was, in fact,
first established in 1683, Sadler's Wells is
the most eclectic modern-dance and ballet
venue in town, with experimental dance
shows of all genres and from all corners of
the globe. The Lilian Baylis Studio stages
smaller productions.

✪ East London

Vortex Jazz Club   Jazz
(Map p255; ☏020-7254 4097; www.vortexjazz.
co.uk; 11 Gillett Sq, N16; ⊗8pm-midnight; 🚇Dal-
ston Kingsland) With a varied menu of jazz,
the Vortex hosts an outstanding line-up of
musicians, singers and songwriters from the
UK, the USA, Europe, Africa and beyond.

Hackney Empire   Theatre
(Map p255; ☏020-8985 2424; www.hackney
empire.co.uk; 291 Mare St, E8; 🚇Hackney Central)
One of London's most beautiful theatres,
this renovated Edwardian music hall offers
an diverse range of performances, from
hard-edged political theatre to musicals,
opera and comedy. It's one of the very best
places to catch a pantomime at Christmas.

✪ Greenwich & South London

O2 Academy Brixton   Live Music
(www.o2academybrixton.co.uk; 211 Stockwell Rd,
SW9; ⊗most nights doors open 7pm; ⊖Brixton)

From left: *Cinderella* at Hackney Empire; Up the Creek
comedy club; the Doobie Brothers at the O2 Arena

It's hard to have a bad night at the Brixton Academy, even if you leave with your soles sticky with beer, as this cavernous former-5000-capacity art deco theatre always thrums with bonhomie. There's a properly raked floor for good views, as well as plenty of bars and an excellent mixed bill of established and emerging talent. Most shows are 14-plus.

O2 Arena
Live Music

(www.theo2.co.uk; Peninsula Sq, SE10; 🕾; 🚇North Greenwich) One of the city's major concert venues, hosting all the biggies – the Rolling Stones, Paul Simon and Sting, One Direction, Ed Sheeran and many others – inside the 20,000-capacity arena. It's also a popular venue for sporting events and you can even climb the roof for ranging views with Up at the O2 (p203).

Up the Creek
Comedy

(Map p256; www.up-the-creek.com; 302 Creek Rd, SE10; tickets £5-15; ⏰7-11pm Thu & Sun, to 2am Fri & Sat; 🚈DLR Cutty Sark) Bizarrely enough, the hecklers can be funnier than the acts at this great club. Mischief, rowdiness and excellent comedy are the norm, with the Blackout

open-mic night on Thursdays (www.the-blackout.co.uk; £5) and Sunday specials (www.sundayspecial.co.uk; £7). There's an after-party disco on Fridays and Saturdays. Check full times of acts on the website.

⊛ Kensington & Hyde Park

Pheasantry
Live Music

(Map p250; ✆020-7351 5031; www.pizzaexpress.com/kings-road; 152-154 King's Rd, SW3; from £12; ⏰11.30am-11pm; 🚇Sloane Sq, South Kensington) Currently run by Pizza Express, the Pheasantry on King's Rd ranges over three floors, with a lovely garden at the front for alfresco dining, but the crowd-puller is the live cabaret and jazz in the basement. A Grade II–listed 19th-century building, the Pheasantry has been a ballet academy, a boho bar and a nightclub (where Lou Reed once sang).

Royal Albert Hall
Concert Venue

(Map p250; ✆0845 401 5034; www.royalalberthall.com; Kensington Gore, SW7; 🚇South Kensington) This splendid Victorian concert hall hosts classical music, rock and other

👍 Theatre

A night out at the theatre is as much a must-do London experience as a trip on the top deck of a double-decker bus. London's Theatreland in the dazzling West End – from Aldwych in the east, past Shaftesbury Ave to Regent St in the west – has a concentration of theatres only rivalled by New York's Broadway. It's a thrillingly diverse scene, encompassing Shakespeare's classics performed with old-school precision, edgy new works, raise-the-roof musicals and some of the world's longest-running shows.

Shaftesbury Theatre

performances, but is famously the venue for the BBC-sponsored Proms. Booking is possible, but from mid-July to mid-September Proms punters queue for £5 standing (or 'promenading') tickets that go on sale one hour before curtain-up. Otherwise, the box office and prepaid-ticket collection counter are through door 12 (south side of the hall).

606 Club — Blues, Jazz
(☎020-7352 5953; www.606club.co.uk; 90 Lots Rd, SW10; ⏰7-11.15pm Sun-Thu, 8pm-12.30am Fri & Sat; 🚇Imperial Wharf) Named after its old address on the King's Rd that cast a spell over jazz lovers London-wide back in the '80s, this fantastic, tucked-away basement jazz club and restaurant gives centre stage to contemporary British-based jazz musicians nightly. The club can only serve alcohol to nonmembers who are dining, and it is advisable to book to get a table.

✪ North London

Jazz Cafe — Live Music
(Map p254; ☎020-7485 6834; www.thejazz cafelondon.com; 5 Parkway, NW1; ⏰live shows from 7pm, club nights 10pm-3am; 🚇Camden Town) The name would have you think jazz is the main staple, but it's only a small slice of what's on offer. The intimate clublike space also serves up funk, hip hop, R & B, soul and rare groove, with big-name acts regularly dropping in. Saturday club night is soul night, with two live sets from the house band.

Cecil Sharp House — Traditional Music
(Map p254; www.cecilsharphouse.org; 2 Regent's Park Rd, NW1; 🚇Camden Town) If you've ever fancied clog stamping, hanky waving or bell jingling, this is the place for you. Home to the English Folk Dance and Song Society, this institute keeps all manner of wacky folk traditions alive, with performances and classes held in its gorgeous mural-covered Kennedy Hall. The dance classes are oodles of fun; no experience necessary.

KOKO — Live Music
(Map p254; www.koko.uk.com; 1a Camden High St, NW1; 🚇Mornington Cres) Once the legendary Camden Palace, where Charlie Chaplin, the Goons and the Sex Pistols performed, and where Prince played surprise gigs, KOKO is maintaining its reputation as one of London's better gig venues. The theatre has a dance floor and decadent balconies, and attracts an indie crowd. There are live bands most nights and hugely popular club nights on Saturdays.

Scala — Live Music
(Map p254; ☎020-7833 2022; www.scala.co.uk; 275 Pentonville Rd, N1; 🚇King's Cross St Pancras) Opened in 1920 as a salubrious golden-age cinema, Scala slipped into porn-movie hell in the 1970s, only to be reborn as a club and live-music venue in the noughties. It's one of the best places in London to catch an intimate gig and is a great dance space too, hosting a diverse range of club nights.

The Viviana Durante Company at the Barbican Centre

Regent's Park
Open Air Theatre   Theatre

(Map p254; ☎0844 826 4242; www.openairthe atre.org; Queen Mary's Gardens, Regent's Park, NW1; ⊙May-Sep; 🌢; ⊖Baker St) A popular and very atmospheric summertime fixture in London, this 1250-seat outdoor auditorium plays host to four productions a year: famous plays, new works, musicals and usually one production aimed at families.

✪ The City

Barbican Centre   Performing Arts

(Map p253; ☎020-7638 8891; www.barbican.org. uk; Silk St, EC2; ⊙box office 10am-8pm Mon-Sat, 11am-8pm Sun; ⊖Barbican) Home to the London Symphony Orchestra and the BBC Symphony Orchestra, the **Barbican** (☎020-7638 4141; tours adult/child £12.50/10; ⊙9am-11pm Mon-Sat, 11am-11pm Sun; ⊖Barbican) also hosts scores of other concerts, focusing in particular on jazz, folk, world and soul artists. Dance is also performed here, while

the cinema screens recent releases as well as film festivals.

✪ The South Bank

Shakespeare's Globe   Theatre

(Map p245; ☎020-7401 9919; www.shake spearesglobe.com; 21 New Globe Walk, SE1; seats £20-45, standing £5; ⊖Blackfriars, London Bridge) If you love Shakespeare and the theatre, the Globe (p85) will knock your theatrical socks off. This authentic Shakespearean theatre is a wooden 'O' without a roof over the central stage area, and although there are covered wooden bench seats in tiers around the stage, many people (there's room for 700) do as 17th-century 'groundlings' did, and stand in front of the stage.

Because the building is quite open to the elements, you may have to wrap up. Groundlings note: umbrellas are not allowed, but cheap raincoats are on sale. Unexpected aircraft noise is unavoidable too.

The theatre season runs from late April to mid-October and includes works by

Shakespeare and his contemporaries, such as Christopher Marlowe.

If you don't like the idea of standing in the rain or sitting in the cold, opt for an indoor candlelit play in the **Sam Wanamaker Playhouse**, a Jacobean theatre similar to the one Shakespeare would have used in winter. The programming also includes opera.

National Theatre — Theatre

(Map p245; Royal National Theatre; ☎020-7452 3000; www.nationaltheatre.org.uk; South Bank, SE1; ⊖Waterloo) England's flagship theatre showcases a mix of classic and contemporary plays performed by excellent casts in three theatres (Olivier, Lyttelton and Dorfman). Artistic director Rufus Norris made headlines in 2016 for announcing plans to stage a Brexit-based drama.

Unicorn Theatre — Theatre

(Map p245; ☎020-7645 0560; www.unicornthe atre.com; 147 Tooley St, SE1; ⊖London Bridge) It seems only natural that one of the first theatres dedicated to young audiences would make its home in a neighbourhood of heavy-hitting theatres. Its rationale is that the best theatre for children should be judged against the same standards as the best theatre for adults. The productions are therefore excellent, wide-ranging and perfectly tailored to their target audience.

Southbank Centre — Concert Venue

(Map p245; ☎0844 875 0073; www.southbank centre.co.uk; Belvedere Rd, SE1; ⊖Waterloo) The Southbank Centre comprises several venues – **Royal Festival Hall** (☎020-7960 4200; 🛜), **Queen Elizabeth Hall** (QEH) and Purcell Room – hosting a wide range of performing arts. As well as regular programming, it organises fantastic festivals, including **London Wonderground** (circus and cabaret), **Udderbelly** (a festival of comedy in all its guises) and **Meltdown** (a music event curated by the best and most eclectic names in music).

Old Vic — Theatre

(Map p245; ☎0844 871 7628; www.oldvicthe atre.com; The Cut, SE1; ⊖Waterloo) American actor Kevin Spacey took the theatrical helm of this London theatre in 2003. He was succeeded in April 2015 by Matthew Warchus

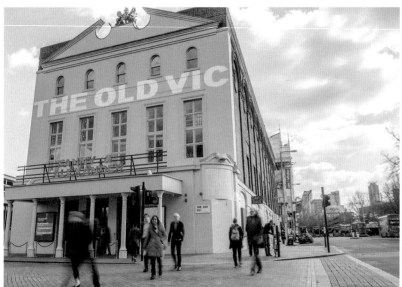

WILLY BARTON / SHUTTERSTOCK ©

(who directed *Matilda the Musical* and the film *Pride*), whose aim is to bring eclectic programming to the theatre: expect new writing, as well as dynamic revivals of old works and musicals.

Young Vic   Theatre
(Map p245; ☎020-7922 2922; www.youngvic.
org; 66 The Cut, SE1; ⊖Southwark, Waterloo) This groundbreaking theatre is as much about showcasing and discovering new talent as it is about people discovering theatre. The Young Vic features actors, directors and plays from across the world, many tackling contemporary political and cultural issues, such as racism or corruption.

✪ The West End

Wigmore Hall   Classical Music
(Map p250; www.wigmore-hall.org.uk; 36 Wigmore St, W1; ⊖Bond St) This is one of the best and most active (more than 400 concerts a year) classical-music venues in town, not only because of its fantastic acoustics, beautiful art nouveau hall and great variety of concerts and recitals, but also because of the sheer standard of the performances. Built in 1901, it has remained one of the world's top places for chamber music.

Pizza Express Jazz Club   Jazz
(Map p248; ☎020-7439 4962; www.pizzaexpress
live.com/venues/soho-jazz-club; 10 Dean St, W1; tickets £15-40; ⊖Tottenham Court Rd) Pizza Express has been one of the best jazz venues in London since opening in 1969. It may be a strange arrangement, in a basement beneath a branch of the chain restaurant, but it's highly popular. Lots of big names perform here, and promising artists such as Norah Jones, Gregory Porter and the late Amy Winehouse played here in their early days.

Royal Opera House   Opera
(Map p248; ☎020-7304 4000; www.roh.org.uk; Bow St, WC2; tickets £4-270; ⊖Covent Garden) Classic opera in London has a fantastic setting on Covent Garden Piazza and coming here for a night is a sumptuous – if pricey –

👍 Live Music

Musically diverse and defiantly different, London is a hot spot of musical innovation and talent. It leads the world in articulate indie rock, in particular, and tomorrow's guitar heroes are right-this-minute paying their dues on sticky-floored stages in Camden Town, Shoreditch and Dalston.

Monster international acts see London as an essential stop on their transglobal stomps, but be prepared for tickets selling out faster than you can find your credit card. The city's beautiful old theatres and music halls play host to a constant roster of well-known names in more intimate settings. In summer giant festivals take over the city's parks, while smaller, more localised events such as the **Dalston Music Festival** (www.dalstonmusicfestival.com) showcase up-and-comers in multiple spaces.

If jazz or blues are your thing, London has some truly excellent clubs and pubs where you can catch classics and contemporary tunes. The city's major jazz event is the **London Jazz Festival** (www.efglondonjazzfestival.org.uk) in November.

affair. Although the program has been fluffed up by modern influences, the main attractions are still the opera and classical ballet – all are wonderful productions and feature world-class performers.

Classical Music, Ballet & Opera

With multiple world-class orchestras and ensembles, quality venues, reasonable ticket prices and performances covering the whole musical gamut from traditional crowd-pleasers to innovative compositions, London will satisfy even the fussiest classical-music buff. The **Southbank Centre** (p192), **Barbican Centre** (p191) and **Royal Albert Hall** (p189) all maintain an alluring roster of performances, further gilding London's outstanding reputation as a cosmopolitan centre for classical music. The Proms is the year's biggest event.

Opera and ballet lovers should make a night at the Royal Opera House a priority – the setting and quality of the programming are truly world-class.

CAIAIMAGE / MARTIN BARRAUD / GETTY IMAGES ©

Prince Charles Cinema   Cinema

(Map p248; www.princecharlescinema.com; 7 Leicester Pl, WC2; tickets £5-16; ⊖Leicester Sq) Leicester Sq cinema-ticket prices are very high, so wait until the first runs have moved to the Prince Charles, central London's cheapest cinema, where nonmembers pay £5 to £12 for new releases. Also presents minifestivals, Q&As with film directors, classics, sleepover movie marathons, and exuberant singalong screenings of films like *Frozen, The Sound of Music* and *Rocky Horror Picture Show* (£16).

Ronnie Scott's   Jazz

(Map p248; ☑020-7439 0747; www.ronniescotts. co.uk; 47 Frith St, W1; ⊘7pm-3am Mon-Sat, 1-4pm & 8pm-midnight Sun; ⊖Leicester Sq, Tottenham Court Rd) Ronnie Scott's jazz club opened in 1965 and became widely known as Britain's best. Support acts are at 7pm, with main gigs at 8.15pm (8pm Sunday) and a second house at 11.15pm Friday and Saturday (check ahead). The more informal Late, Late Show runs from 1am to 3am. Expect to pay from £25; the Late, Late Show and Sunday lunch shows are just £10.

Comedy Store   Comedy

(Map p248; ☑0844 871 7699; www.thecomedy store.co.uk; 1a Oxendon St, SW1; tickets £8-22.50; ⊖Piccadilly Circus) This is one of the first (and still one of the best) comedy clubs in London. Wednesday and Sunday night's Comedy Store Players is the most famous improvisation outfit in town, with the wonderful Josie Lawrence, now a veteran of two decades. On Thursdays, Fridays and Saturdays, Best in Stand Up features the best on London's comedy circuit.

Borderline   Live Music

(Map p248; ☑020-7734 5547; http://borderline. london; Orange Yard, off Manette St, W1; ⊖Tottenham Court Rd) Through the hard-to-find entrance off Orange Yard and down into the basement you'll find a packed, 275-capacity venue that really punches above its weight. Read the gig list: Ed Sheeran, REM, Blur, Counting Crows, PJ Harvey, Lenny Kravitz and Pearl Jam, plus many anonymous indie outfits, have all played here.

Amused Moose Soho   Comedy

(Map p248; ☑box office 020-7287 3727; www. amusedmoose.com; Sanctum Soho Hotel, 20 Warwick St, W1; ⊖Piccadilly Circus, Oxford Circus) One of the city's best clubs, the peripatetic Amused Moose (the cinema in the Sanctum Soho Hotel is just one of its hosting venues) is popular with audiences and comedians alike, perhaps helped along by the fact that heckling is 'unacceptable' and all the acts are 'first-date friendly' (ie unlikely to humiliate the front row). Shows are usually at 8.15pm on Saturday.

WILLY BARTON / SHUTTERSTOCK ©

❂ West London

Bush Theatre — Theatre
(☎020-8743 5050; www.bushtheatre.co.uk;
7 Uxbridge Rd, W12; ⊙10am-11pm Mon-Sat;
⊖Shepherd's Bush) This rehoused and rein-
vigorated West London theatre is renowned
for encouraging new talent and independent, new playwriting. Its success since 1972
is down to strong writing from the likes
of Jonathan Harvey, Conor McPherson,
Stephen Poliakoff and Mark Ravenhill. It
also has an excellent cafe and bar. The
theatre hosts the three-day **Shubbak
Festival**, London's largest biennial festival
of contemporary Arab culture.

Puppet Theatre
Barge — Puppet Theatre
(Map p250; ☎020-7249 6876; www.puppetbarge.
com; 35 Blomfield Rd, W9; adult/child £12/8.50;
⊖Warwick Avenue) This utterly charming
marionette (aka puppet) theatre can be
found in a converted barge moored in Little
Venice – an area as pretty as it sounds. The
theatre has been there for almost 40 years

and holds regular performances during
weekends and school holidays.

Gate Picturehouse — Cinema
(Map p250; ☎0871 902 5731; www.picture
houses.co.uk; 87 Notting Hill Gate, W11; tickets
£7-13.50; ⊖Notting Hill Gate) Opened in
1911, the Gate's single screen has one of
London's most charming art deco cinema
interiors. There are director Q&As and a
wealth of cinema clubs, including the E4
Slackers Club (students) and Silver Screen
(over-60s). Cheapest tickets on Mondays.
Sink a drink in the foyer bar before or after
your film.

Electric Cinema — Cinema
(Map p250; ☎020-7908 9696; www.electric
cinema.co.uk; 191 Portobello Rd, W11; tickets
£8-22.50; ⊖Ladbroke Grove) Having notched
up its centenary in 2011, the Electric is one
of the UK's oldest cinemas, updated. Avail
yourself of the luxurious leather armchairs,
sofas, footstools and tables for food and
drink in the auditorium, or select one of
the six front-row double beds! Tickets are
cheapest on Mondays.

ACTIVE LONDON

Exploring the city on two wheels and more

Active London

London boasts a well-developed infrastructure for participatory and spectator sports, with world-famous venues scattered around the city and a surprisingly large amount of green space for weekend warriors to work up a sweat in.

Many big sporting events are free to watch; and if you've missed out on expensive ones, you can always fall back on the pub, or in spring and summer, the many big screens dotted around town.

In This Section

What to Watch

Rugby The Six Nations, rugby's annual competition between England, Wales, Scotland, Ireland, France and Italy, runs across five weekends in February and March.

Tennis London is gripped by Wimbledon fever in July.

Football The season runs from August to May.

BIKEWORLDTRAVEL / SHUTTERSTOCK ©

London Marathon

The Best...

Free Spectator Sports

London Marathon (April) Watch runners pound the pavement from Blackheath to Buckingham Palace.

Oxford & Cambridge Boat Race (early April) Features the arch-rival universities on a course from Putney to Mortlake.

London Marathon (April) Watch runners pound the pavement from Blackheath to Buckingham Palace.

Big-Screen Locations

Outdoor screens usually operate from April to October.

Trafalgar Square (p56) If there is anything big happening, you can be guaranteed there will be a big screen to watch it on London's prime square.

Queen Elizabeth Olympic Park (p202) Given its legacy, it's hardly surprising big sporting events are broadcast here.

🕀 Walking Tours

Guide London   Tours
(Association of Professional Tourist Guides; 020-7611 2545; www.guidelondon.org.uk; half-/full day £165/270) Hire a prestigious Blue Badge Tourist Guide, know-it-all guides who have studied for two years and passed a dozen written and practical exams to do their job. They can tell you stories behind the sights that you'd only hear from them or whisk you on a themed tour, from royalty and The Beatles to parks and shopping. Go by car, public transport, bike or on foot.

Unseen Tours   Walking
(07514 266774; www.sockmobevents.org.uk; tours £12) See London from an entirely different angle on one of these award-winning neighbourhood tours led by the London homeless covering Covent Garden, Camden Town, Brick Lane, Shoreditch and London Bridge. Sixty percent of the tour price goes to the guide.

London Walks   Walking
(020-7624 3978; www.walks.com; adult/child £10/free) A huge choice of themed walks, including Jack the Ripper, the Beatles, Sherlock Holmes, Harry Potter and ghost walks. Check the website for schedules.

🕀 Bus Tours

Original Tour   Bus
(www.theoriginaltour.com; adult/child £32/15; 8.30am-8.30pm) A 24-hour hop-on, hop-off bus service with a river cruise thrown in, as well as three themed walks: Changing of the Guard, Rock 'n' Roll and Jack the Ripper. Buses run every five to 20 minutes; you can buy tickets on the bus or online. There's also a 48-hour ticket available (adult/child £41/19.50), with an extended river cruise.

Big Bus Tours   Bus
(020-7808 6753; www.bigbustours.com; adult/child £35/18; every 20min 8.30am-6pm Apr-Sep, to 5pm Oct & Mar, to 4.30pm Nov-Feb) Informative commentaries in 12 languages.

Double-decker tour bus

RON ELLIS / SHUTTERSTOCK ©

The ticket includes a free river cruise with City Cruises and three thematic walking tours (royal London, film locations, mysteries). Good online booking discounts available. Onboard wi-fi. The ticket is valid for 24 hours; for an extra £8 (£4 for children), you can upgrade to a 48-hour ticket.

🜛 Boat Tours

London Waterbus Company   Cruise
(Map p250; ☎020-7482 2550; www.londonwater bus.com; 32 Camden Lock Pl, NW1; adult/child one-way £9/7.50, return £14/12; ⊙hourly 10am-5pm Apr-Sep, weekends only & less frequent departures other months; ⊖Warwick Ave, Camden Town) This enclosed barge runs enjoyable 50-minute trips on Regent's Canal between Little Venice and Camden Lock, passing by Regent's Park and stopping at London Zoo. There are fewer departures outside high season; check the website for schedules. One-way tickets (adult/child £27/21), including entry to London Zoo, allowing passengers to disembark within the zoo grounds are available. Buy tickets aboard the narrowboats.

Thames River Services   Boating
(Map p256; ☎020-7930 4097; www.thamesriver services.co.uk; adult/child one-way £12.50/6.25, return £16.50/8.25) These cruise boats leave Westminster Pier for Greenwich, stopping at the Tower of London. Every second service from April to October continues on from Greenwich to the Thames Barrier (from Westminster, one-way adult/child £14/7, return £17/8.50, hourly 11.30am to 3.30pm) but does not land there, passing the O2 (p203) along the way.

Thames Rockets   Boating
(Map p245; ☎020-7928 8933; www.thamesrock ets.com; Boarding Gate 1, London Eye, Waterloo Millennium Pier, Westminster Bridge Rd, SE1; adult/child from £43.50/29.50; ⊙10am-6pm; 🖝) Feel like James Bond on this high-speed inflatable boat that flies down the Thames at 30 knots. Tours depart from the London

🎾 Football

Football is at the very heart of English sporting culture, with about a dozen league teams in London. London had five teams in the Premier League (www.premierleague.com) in 2017–2018: Arsenal, Chelsea, Crystal Palace, Tottenham Hotspur and West Ham United. The competition runs from August to May, although it's extremely difficult for visitors to secure tickets to matches (they are usually all snapped up by season-ticket holders). Consider taking a tour at **Wembley** (☎0800 169 9933; www.wembleystadium.com; tours adult/child £20/12; ⊖Wembley Park), **London Stadium** (☎020-8522 6157; www.london-stadium.com; Queen Elizabeth Olympic Park, E20; tours adult/child £19/11; ⊙tours 10am-4.15pm; ⊟DLR Pudding Mill Lane) or **Arsenal Emirates Stadium** (☎020-7619 5000; www.arsenal.com/tours; Hornsey Rd, N5; tours self-guided adult/child £22/14, guided £40; ⊙10am-6pm Mon-Sat, to 4pm Sun; ⊖Holloway Rd) instead.

Alternatively, numerous pubs across the capital show Premier League games (as well as international fixtures) and watching a football game in a pub is an experience in itself.

Football match at Wembley stadium
COSMINLFTODE / SHUTTERSTOCK ©

Eye or St Katharine Pier, including the 50-minute Ultimate London Adventure (adult/child £43.50/29.50), the 80-minute Thames Barrier Explorer's Voyage (adult/child £54.50/39.50) or Thames Lates, a

 Santander Cycles

London's cycle-hire scheme is called **Santander Cycles** (☏0343 222 6666; www.tfl.gov.uk/modes/cycling/santander-cycles), also referred to as 'Boris Bikes' after their former sponsor and the city's former mayor (and current Foreign Secretary) Boris Johnson, who launched the initiative. The bikes have proved as popular with visitors as with Londoners.

The idea is simple: pick up a bike from one of the 750 docking stations dotted around the capital. Cycle. Drop it off at another docking station.

The access fee is £2 for 24 hours. All you need is a credit or debit card. The first 30 minutes are free. It's then £2 for any additional period of 30 minutes.

You can take as many bikes as you like during your access period (24 hours), leaving five minutes between each trip.

The pricing structure is designed to encourage short journeys rather than longer rentals; for those, go to a hire company. You'll also find that although easy to ride, the bikes only have three gears and are quite heavy. You must be aged 18 to buy access and at least 14 to ride a bike.

Santander Cycles hire station, Soho
TUPUNGATO / SHUTTERSTOCK ©

50-minute sunset trip with a cocktail on board (adults only £39.50).

Lee & Stort Boats   Cruise
(Map p255; ☏0845 116 2012; www.leeandstort boats.co.uk; Stratford waterfront pontoon, E20;

adult/child £9/4; ⊘daily Apr-Sep, Sat & Sun Mar & Oct; ⊕Stratford) Lee & Stort offers 45-minute tours on the waterways through Queen Elizabeth Olympic Park. Check the display boards in the park for departure times, which are usually on the hour from midday onwards.

⊙ Swimming & Spas

**Hampstead Heath
Ponds**   Swimming
(www.cityoflondon.gov.uk; Hampstead Heath, NW5; adult/child £2/1; ⊕Hampstead Heath) Set in the midst of the gorgeous heath, Hampstead's three bathing ponds (men's, women's and mixed) offer a cooling dip in murky brown water. Despite what you might think from its appearance, the water is tested daily and meets stringent quality guidelines.

Porchester Spa   Spa
(Map p250; ☏020-7313 3858; www.porchester spatreatments.co.uk; Porchester Centre, Queensway, W2; admission £28.90; ⊘10am-10pm; ⊕Bayswater, Royal Oak) Housed in a gorgeous, art deco building, the Porchester is a no-frills spa run by Westminster Council. With a 30m swimming pool, a large Finnish-log sauna, two steam rooms, three Turkish hot rooms and a massive plunge pool, there are plenty of affordable treatments on offer, including massages and male and female pampering/grooming sessions.

It's women only on Tuesdays, Thursdays and Fridays all day and between 10am and 2pm on Sundays; men only on Mondays, Wednesdays and Saturdays. Couples are welcome from 4pm to 10pm on Sundays.

**London Aquatics
Centre**   Swimming
(☏020-8536 3150; www.londonaquatics centre.org; Carpenters Rd, E20; adult/child from £5.20/3; ⊘6am-10.30pm; ⊕Stratford) The sweeping lines and wavelike movement of Zaha Hadid's award-winning Aquatics Centre make it the architectural highlight of **Queen Elizabeth Olympic Park** (Map

p255; www.queenelizabetholympicpark.co.uk; E20; 🚇Stratford). Bathed in natural light, the 50m competition pool beneath the huge undulating roof (which sits on just three supports) is an extraordinary place to swim. There's also a second 50m pool, a diving area, a gym, a creche and a cafe.

Serpentine Lido Swimming
(Map p250; 📞020-7706 3422; Hyde Park, W2; adult/child £4.80/1.80; ⏰10am-6pm daily Jun-Aug, to 6pm Sat & Sun May; 🚇Hyde Park Corner, Knightsbridge) Perhaps the ultimate London pool is inside the Serpentine lake. This fabulous lido is open May to August. Sun loungers are available for £3.50 for the whole day.

🚴 Cycling

Lee Valley VeloPark Cycling
(Map p255; 📞0300 003 0613; www.visitlee valley.org.uk/velopark; Abercrombie Rd, E20; 1hr taster £40, pay & ride from £4, bike & helmet hire adult/child from £12/8; ⏰9am-10pm; 🚇DLR Stratford International) The beautifully designed, cutting-edge Queen Elizabeth Olympic Park velodrome is open to the public – either to wander through and watch the pros tear around the steep-sloped circuit, or to have a go yourself. Both the velodrome and the attached BMX park offer taster sessions. Mountain bikers and road cyclists can attack the tracks on a pay-and-ride basis.

London Bicycle Tour Cycling
(Map p245; 📞020-7928 6838; www.london bicycle.com; 1 Gabriel's Wharf, 56 Upper Ground, SE1; tour incl bike from adult/child £24.95/21.95, bike hire per day £20; 🚇Southwark, Waterloo) Three-hour tours begin in the South Bank and take in London's highlights on both sides of the river; the classic tour is available in eight languages. A night ride is available. You can also hire traditional or speciality bikes, such as tandems and folding bikes, by the hour or day.

🎾 Tennis

Wimbledon
Championships Spectator Sport
(📞020-8944 1066; www.wimbledon.com; Church Rd, SW19; grounds admission £8-25, tickets £41-190) For a few weeks each June and July, the sporting world's attention is fixed on the quiet southern suburb of Wimbledon, as it has been since 1877. Most show-court tickets for the Wimbledon Champion-ships are allocated through public ballot, applications for which usually begin in early August of the preceding year and close at the end of December.

Entry into the ballot does not mean entrants will get a ticket. A quantity of show-court, outer-court, ground and late-entry tickets are also available if you queue on the day of play, but if you want a show-court ticket it is recommended you camp the night before in the queue. See the website for details.

🧗 Climbing

Up at The O2 Adventure Sports
(www.theo2.co.uk/upattheo2; The O2, Greenwich Peninsula, SE10; from £30; ⏰hours vary; 🚇North Greenwich) London isn't exactly your thrill-seeking destination, but this terrific ascent of the O2 (p189) is tons of fun. Equipped with climbing suit and harness, you'll scale the famous entertainment venue to reach a viewing platform perched 52m above the Thames with sweeping views of Canary Wharf, the river, Greenwich and beyond. Hours vary depending on the season (sunset and twilight climbs also available).

REST YOUR HEAD

Top tips for the best accommodation

Rest Your Head

Landing the right accommodation is integral to your London experience, and there's no shortage of choice. There's some fantastic accommodation, from party-oriented hostels to stately top-end hotels.

Budget is likely to be your main consideration, given how pricey London accommodation is, but you should also think about the neighbourhood you'd like to stay in. Are you a culture vulture? Do you want to walk (or take a quick cab ride) home after a night out? Are you after village charm or cool cachet? Think your options through and book ahead: London is busy year-round.

In This Section

Prices & Tipping

A 'budget hotel' in London generally costs up to £100 for a standard double room with bathroom. For a midrange option, plan on spending £100 to £200. Luxury options run £200 and higher.

Tipping isn't expected in hotels in London, except perhaps for porters in top-end hotels (although it remains discretionary).

S.SOKOLOV / SHUTTERSTOCK ©

Reservations

○ Book rooms as far in advance as possible, especially for weekends and holiday periods.

○ Visit London (www.visitlondon.com) offers a free accommodation booking service and has a list of family-friendly accommodation.

○ Most hotels will match prices on booking sites if you book directly, and this may come with extra perks such as free breakfast or late checkout.

Useful Websites

Lonely Planet (www.lonelyplanet.com/london) Hundreds of properties, from budget hostels to luxury apartments.

London Town (www.londontown.com) Excellent last-minute offers on boutique hotels and B&Bs.

Alastair Sawdays (www.sawdays.co.uk) Hand-picked selection of bolt-holes in the capital.

Good to Know

Value-added tax (VAT; 20%) is added to hotel rooms. Some hotels include this in their advertised rates, some don't.

Breakfast may be included in the room rate. Sometimes this is a continental breakfast; full English breakfast might cost extra.

Hotels

London has a grand roll call of stately hotels and many are experiences in their own right. Standards across the top end and much of the boutique bracket are high, but so are prices. Quirkiness and individuality can be found in abundance, alongside dyed-in-the-wool traditionalism. A wealth of budget boutique hotels has exploited a lucrative niche, while a rung or two down in overall quality and charm, midrange chain hotels generally offer good locations and dependable comfort. Demand can often outstrip supply – especially on the bottom step of the market – so book ahead, particularly during holiday periods and in summer.

B&Bs

Housed in good-looking old properties, bed and breakfasts come in a tier below hotels, often promising boutique-style charm and a more personal level of service. Handy B&B clusters appear in Paddington, South Kensington, Victoria and Bloomsbury.

Hostels

The cheapest form of accommodation is hostels, both the official Youth Hostel Association (YHA) ones and the usually hipper, more party-oriented independent ones. Hostels vary in quality so select carefully; most offer twins as well as dorms.

Rates & Booking

Deluxe hotel rooms will cost from around £350 per double but there's good variety at the top end, so you should find a room from about £200 offering superior comfort without the prestige. Some boutique hotels also occupy this bracket. There's a noticeable dip in quality below this price. Under £100 and you're at the more serviceable, budget end of the market. Look out for weekend deals that can put a better class of hotel within reach. Rates often slide in winter. Book through the hotels' websites for the best online deals or promotional rates.

Long-Term Rentals

If you're in London for a week or more, try a short-term or serviced apartment; rates at the bottom end are comparable to a B&B, you can manage your budget more carefully by eating in, and you'll feel like a local.

Neighbourhoods with a great vibe include Notting Hill, Hackney, Bermondsey, Pimlico and Camden, where you'll find plenty of food markets, great local pubs and lots of boutiques. Traditional accommodations can be limited in some areas, but many travellers can find places to stay on the usual home-sharing services.

For something a little more hotel-like, serviced apartments are a great option. The following are in the centre: **Cheval Three Quays** (☎020-3725 5333; www.cheval residences.com; 40 Lower Thames St, EC3; apt from £369; ❄🖥; ⊖Tower Hill), **No 5 Maddox Street** (☎020-7647 0200; www.living-rooms. co.uk/hotel/no-5-maddox-st; 5 Maddox St, W1; ste £250-925; ❄🖥; ⊖Oxford Circus) and **Beaufort House** (Map p250; ☎020-7584 2600; www.beauforthouse.co.uk; 45 Beaufort Gardens, SW3; 1-4 bedroom apt £443-1350; ❄🖥; ⊖Knightsbridge).

Where to Stay

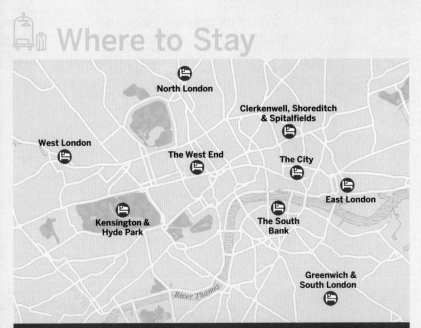

Neighbourhood	Atmosphere
The West End	At the heart of London, with excellent transport links. Fantastic range of options, but expensive and busy. Numerous eating and nightlife options.
The City	Central and well connected, but geared towards business clientele; very quiet at weekends. Expensive on week nights, but good deals to be found at weekends.
The South Bank	Cheaper than the West End, but choice and transport connections more limited. Close to great sights such as the Tate Modern and Borough Market.
Kensington & Hyde Park	Stylish area, with gorgeous hotels, but expensive and with limited nightlife. Good transport links and easy connection to Heathrow.
Clerkenwell, Shoreditch & Spitalfields	Trendy area with great boutique hotels; excellent for restaurants and nightlife, but few top sights and transport options somewhat limited.
East London	Limited sleeping options, but great multicultural local feel; some areas less safe at night.
North London	Leafy area, with great sleeping options and a vibrant nightlife, but further from main sights and with fewer transport options.
West London	Lovely neighbourhood with village charm, great vibe at weekends; plenty of cheap but average hotels. Light on top sights.
Greenwich & South London	Village-like feel, but limited sleeping and transport options; great for Greenwich sights, but inconvenient for everything else.
Richmond, Kew & Hampton Court	Smart riverside hotels, semirural pockets, but sights spread out and far from central London.

Tower Bridge (p80) and the River Thames

In Focus

King's Cross station

London Today

Britain's exit from the EU (Brexit) has put a damper on London's spirit. With its multicultural population, thriving financial sector and firm links with the continent, the capital seems ideologically at odds with the rest of the country. Its energy, however, remains second to none, with its creative juices in full flow and a lot of exciting developments, such as the Crossrail line and Battersea and King's Cross regeneration.

London versus the Rest?

London is the world's leading financial centre for international business and commerce and the fifth-largest city economy in the world. As the economic downturn of the last decade fades into memory, the UK is increasingly a nation of two halves: London (and the southeast) and the rest of the country. The capital generates more than 20% of Britain's income, a percentage that has been rising over the last 10 years. Employment in London is rosier than the rest of the nation, with the jobless rate at just under 6%; the price of property is double the national average; and incomes are 30% higher in London than elsewhere in the country. And tourism continues to grow at 3.5% a year. But there's a flip side: 28% of Londoners are living in poverty compared with just 21% in the rest of England.

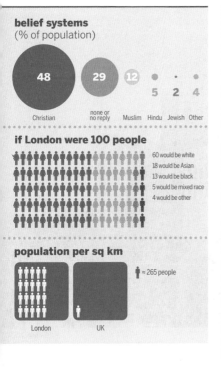

belief systems
(% of population)

48 Christian
29 none or no reply
12 Muslim
5 Hindu
2 Jewish
4 Other

if London were 100 people

60 would be white
18 would be Asian
13 would be black
5 would be mixed race
4 would be other

population per sq km

♟ ≈ 265 people

London   UK

Ethnicity & Multiculturalism

London is one of the most cosmopolitan places in which to live. According to the last census (2011), almost 37% of London's population is born overseas – with almost a quarter born outside Europe. Today an estimated 270 different ethnic groups speak 300 different languages and, despite some tensions, most get along well.

Building Boom

The huge rise in population – London is expected to have nine million inhabitants by 2020, up from 7.8 million in 2010 – has led to a building boom not seen since the end of WWII. Church spires are now dwarfed by a forest of construction cranes working to build high-rise apartments and office buildings. East London is where most of the activity is taking place, but the boom is evident along the entire stretch of the Thames. Keeping pace with the rising skyline are property prices: London is now the world's most expensive city for property, with the average price of a one-bedroom apartment a huge £1.1 million in Kensington and Chelsea.

Goodbye to Europe

On 24 June 2016, London awoke to monumental news. By a slim referendum vote the UK had opted to leave the EU, cutting ties stretching back 43 years. Nationally, the referendum result was close: 52% voted to leave the EU against 48% for remain, although, unsurprisingly, the capital was strongly in favour of 'remain' (60%).

Brexit became law in March 2017, when Prime Minister Theresa May formally launched the two-year disentanglement process. Depending on the outcome of the negotiations, Brexit could have an enormous impact on London, especially the financial-services industry and the millions of EU nationals living in the capital. Brexit comes into force in April 2019.

All Change in Politics

The 'leave' vote in the Brexit referendum appeared to surprise both camps. David Cameron resigned as prime minister and was succeeded by Theresa May. After less than a year in office, May called a snap election that resulted in a hung parliament, with no overall majority, leaving her a weakened figure.

Closer to home, the mayor of London, Boris Johnson, left office after two terms to join May's Cabinet as foreign secretary. Less than impressed by Johnson's second term, the capital rejected his party's candidate, Zac Goldsmith, in favour of Sadiq Khan, a Labour MP who was born in Tooting, South London, to a working-class British Pakistani family and is a practising Muslim, making him the world's first elected leader of that faith in any Western city.

Hampton Court Palace (p110)

KIEV.VICTOR / SHUTTERSTOCK ©

History

London's history is a long and turbulent narrative spanning more than two millenniums. Over those years there have been good times of strength and economic prosperity and horrific times of plague, fire and war. But even when down on its knees, London has always been able to get up, dust itself off and move on, constantly reinventing itself along the way.

AD 43	852	1066
The Romans invade Britain, led by Emperor Claudius; they mix with the local Celtic tribespeople and stay for almost four centuries.	Vikings settle in London; a period of great struggle between the kingdoms of Wessex and Denmark begins.	Following his decisive victory at the Battle of Hastings, William, Duke of Normandy, is crowned in Westminster Abbey.

Westminster Abbey (p36)

Londinium

The Celts were the first to arrive in the area that is now London, some time around the 4th century BC. It was the Romans, however, who established a real settlement in AD 43, the port of Londinium. They slung a wooden bridge over the Thames (near the site of today's London Bridge) and created a thriving colonial outpost before abandoning British soil for good in 410.

Saxon & Norman London

Saxon settlers, who colonised the southeast of England from the 5th century onwards, established themselves outside the city walls due west of Londinium in Lundenwic. This trading community grew in importance and attracted the attention of the Vikings in Denmark. They attacked in 842 and again nine years later, burning Lundenwic to the ground.

1215
King John signs the Magna Carta, an agreement forming the basis of constitutional law in England.

1348
Rats on ships from Europe bring the 'Black Death', a plague that eventually wipes out almost two-thirds of the city's residents.

1605
A Catholic plot to blow up James I is foiled; Guy Fawkes, one of the alleged plotters, is executed the following year.

Kensington Palace (p98)

LEONID ANDRONOV / SHUTTERSTOCK ©

Under the leadership of King Alfred the Great of Wessex, the Saxon population fought back, driving the Danes out in 886.

Saxon London grew into a prosperous and well-organised town segmented into 20 wards, each with its own alderman and resident colonies of German merchants and French vintners. But attacks by the Danes continued apace, and the Saxon leadership was weakening; in 1016 Londoners were forced to accept the Danish leader Canute as king of England. With the death of Canute's brutal son Harthacanute in 1042, the throne passed to the Saxon Edward the Confessor, who went on to found a palace and an abbey at Westminster.

On his deathbed in 1066, Edward anointed Harold Godwinson, the Earl of Wessex, as his successor. This enraged William, Duke of Normandy, who claimed that Edward had promised him the throne. William mounted a massive invasion from France, and on 14 October defeated (and killed) Harold at the Battle of Hastings, before marching on London to claim his prize. William, now dubbed 'the Conqueror', was crowned king of England in Westminster Abbey on 25 December 1066, ensuring the Norman conquest was complete.

Medieval & Tudor London

Successive medieval kings were happy to let the City of London keep its independence as long as its merchants continued to finance their wars and building projects. During the Tudor dynasty, which coincided with the discovery of the Americas and thriving world trade, London became one of the largest and most important cities in Europe. Henry VIII reigned from 1509 to 1547, built palaces at Whitehall and St James's, and bullied his lord chancellor, Cardinal Thomas Wolsey, into giving him the one Wolsey had built at Hampton Court.

The most momentous event of his reign, however, was his split from the Catholic Church in 1534 after the Pope refused to annul his marriage to Catherine of Aragon, who had borne him only one surviving daughter after 24 years of marriage.

The 45-year reign (1558–1603) of Henry's daughter Elizabeth I is still regarded as one of the most extraordinary periods in English history. During these four decades English literature reached new heights, and religious tolerance gradually grew. With the defeat

1666	1708	1838
The Great Fire of London burns for five days, leaving four-fifths of the metropolis in smoking ruins.	The last stone of Sir Christopher Wren's masterpiece, St Paul's Cathedral, is laid by his son and the son of his master mason.	The coronation of Queen Victoria ushers in a new era for London; the British capital becomes the economic centre of the world.

of the Spanish Armada in 1588, England became a naval superpower, and London established itself as the premier world trade market with the opening of the Royal Exchange in 1570.

Civil Wars, Plague & Fire

Elizabeth was succeeded by her second cousin James I, and then his son Charles I. The latter's belief in the 'divine right of kings' set him on a collision course with an increasingly confident parliament at Westminster and a powerful City of London. The latter two rallied behind Oliver Cromwell against royalist troops. Charles was defeated in 1646 and executed in 1649.

Cromwell ruled the country as a republic for the next 11 years. Under the Commonwealth of England, as the English republic was known, Cromwell banned theatre, dancing, Christmas and just about anything remotely fun.

After Cromwell's death, parliament restored the exiled Charles II to the throne in 1660. Charles II's reign witnessed two great tragedies in London: the Great Plague of 1665, which decimated the population, and the Great Fire of London, which swept ferociously through the city's densely packed streets the following year. The wreckage of the inferno at least allowed master architect Christopher Wren to build his 51 magnificent churches. The crowning glory of the 'Great Rebuilding' was his St Paul's Cathedral, completed in 1708.

What's in the Name?

Many of London's street names, especially in the City, recall the goods that were traded there: Poultry, Cornhill, Sea Coal Lane, Milk and Bread Sts, and the more cryptic Friday St, where you bought fish for that fasting day. Other meanings are not so obvious. The '-wich' or '-wych' in names such as Greenwich, Aldwych and Dulwich come from the Saxon word *wic,* meaning 'settlement'. *Ea* or *ey* is an old word for 'island' or 'marsh'; thus Chelsea (Island of Shale), Bermondsey (Bermond's Island), Battersea (Peter's Island) and Hackney (Haca's Marsh). In Old English *ceap* meant 'market'; hence Eastcheap is where the common people shopped, while Cheapside (originally Westcheap) was reserved for the royal household. 'Borough' comes from *burg,* Old English for 'fort' or 'town'. And the odd names East Ham and West Ham come from the Old English *hamm* or 'hem'; they were just bigger enclosed (or 'hemmed-in') settlements than the more standard hamlets.

Georgian & Victorian London

While the achievements of the 18th-century Georgian kings were impressive (though 'mad' George III will forever be remembered as the king who lost the American colonies), they were overshadowed by those of the dazzling Victorian era, dating from Queen Victoria's ascension to the throne in 1837.

1851
The Great Exhibition, the brainchild of Victoria's consort, Albert, opens to great fanfare in the Crystal Palace in Hyde Park.

1940–41
London is devastated by the Blitz, although St Paul's Cathedral and the Tower of London escape largely unscathed.

1953
Queen Elizabeth II's coronation is broadcast live around the world on television; many English families buy their first TV.

Great Fire of London

The Great Fire of London broke out in Thomas Farriner's bakery in Pudding Lane on the evening of 2 September 1666. Initially dismissed by London's lord mayor as 'something a woman might pisse out', the fire spread uncontrollably and destroyed 89 churches and more than 13,000 houses, raging for days. Amazingly, fewer than a dozen people died. The fire destroyed medieval London, changing the city forever. Many Londoners left for the countryside or to seek their fortunes in the New World, while the city itself rebuilt its medieval heart with grand buildings such as Christopher Wren's St Paul's Cathedral. Wren's magnificent Monument (1677) near London Bridge stands as a memorial to the fire and its victims.

During the Industrial Revolution, London became the nerve centre of the largest and richest empire the world had ever witnessed, in an imperial expansion that covered a quarter of the earth's surface area and ruled over more than 500 million people. Queen Victoria lived to celebrate her Diamond Jubilee in 1897, but died four years later aged 81 and was laid to rest beside her beloved consort, Prince Albert, at Windsor. Her reign is seen as the climax of Britain's world supremacy, when London was the de facto capital of the world.

The World Wars

Later known as the Great War, WWI broke out in August 1914, and the first German bombs fell from zeppelins near the Guildhall a year later, killing 39 people. Planes were soon dropping bombs on the capital, killing in all some 670 Londoners (half the national total of civilian deaths).

In the 1930s Prime Minister Neville Chamberlain's policy of appeasing Adolf Hitler eventually proved misguided, as the German führer's lust for expansion appeared insatiable. When Nazi Germany invaded Poland on 1 September 1939, Britain declared war, having signed a mutual-assistance pact with that country only a few days before. World War II (1939–45), which would prove to be Europe's darkest hour, had begun.

Winston Churchill, prime minister from 1940, orchestrated much of the nation's war strategy from the Cabinet War Rooms deep below Whitehall, lifting the nation's spirit from here with his stirring wartime speeches. By the time Nazi Germany capitulated in May 1945, up to a third of the East End and the City of London had been flattened, almost 30,000 Londoners had been killed and a further 50,000 seriously wounded.

Postwar London

Once the celebrations of Victory in Europe (VE) day had died down, the nation began to confront the war's appalling toll and to rebuild. The years of austerity had begun, with rationing of essential items and high-rise residences sprouting up from bombsites. Rationing

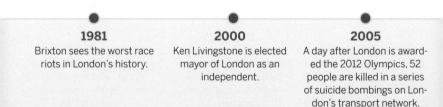

1981
Brixton sees the worst race riots in London's history.

2000
Ken Livingstone is elected mayor of London as an independent.

2005
A day after London is awarded the 2012 Olympics, 52 people are killed in a series of suicide bombings on London's transport network.

of most goods ended in 1953, the year Elizabeth II was crowned following the death the year before of her father King George VI.

Immigrants from around the world – particularly the former colonies – flocked to postwar London, where a dwindling population had generated labour shortages, and the city's character changed forever. The place to be during the 1960s, 'Swinging London' became the epicentre of cool in fashion and music, its streets awash with colour and vitality.

The ensuing 1970s brought glam rock, punk, economic depression and the country's first female prime minister in 1979. In power for the entire 1980s and pushing an unprecedented program of privatisation, the late Margaret Thatcher is easily the most significant of Britain's postwar leaders. Opinions about 'Maggie' still polarise the Brits today.

While poorer Londoners suffered under Thatcher's significant trimming back of the welfare state, things had rarely looked better for the wealthy, as London underwent explosive economic growth. In 1992, much to the astonishment of most Londoners, the Conservative Party was elected for their fourth successive term in government, despite Mrs Thatcher being jettisoned by her party a year and a half before. By 1995 the writing was on the wall for the Conservative Party, as the Labour Party, apparently unelectable for a decade, came back with a new face.

London in the New Century

Invigorated by its sheer desperation to return to power, the Labour Party elected the thoroughly telegenic Tony Blair as its leader, who in turn managed to ditch some of the more socialist-sounding clauses in its party credo and reinvent it as New Labour, leading to a huge landslide win in the May 1997 general election. The Conservatives atomised nationwide; the Blair era had begun in earnest.

Most importantly for London, Labour recognised the demand the city had for local government, and created the London Assembly and the post of mayor. In Ken Livingstone, London elected a mayor who introduced a congestion charge and sought to update the ageing public-transport network. In 2008 he was defeated by his arch-rival, Conservative Boris Johnson.

Johnson won his second term in 2012, the year of the Olympic Games (overwhelmingly judged an unqualified success) and the Queen's Diamond Jubilee (the 60th anniversary of her ascension to the throne).

Since the Olympics, both the nation and the city have changed leadership (Theresa May replacing David Cameron as prime minister, Sadiq Khan taking over as mayor from Boris Johnson), and the Brexit referendum is blowing a wind of change (panic?) through the city.

2008
Boris Johnson, a Conservative MP and journalist, beats Ken Livingstone to become London's new mayor.

2012
London hosts the 2012 Olympics and Paralympics.

2017
A fire in West London's public-housing Grenfell Tower kills 71 people, symbolising the capital's growing inequality.

The Shard (p79) and Tower Bridge (p80) at sunset

PIOTREKNIK / SHUTTERSTOCK ©

Architecture

Unlike many other world-class cities, London has never been methodically planned. Rather, it has developed in an organic fashion. London retains architectural reminders from every period of its long history. This is a city for explorers; seek out part of a Roman wall enclosed in the lobby of a modern building, for example, or a coaching inn dating to the Restoration tucked away in a courtyard off Borough High St.

Ancient London Architecture

Traces of medieval London are hard to find thanks to the devastating Great Fire of 1666, but several works by the architect Inigo Jones (1573–1652) have endured, including Covent Garden Piazza in the West End.

There are a few even older treasures scattered around, including the mighty Tower of London in the City, parts of which date back to the late 11th century. Westminster Abbey and Temple Church are 12th- to 13th-century creations. Few Roman traces survive outside museums, though the Temple of Mithras, built in AD 240, was relocated to the eastern end of Queen Victoria St in the City when the Bloomberg headquarters were completed at Walbrook Sq in 2016. Stretches of the Roman wall remain as foundations to a medieval wall outside Tower Hill tube station and in a few sections below Bastion high walk, next to the Museum of London, all in the City.

The Saxons, who moved into the area after the decline of the Roman Empire, found Londinium too small, ignored what the Romans had left behind and built their communities further up the Thames. The best place to see in situ what the Saxons left behind is the church of All Hallows by the Tower (northwest of the Tower of London), which boasts an important archway, the walls of a 7th-century Saxon church and fragments from a Roman pavement.

Noteworthy medieval secular structures include the 1365 Jewel Tower, opposite the Houses of Parliament, and Westminster Hall, both surviving chunks of the medieval Palace of Westminster.

After the Great Fire

After the 1666 fire, Sir Christopher Wren was commissioned to oversee reconstruction, but his vision of a new city layout of broad, symmetrical avenues never made it past the planners. His legacy lives on, however, in St Paul's Cathedral (1708), in the maritime precincts at Greenwich and in numerous City churches.

Nicholas Hawksmoor joined contemporary James Gibb in taking Wren's English baroque style even further; one great example is St Martin-in-the-Fields in Trafalgar Sq.

Like Wren before him, Georgian architect John Nash aimed to impose some symmetry on unruly London and was slightly more successful in achieving this, through grand creations such as Trafalgar Sq and the elegantly curving arcade of Regent St. Built in similar style, the surrounding squares of St James's remain some of the finest public spaces in London – little wonder then that Queen Victoria decided to move into the recently vacated Buckingham Palace in 1837.

Towards Modernity

The Victorians replaced grand vision with pragmatism; they desired ornate civic buildings that reflected the glory of empire but were open to the masses too. The Victorian style's turrets, towers and arches are best exemplified by the flamboyant Natural History Museum (Alfred Waterhouse), St Pancras Chambers (George Gilbert Scott) and the Houses of Parliament (Augustus Pugin and Charles Barry), the latter replacing the Palace of Westminster that had largely burnt down in 1834.

The Victorians and Edwardians were also ardent builders of functional and cheap terraced houses, many of which became slums, but today house London's urban middle classes.

A flirtation with art deco and the great suburban residential building boom of the 1930s was followed by a utilitarian modernism after WWII, as the city rushed to build new housing to replace terraces lost in the Blitz. Low-cost developments and unattractive high-rise housing were thrown up on bombsites; many of these blocks still fragment the London horizon today.

Brutalism – a hard-edged and uncompromising architectural style that flourished from the 1950s to the 1970s, favouring concrete and reflecting socialist utopian principles – worked better on paper than in real life, but made significant contributions to London's architectural melange. Denys Lasdun's National Theatre, begun in 1966, is representative of the style.

★ **Best Modern Architecture**

Shard (p79)

Tate Modern (p82)

30 St Mary Axe (p69)

Millennium Bridge (p91)

London Aquatics Centre (p202)

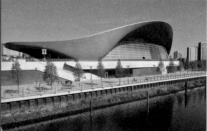

London Aquatics Centre (p202)

RON ELLIS / SHUTTERSTOCK ©

Postmodernism & Beyond

The next big wave of development arrived in the derelict wasteland of the former London docks, which were emptied of their terraces and warehouses and rebuilt as towering skyscrapers and 'loft' apartments. Taking pride of place in the Docklands was Cesar Pelli's 244m-high 1 Canada Square (1991), commonly known as Canary Wharf and easily visible from central London. The City was also the site of architectural innovation, including the centrepiece 1986 Lloyd's of London, Sir Richard Rogers' 'inside-out' masterpiece of ducts, pipes, glass and stainless steel.

Contemporary Architecture

There followed a lull in new construction until around 2000, when a glut of millennium projects unveiled new structures and rejuvenated others: the London Eye, Tate Modern and the Millennium Bridge all spiced up the South Bank, while Norman Foster's iconic 30 St Mary Axe, better known as the Gherkin, started a new wave of skyscraper construction in the City. Even the once-mocked Millennium Dome won a new lease of life as the O2 concert and sports hall.

By the middle of the decade, London's biggest urban-development project ever was under way, the 200-hectare Queen Elizabeth Olympic Park in the Lea River Valley near Stratford in East London, where most of the events of the 2012 Summer Olympics and Paralympics took place. But the park would offer few architectural surprises – except for Zaha Hadid's stunning London Aquatics Centre, a breathtaking structure suitably inspired by the fluid geometry of water; and the ArcelorMittal Orbit, a zany public work of art with viewing platforms, designed by the sculptor Anish Kapoor.

The spotlight may have been shining on East London, but the City and South London have also undergone energetic developments. Most notable is the so-called Shard, at 310m the EU's tallest building, completed in 2012. In the City, the Walkie Talkie has divided opinions, but its junglelike Sky Garden on levels 35 to 37 are universally loved.

In the City, 1 Undershaft will become the second-tallest building in London (sometime around 2023) after the Shard, and the tallest in the Square Mile at 73 floors.

British Library (p118)

MARK CHILVERS / LONELY PLANET ©

Literary London

For over six centuries, London has been the setting for works of prose. Indeed, the capital has been the inspiration for the masterful imaginations of such eminent wordsmiths as Shakespeare, Defoe, Dickens, Orwell, Conrad, Eliot, Greene and Woolf (even though not all were native to the city, or even British).

It's hard to reconcile the bawdy portrayal of London in Geoffrey Chaucer's *Canterbury Tales* with Charles Dickens' bleak hellhole in *Oliver Twist*, let alone Daniel Defoe's plague-ravaged metropolis in *Journal of the Plague Year* with Zadie Smith's multiethnic romp *White Teeth*. Ever-changing, yet somehow eerily consistent, London has left its mark on some of the most influential writing in the English language.

Chaucerian London

The first literary reference to London appears in Chaucer's *Canterbury Tales*, written between 1387 and 1400: the 29 pilgrims of the tale gather for their trip to Canterbury at the

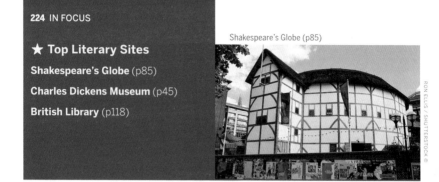

★ **Top Literary Sites**

Shakespeare's Globe (p85)

Charles Dickens Museum (p45)

British Library (p118)

Shakespeare's Globe (p85)

RON ELLIS / SHUTTERSTOCK ©

Tabard Inn in Talbot Yard, Southwark, and agree to share stories on the way there and back. The inn burned down in 1676; a blue plaque marks the site of the building today.

Shakespearian London

Born in Warwickshire, William Shakespeare (1564–1616) spent most of his life as an actor and playwright in London around the turn of the 17th century. He trod the boards of several theatres in Shoreditch and Southwark and wrote his greatest tragedies, among them *Hamlet, Othello, Macbeth* and *King Lear,* for the original Globe theatre on the South Bank. Although London was his home for most of his life, Shakespeare set nearly all his plays in foreign or imaginary lands. Only *Henry IV: Parts I & II* include a London setting – a tavern called the Boar's Head in Eastcheap.

Dickensian & 19th-Century London

Two early 19th-century Romantic poets drew inspiration from London. John Keats, born above a Moorgate public house in 1795, wrote 'Ode to a Nightingale' while living near Hampstead Heath in 1819 and 'Ode on a Grecian Urn' reportedly after viewing the Parthenon frieze in the British Museum the same year. William Wordsworth discovered inspiration for the poem 'Upon Westminster Bridge' while visiting London in 1802.

Charles Dickens was the definitive London author. When his father and family were interned at Marshalsea Prison in Southwark for not paying their debts, 12-year-old Charles was forced to fend for himself on the streets. That grim period provided a font of experiences from which to draw. His novels most closely associated with London are *Oliver Twist,* with its gang of thieves led by Fagin in Clerkenwell, and *Little Dorrit,* whose hero was born in the Marshalsea. The house in Bloomsbury where he wrote *Oliver Twist* and two other novels now houses the expanded Charles Dickens Museum.

Sir Arthur Conan Doyle (1858–1930) portrayed a very different London, his pipe-smoking, cocaine-snorting sleuth, Sherlock Holmes, coming to exemplify a cool and unflappable Englishness. Letters to the mythical hero and his admiring friend, Dr Watson, still arrive at 221b Baker St, where there's a museum dedicated to everyone's favourite Victorian **detective** (Map p254; ☑020-7935 8866; www.sherlock-holmes.co.uk; 221b Baker St, NW1; adult/child £15/10; ☺9.30am-6pm; ☻Baker St).

London at the end of the 19th century appears in many books, but especially those of Somerset Maugham. His first novel, *Liza of Lambeth,* was based on his experiences as an intern in the slums of South London, while *Of Human Bondage* provides a portrait of late-Victorian London.

American Writers & London in the 20th Century

Of Americans who wrote about London at the turn of the century, Henry James, who settled here, stands supreme with his *Daisy Miller* and *The Europeans*. St Louis–born TS Eliot moved to London in 1915, where he published his poems 'The Love Song of J Alfred Prufrock' and 'The Waste Land', in which London is portrayed as an 'unreal city'.

Interwar Developments

Between the world wars, PG Wodehouse depicted London high life with his hilarious lampooning of the English upper classes in the Jeeves stories. George Orwell's experience of living as a beggar in London's East End coloured his book *Down and Out in Paris and London* (1933).

The Modern Age

This period is marked by the emergence of multicultural voices. Hanif Kureishi explored London from the perspective of young Pakistanis in his best-known novels *The Black Album* and *The Buddha of Suburbia*, while Timothy Mo's *Sour Sweet* is a poignant and funny account of a Chinese family in the 1960s trying to adjust to English life.

The decades leading up to the turn of the millennium were great ones for British literature, bringing a dazzling new generation of writers to the fore, such as Martin Amis *(Money, London Fields)*, Julian Barnes *(Metroland, Talking it Over)*, Ian McEwan *(Enduring Love, Atonement)* and Salman Rushdie *(Midnight's Children, The Satanic Verses)*.

Millennium London

Helen Fielding's *Bridget Jones's Diary* and its sequel, *Bridget Jones: The Edge of Reason*, launched the 'chick lit' genre, one that transcended the travails of a young single Londoner to become a worldwide phenomenon.

Peter Ackroyd named the city as the love of his life; *London: the Biography* was his inexhaustible paean to the capital.

New, diverse voices also emerged, including Monica Ali, who brought the East End to life in *Brick Lane*, and Zadie Smith, whose incisive wit and wacky East London characters in *White Teeth* conquered millions.

The Current Scene

Home to most of the UK's major publishers and its best bookshops, London remains a vibrant place for writers and readers alike. 'Rediscovered' author Howard Jacobson, variously called the 'Jewish Jane Austen' and the 'English Philip Roth', won the Man Booker Prize in 2010 for *The Finkler Question*, the first time the prestigious award had gone to a comic novel in 25 years. Literary titan and huge commercial success Hilary Mantel, author of *Wolf Hall*, won the same award for her historical novel *Bring up the Bodies* two years later.

London continues to inspire Zadie Smith with *NW* (2012), which chronicles the life of four characters in northwest London, and *Swing Time* (2016), which recounts the tale of two mixed-race girls from North London. Elif Shafak's *Honour* tells of how traditional practices shatter and transform the lives of Turkish immigrants in 1970s East London, while Jake Arnott's *The Long Firm* is an intelligent Soho-based gangster yarn.

Every bookshop in town has a London section, where you will find many of these titles and lots more.

Tate Britain (p52)

KIEV.VICTOR / SHUTTERSTOCK ©

Art

When it comes to art, London has traditionally been overshadowed by other European capitals. Yet many of history's greatest artists have spent time in London, including the likes of Monet and Van Gogh, and in terms of contemporary art, there's a compelling argument for putting London at the very top of the European pack.

Holbein to Turner

It wasn't until the rule of the Tudors that art began to take off in London. The German Hans Holbein the Younger (1497–1543) was court painter to Henry VIII, and one of his finest works, *The Ambassadors* (1533), hangs in the National Gallery. A batch of great portrait artists worked at court during the 17th century, the best being Anthony Van Dyck (1599–1641), who painted *Charles I on Horseback* (1638), also in the National Gallery.

Local artists began to emerge in the 18th century, including landscapists Thomas Gainsborough (1727–88) and John Constable (1776–1837).

JMW Turner (1775–1851), equally at home with oils and watercolours, represented the pinnacle of 19th-century British art. His later works, including *Snow Storm – Steam-boat off a Harbour's Mouth* (1842) and *Rain, Steam and Speed – the Great Western Railway*

(1844), now in the Tate Britain and the National Gallery respectively, later inspired the Impressionist works of Claude Monet.

The Pre-Raphaelites to Hockney

The brief but splendid flowering of the Pre-Raphaelite Brotherhood (1848–54) with the likes of William Holman Hunt and John Everett Millais took its inspiration from the Romantic poets. Tate Britain has the best selection of works from this period.

Sculptors Henry Moore (1898–1986) and Barbara Hepworth (1903–1975) both typified the modernist movement in British sculpture (you can see examples of their work in Kensington Gardens).

After WWII, art transformed yet again. In 1945, the tortured, Irish-born painter Francis Bacon (1909–92) caused a stir when he exhibited his *Three Studies for Figures at the Base of a Crucifixion* – now on display at the Tate Britain – and afterwards continued to spook the art world with his repulsive yet mesmerising visions.

Australian art critic Robert Hughes once eulogised Bacon's contemporary, Lucian Freud (1922–2011), as 'the greatest living realist painter'. Freud's early work was often surrealist, but from the 1950s the bohemian Freud exclusively focused on pale, muted portraits.

London in the swinging 1960s was perfectly encapsulated by pop art, its vocabulary best articulated by the brilliant David Hockney (b 1937). Two of his most famous works, *Mr and Mrs Clark and Percy* (1971) and *A Bigger Splash* (1974), are displayed at the Tate Britain.

★ Best for British Art

Tate Britain (p52)

National Gallery (p54)

National Portrait Gallery (p55)

Summer Exhibition, Royal Academy of Arts (p49)

Brit Art & Beyond

Brit Art sprang from a show called *Freeze*, which was staged in a Docklands warehouse in 1988, organised by artist and showman Damien Hirst and largely featuring his fellow graduates from Goldsmiths College. Influenced by pop culture and punk, Brit Art was brash, decadent, ironic, easy to grasp and eminently marketable. Hirst's *Mother & Child (Divided)*, a cow and her calf sliced into sections and preserved in formaldehyde, and Tracey Emin's *My Bed*, the artist's unmade bed and the mess next to it, are seminal works from this era.

The best way to take the pulse of the British contemporary-art scene is to attend the annual Summer Exhibition at the Royal Academy of Arts, which features works by established as well as unknown artists.

Big names to look out for across the capital include Anthony Gormley, whose *Planets* is outside the British Library, and *Quantum Cloud* below the Emirates Air Line cable car in the Docklands; Anish Kapoor, whose ArcelorMittal Orbit towers over the Queen Elizabeth Olympic Park, and Banksy, whose graffiti adorns many a street in the capital.

St Pancras Station (p119)

JUSTIN FOULKES / LONELY PLANET ©

Survival Guide

Directory A–Z

Customs Regulations

Until Brexit comes into force, the UK distinguishes between goods bought duty-free outside the EU and those bought in another EU country, where taxes and duties will have already been paid.

If you exceed your duty-free allowance, you will have to pay tax on the items. For European goods, there is officially no limit to how much you can bring but customs uses certain guidelines to distinguish between personal and commercial use.

Discount Cards

London Pass (☏020-7293 0972; www.londonpass. com; 1/2/3/6/10 days £66/91/109/149/179) is worthwhile for visitors who want to take in lots of paid sights in a short time. The pass offers free entry and queue-jumping to all major attractions, and can be adapted to include use of the Underground and buses. Child passes are available too. Check the website for details.

You can download the app to your smartphone or collect your pass from the **London Pass Redemption Desk** (www.londonpass.com; 11a Charing Cross Rd, WC2; ⊙10am-4.30pm; ⊕Leicester Sq), near Leicester Sq.

Electricity

Type G
230V/50Hz

Emergency

Dial ☏999 to call the police, fire brigade or an ambulance.

Entry & Exit Formalities

UK immigration authorities are stringent and methodical, so queues can get long at passport control.

Etiquette

Although largely informal in their everyday dealings, Londoners do observe some (unspoken) rules of etiquette.

Strangers Unless asking for directions, British people generally won't start a conversation at bus stops or on underground (tube) platforms. More latitude is given to non-British people.

Greetings When meeting someone formally for the first time, shake hands.

Queues The British don't tolerate queue jumping. Any attempt to do so will receive tutting and protest.

Tube Stand on the right and pass on the left while riding an Underground escalator.

Apologise The British love apologising. If you bump into someone on the tube, say sorry; they may apologise back, even if you are to blame.

LGBT+ Travellers

Protection from discrimination is enshrined in law and same-sex couples have the right to marry. That's not to say that homophobia does not exist. Always report homophobic crimes to the **police** (☏999).

Useful Resources

60by80 (www.60by80.com/london) Gay travel information.

Boyz (www.boyz.co.uk) Weekly magazine covering the bar and club scenes.

Diva (www.divamag.co.uk) Monthly lesbian magazine.

Gay Times (www.gaytimes.co.uk) Long-standing monthly gay men's mag.

Pride Life (www.pridelife.com) Quarterly news and lifestyle magazine.

QX (www.qxmagazine.com) Another weekly mag devoted mainly to men's venues.

Book Your Stay Online

For more accommodation reviews by Lonely Planet authors, check out http://hotels.lonelyplanet.com/london. You'll find independent reviews, as well as recommendations on the best places to stay. Best of all, you can book online.

Time Out London LGBT (www.timeout.com/london/lgbt) Bar, club and events listings.

Health

EU nationals can obtain free emergency treatment (and, in some cases, reduced-cost health care) on presentation of a **European Health Insurance Card** (www.ehic.org.uk). It's still too early to say what will happen to the EHIC card after the UK leaves the EU, but it would be advisable to check before travelling to London.

Reciprocal arrangements with the UK allow Australians, New Zealanders and residents and nationals of several other countries to receive free emergency medical treatment and subsidised dental care through the **National Health Service** (NHS; ☏111; www.nhs.uk). They can use hospital emergency departments, GPs and dentists. For a full list visit the 'Services near you' section of the NHS website.

Hospitals

A number of hospitals have 24-hour accident- and emergency-departments. Centrally located hospitals:

Guy's Hospital (☏020-7188 7188; www.guysandstthomas.nhs.uk; Great Maze Pond, SE1; ☺London Bridge)

University College London Hospital (☏020-3456 7890; www.uclh.nhs.uk; 235 Euston Rd, NW1; ☺Warren St, Euston)

Insurance

Travel insurance is advisable as it offers greater flexibility over where and how you're treated and covers expenses for an ambulance and repatriation that will not be picked up by the NHS.

It will also cover mishaps such as loss of baggage, cancelled flights and so forth.

Pharmacies

The main pharmacy chains in London are Boots and Superdrug; a branch of either – or both – can be found on virtually every high street.

The **Boots** (☏020-7734 6126; www.boots.com; 44-46 Regent St, W1; ☺8am-11pm Mon-Fri, 9am-11pm Sat, 12.30-6.30pm Sun; ☺Piccadilly Circus) in Piccadilly Circus is one of the biggest and most centrally located and has extended opening times.

Internet Access

° Virtually every hotel in London now provides wi-fi free of charge.

° A huge number of cafes, and many restaurants, offer free wi-fi to customers, including major chain cafes. Cultural venues such as the Barbican and the Southbank Centre also have free wi-fi.

Legal Matters

Should you face any legal difficulties while in London, visit a branch of the Citizens Advice Bureau (www. citizensadvice.org.uk), or contact your embassy.

Drugs

Illegal drugs of every type are widely available in London, especially in clubs. Nonetheless, all the usual drug warnings apply. If you're caught with pot today, you're likely to be arrested. Possession of harder drugs, including heroin and cocaine, is always treated seriously. Searches on entering clubs are common.

Fines

In general you rarely have to pay on the spot for an offence. The exceptions are trains, the tube and buses, where people who can't produce a valid ticket for the journey when asked to by an inspector can be fined there and then.

Money

ATMs are widespread. Major credit cards are accepted everywhere. The best place to change money is in post-office branches, which do not charge a commission.

Practicalities

Weights & Measures The UK uses a confusing mix of metric and imperial systems.

Smoking & Vaping Smoking is forbidden in all enclosed public places. Most pubs have some sort of smoking area outside. Some pubs and restaurants have a no-vaping policy; vaping is not allowed on buses, the tube or trains.

Currency

The pound sterling (£) is the unit of currency. One pound sterling is made up of 100 pence (called 'pee', colloquially).

Notes come in denominations of £5, £10, £20 and £50, while coins are 1p ('penny'), 2p, 5p, 10p, 20p, 50p, £1 and £2.

Credit & Debit Cards

○ Credit and debit cards are accepted almost universally in London, from restaurants and bars to shops and even by some taxis.

○ American Express and Diners Club are far less widely used than Visa and MasterCard.

○ Contactless cards and payments (which do not require a chip and pin or a signature) are increasingly widespread (watch for the wi-fi-like symbol on cards, shops, taxis, buses, the Underground, rail services and other transport options). Transactions are limited to a maximum of £30.

Opening Hours

The following are standard opening hours.

Banks 9am–5pm Monday–Friday

Pubs and bars 11am–11pm (many are open later)

Restaurants noon–2.30pm and 6pm–11pm

Sights 10am–6pm

Shops 9am–7pm Monday–Saturday, noon–6pm Sunday

Public Holidays

Most attractions and businesses close for a couple of days over Christmas and sometimes Easter. Places that normally shut on Sunday will probably close on bank-holiday Mondays.

New Year's Day 1 January

Good Friday Late March/April

Easter Monday Late March/April

May Day Holiday First Monday in May

Spring Bank Holiday Last Monday in May

Summer Bank Holiday Last Monday in August

Christmas Day 25 December

Boxing Day 26 December

Safe Travel

London is a fairly safe city for its size, but exercise common sense.

○ Several high-profile terrorist attacks have afflicted London in recent years, but the risk to individual visitors is remote. Report anything suspicious to the police by calling ☎999 (emergency) or ☎101 (nonemergency).

○ Keep an eye on your handbag and wallet, especially in bars and nightclubs, and in crowded areas such as the Underground.

○ Be discreet with your tablet or smartphone – snatching happens.

○ If you're getting a cab after a night's clubbing, go for a black taxi or a licensed minicab firm.

Telephone

Buy local SIM cards for European and Australian phones, or a pay-as-you-go phone. Set other phones to international roaming.

Useful Numbers

London's area code	☎020
International access code	☎00
Police, fire or ambulance	☎999
Reverse charge/ collect calls	☎155

Toilets

Train stations, bus terminals and attractions generally have good facilities, providing also for people with disabilities and those with babies. You'll also find public toilets across the city; most charge 50p. Department stores and museums generally have toilets. It's an offence to urinate in the streets.

Tourist Information

Visit London (www.visitlondon.com) can fill you in on everything from attractions and events to tours and accommodation. Kiosks are dotted about the city and can also provide maps and brochures; some branches are able to book theatre tickets.

Heathrow Airport (Terminal 1, 2 & 3 Underground station concourse; ☺7.30am-8.30pm)

King's Cross St Pancras Station (Western Ticket Hall, Euston Rd N1; ☺8am-6pm)

Liverpool Street Station (Liverpool St Station; ☺8am-6pm; ⊖Liverpool St)

Piccadilly Circus Underground Station (Piccadilly Circus Underground Station; ☺9am-4pm)

Victoria Station (Victoria Station; ☺8am-6pm; ⊖Victoria)

Travellers with Disabilities

For travellers with access needs, London is a frustrating mix of user-friendliness and head-in-the-sand disinterest. New hotels and modern tourist attractions are legally required to be accessible to people in wheelchairs, but many historic buildings, B&Bs and guesthouses are in older buildings, which are hard or prohibitively expensive to adapt. Similarly, visitors with vision, hearing or cognitive impairments will find their needs met in a piecemeal fashion.

Transport can be hit-and-miss too:

○ Around a quarter of tube stations, half of overground stations and all DLR stations have step-free access.

○ Buses can be lowered to street level when they stop and wheelchair users travel free.

○ All black cabs are wheelchair-accessible.

○ Guide dogs are universally welcome on public

transport and in hotels, restaurants, attractions etc.

Useful Resources

Accessible London (http://www.disabledgo.com/accessible-london-visit-london) Professionally audited guide, produced by DisabledGo, to access in the city.

Transport for London (www.tfl.gov.uk/transport-accessibility/) All the information you'll need to get around London on public transport.

VisitLondon (www.visitlondon.com/traveller-information/essential-information/accessible-london) The tourist board's accessible-travel page has useful links and information on accessible shops, hotels and toilets.

Visas

Not required for Australian, Canadian, New Zealand and US visitors, as well as several other nations, for stays of up to six months.

Immigration to the UK is becoming tougher, particularly for those seeking to work or study. The exit of the UK from the EU is planned for 2019 and entry requirements for EU nationals may change. Make sure you check the website of the UK Border Agency (www.gov.uk/check-uk-visa) or with your local British embassy or consulate for the most up-to-date information.

Women Travellers

Female visitors to London are unlikely to have many problems, provided they take the usual big-city precautions. Don't get into an Underground carriage with no one else in it or with just one or two men. And if you feel unsafe, you should take a taxi or licensed minicab.

Transport

Arriving in London

Most people arrive in London by air, but an increasing number of visitors coming from Europe let the *Eurostar* (the Channel Tunnel train) take the strain, while buses from the continent are a further option.

The city has five airports: Heathrow, which is the largest, to the west; Gatwick to the south; Stansted to the northeast; Luton to the northwest; and London City in the Docklands.

Flights, cars and tours can be booked online at lonelyplanet.com.

Heathrow Airport

Some 15 miles west of central London, **Heathrow Airport** (LHR; www.heathrowairport.com) is one of the world's busiest international airports; it has four terminals, numbered 2 to 5.

Train

Three Underground stations on the Piccadilly line serve Heathrow: one for Terminals 2 and 3, another for Terminal 4, and the terminus for Terminal 5. The Underground, commonly referred to as 'the tube', is the cheapest way of getting to Heathrow (from central London, one hour, with trains every three to nine minutes). It runs from around 5am to midnight. Buy tickets at the station.

Heathrow Express (www.heathrowexpress.com; one-way/return £27/42; ☎), every 15 minutes, and the new Elizabeth Line, every 5 minutes, link Heathrow with Paddington train station. Heathrow Express trains take a mere 15 minutes to reach Paddington, the Elizabeth Line 30 minutes. Trains on each service run from around 5am to between 11pm and midnight.

Bus

National Express (www.nationalexpress.com) coaches (one way from £6, 35 to 90 minutes, every 30 minutes to one hour) link the Heathrow Central bus station with London Victoria Coach Station.

Taxi

A metered black-cab trip to/from central London will

cost between £48 and £90 and take 45 minutes to an hour, depending on traffic and your departure point.

Gatwick Airport

Located some 30 miles south of central London, **Gatwick** (LGW; www.gatwick airport.com) is smaller than Heathrow and is Britain's number-two airport, mainly for international flights. The North and South Terminals are linked by a 24-hour shuttle train, with the journey time about three minutes.

Train

National Rail (www.nation alrail.co.uk) Regular train services to/from London Bridge (30 minutes, every 15 to 30 minutes), London King's Cross (55 minutes, every 15 to 30 minutes) and London Victoria (30 minutes, every 10 to 15 minutes). Fares vary depending on the time of travel and the

train company, but allow £10 to £20 for a single trip.

Gatwick Express (www.gatwickexpress.com; one-way/return adult £19.90/35.60, child £9.95/17.75) Trains run every 15 minutes from the station near the Gatwick South Terminal to London Victoria. Services run from around 5am to about 11pm. The journey takes 30 minutes; book online for the best deals.

Bus

National Express (www.nationalexpress.com) coaches run throughout the day from Gatwick to London Victoria Coach Station (one-way from £8). Services depart hourly around the clock. Journey time is between 80 minutes and two hours, depending on traffic.

Taxi

A metered black-cab trip to/from central London costs around £100 and takes just

over an hour. Minicabs are usually cheaper.

Stansted Airport

Stansted (STN; www.stanstedairport.com) is 35 miles northeast of central London in the direction of Cambridge. An international airport, Stansted serves a multitude of mainly European destinations and is served primarily by low-cost carriers such as Ryanair.

Train

Stansted Express (☎0345 600 7245; www.stanstedexpress.com; one-way/return £17/29) Rail service (45 minutes, every 15 to 30 minutes) links the airport and Liverpool St station. From the airport, the first train leaves at 5.30am, the last at 12.30am. Trains depart Liverpool St station from 3.40am to 11.25pm.

Bus

National Express coaches run around the clock, offering more than 100 services per day.

Airbus A6 Runs to Victoria Coach Station (around one hour to 1½ hours, every 20 minutes) via Marble Arch, Paddington, Baker St and Golders Green (one way from £10).

Airbus A7 Also runs to Victoria Coach Station (around one hour to 1½ hours, every 20 minutes), via Waterloo and Southwark (one-way from £10).

Airbus A8 Runs to Liverpool St station (one-way from £6, 60 to 80 minutes, every 30 minutes), via Bethnal Green, Shoreditch High St and Mile End.

Climate Change & Travel

Every form of transport that relies on carbon-based fuel generates CO_2, the main cause of human-induced climate change. Modern travel is dependent on aeroplanes, which might use less fuel per kilometre per person than most cars but travel much greater distances. The altitude at which aircraft emit gases (including CO_2) and particles also contributes to their climate change impact. Many websites offer 'carbon calculators' that allow people to estimate the carbon emissions generated by their journey and, for those who wish to do so, to offset the impact of the greenhouse gases emitted with contributions to portfolios of climate-friendly initiatives throughout the world. Lonely Planet offsets the carbon footprint of all staff and author travel.

EasyBus (www.easybus.co.uk) Runs services to Baker St and Old St tube stations every 15 minutes. The journey (one-way from £4.95) takes one hour from Old St, 1¼ hours from Baker St.

Terravision (www.terravision. eu) Links Stansted to Liverpool St station (one-way from £9, 55 minutes), King's Cross (from £9, 75 minutes) and Victoria Coach Station (from £10, two hours) every 20 to 40 minutes between 6am and 1am. All buses have wi-fi.

Taxi

A metered black-cab trip to/ from central London costs around £130. Minicabs are cheaper.

Luton Airport

A smallish airport 32 miles northwest of London, **Luton** (LTN; www.london-luton.co.uk) generally caters for cheap charter flights and discount airlines.

Train

National Rail (www.national rail.co.uk) has 24-hour services (one-way from £14, 26 to 50 minutes, departures every six minutes to one hour) from London St Pancras International to Luton Airport Parkway station, from where an airport shuttle bus (one-way/return £2.20/3.50) will take you to the airport in 10 minutes.

Bus

Airbus A1 (www.national express.com; one-way from £5)

Runs over 60 times daily to London Victoria Coach Station, via Portman Sq, Baker St, St John's Wood, Finchley Rd and Golders Green. It takes around 1½ hours.

Green Line Bus 757 (☎0344 800 4411; www.greenline.co.uk; one-way/return £10/17) Runs to Luton Airport from London Victoria Coach Station every 30 minutes on a 24-hour service via Marble Arch, Baker St, Finchley Rd and Brent Cross.

Taxi

A metered black-cab trip to/ from central London costs about £110.

London City Airport

Its proximity to central London, which is just 6 miles to the west, as well as to the commercial district of the Docklands, means **London City Airport** (LCY; www.londoncityairport. com) is predominantly a gateway airport for business travellers.

Train

Docklands Light Railway (DLR; www.tfl.gov.uk/dlr) Stops at the London City Airport station (one-way £2.80 to £3.30). The journey to Bank takes just over 20 minutes.

Taxi

A metered black-cab trip to the City/Oxford St/ Earl's Court costs about £25/35/50.

St Pancras International Train Station

The arrival point for the Eurostar (www.eurostar. com) trains to/from Europe is connected by many Underground lines to the rest of the city.

Getting Around

The tube, DLR and Overground network are ideal for zooming across the city; buses, cycling or walking are great for shorter journeys.

Underground

The London Underground is part of an integrated-transport system that also includes the **Docklands Light Railway** (DLR; www. tfl.gov.uk/dlr), a driverless overhead train operating in the eastern part of the city, and Overground network (mostly outside of Zone 1 and sometimes underground). It is overall the quickest and easiest way of getting around the city, if not the cheapest.

The first trains operate from around 5.30am Monday to Saturday and 6.45am Sunday. The last trains leave around 12.30am Monday to Saturday and 11.30pm Sunday.

Additionally, selected lines (the Victoria and Jubilee lines, plus most of the Piccadilly, Central and Northern lines) run all night

Oyster Card

The Oyster Card is a smart card on which you can store credit towards 'prepay' fares, as well as Travelcards. Oyster Cards are valid across the entire public-transport network in London.

All you need to do when entering a station is touch your card on a reader (which has a yellow circle with the image of an Oyster Card on it) and then touch again on your way out. The system will then deduct the appropriate amount of credit from your card. For bus journeys, you only need to touch once upon boarding.

Oyster Cards ensure you will never pay more than the appropriate Travelcard (peak or off-peak) once the daily 'price cap' has been reached.

Oyster Cards can be bought (£5 refundable deposit required) and topped up at any Underground station, travel information centre or shop displaying the Oyster logo. To get your deposit back along with any remaining credit, simply return your Oyster Card at a ticket booth.

Contactless cards (which do not require chip and pin or a signature) can now be used directly on Oyster Card readers and are subject to the same Oyster fares. Foreign visitors should bear in mind the cost of card transactions.

on Friday and Saturday to get revellers home (on what is called the 'Night Tube'), with trains every 10 minutes or so. Fares are off-peak.

During weekend closures, schedules, maps and alternative-route suggestions are posted in every station, and staff are at hand to help redirect you.

Some stations, most famously Leicester Sq and Covent Garden, are much closer in reality than they appear on the map.

Fares

○ London is divided into nine concentric fare zones.

○ It will always be cheaper to travel with an Oyster Card or a contactless card than a paper ticket.

○ Children under the age of 11 travel free; 11- to 15-year-olds are half-price if registered on an accompanying adult's Oyster Card (register at Zone 1 or Heathrow tube stations).

Bus

London's ubiquitous red double-decker buses afford great views of the city, but be aware that the going can be slow, thanks to traffic jams and dozens of commuters getting on and off at every stop.

There are excellent bus maps at every stop detailing all routes and destinations served from that particular area (generally a few bus stops within a two- to three-minute walk, shown on a local map).

Bus services normally operate from 5am to 11.30pm.

Night Bus

○ More than 50 night-bus routes (prefixed with the letter 'N') run from around 11.30pm to 5am.

○ There are also another 60 bus routes operating 24 hours; the frequency decreases between 11pm and 5am.

Fares

○ Cash cannot be used on London's buses. Instead you must pay with an Oyster Card, Travelcard or a contactless payment card. Bus fares are a flat £1.50, no matter the distance travelled.

○ Children aged under 11 years travel free; 11- to 15-year-olds are half-price if registered on an accompanying adult's Oyster Card (register at Zone 1 or Heathrow tube stations).

Taxis

Black Cabs

The black cab is as much a feature of the London cityscape as the red double-decker bus.

○ Cabs are available for hire when the yellow sign above the windscreen is lit; just stick your arm out to signal one.

○ Fares are metered, with a flag-fall charge of £2.60 (covering the first 235m during a weekday), rising by increments of 20p for each subsequent 117m.

○ Fares are more expensive in the evenings and overnight.

○ Apps such as mytaxi (https://uk.mytaxi.com) use your smartphone's GPS to locate the nearest black cab. You only pay the metered fare.

Minicabs

○ Minicabs, which are licensed, are cheaper (usually) competitors of black cabs.

○ Unlike black cabs, minicabs cannot legally be hailed on the street; they must be hired by phone or directly from one of the minicab offices (every high street has at least one and most clubs work with a minicab firm to send revellers home safely).

○ Don't accept unsolicited offers from individuals claiming to be minicab drivers – they are just guys with cars.

○ Minicabs don't have meters; there's usually a fare set by the dispatcher. Make sure you ask before setting off.

○ Your hotel or host will be able to recommend a reputable minicab company in the neighbourhood; every Londoner has the number of at least one company. Or phone a large 24-hour operator such as **Addison Lee** (☏020-7387 8888; www. addisonlee.com).

○ Apps such as Uber or Kabbee allow you to book a minicab in double-quick time and can save you money.

Boat

Thames Clippers (www. thamesclippers.com; all zones adult/child £9.90/4.95) One of several companies operating boats along the River Thames, Thames Clippers offers proper commuter services. It's fast, pleasant and you're almost always guaranteed a seat and a view. Boats run every 20 minutes from 6am to between 10pm and 11pm. The route goes from London Eye Millennium Pier to Woolwich Arsenal Pier, with boats west to Putney too.

Cycling

The **Santander Cycle**
(☏0343 222 6666; www.tfl.gov. uk/modes/cycling/santander-cycles) scheme is a great, affordable and fun way to get around London. For more information, see p202.

Walking

You can't beat walking for neighbourhood exploration. There are plenty of bridges across the Thames and a couple of pedestrian tunnels beneath the river too.

Behind the Scenes

Acknowledgements

Climate map data adapted from Peel MC, Finlayson BL & McMahon TA (2007) 'Updated World Map of the Köppen-Geiger Climate Classification', Hydrology and Earth System Sciences, 11, 16-3344.

This Book

This 3rd edition guidebook was curated by Emilie Filou, who also wrote and researched it along with Damian Harper, Peter Dragicevich and Steve Fallon. The previous edition was also written by Emilie, Peter, Steve and Damian.

This guidebook was produced by the following:

Destination Editor Clifton Wilkinson

Senior Product Editor Genna Patterson

Product Editor Ross Taylor

Senior Cartographer Mark Griffiths

Book Designer Wibowo Rusli

Assisting Editors Ronan Abayawickrema, Barbara Delissen, Victoria Harrison, Kristin Odijk, Charlotte Orr

Cover Researcher Brendan Dempsey-Spencer

Thanks to Hannah Cartmel, Anne Mason, Tony Wheeler

Send Us Your Feedback

We love to hear from travellers – your comments keep us on our toes and help make our books better. Our well-travelled team reads every word on what you loved or loathed about this book. Although we cannot reply individually to postal submissions, we always guarantee that your feedback goes straight to the appropriate authors, in time for the next edition. Each person who sends us information is thanked in the next edition, the most useful submissions are rewarded with a selection of digital PDF chapters.

Visit lonelyplanet.com/contact to submit your updates and suggestions or to ask for help. Our award-winning website also features inspirational travel stories, news and discussions.

Note: We may edit, reproduce and incorporate your comments in Lonely Planet products such as guidebooks, websites and digital products, so let us know if you don't want your comments reproduced or your name acknowledged. For a copy of our privacy policy visit lonelyplanet.com/privacy.

Index

Christmas at Covent Garden (p60)

London Maps

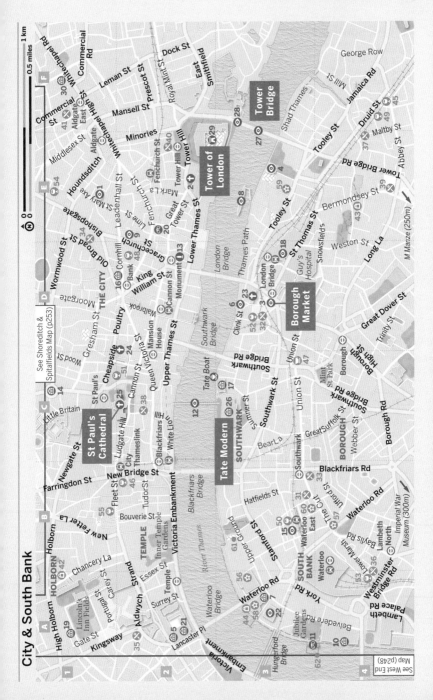

City & South Bank

HOLBORN

Holborn

High Holborn

Chancery La

Lincoln's Inn Fields

Gate St

Kingsway

New Fetter La

Bouverie St

TEMPLE

Inner Temple Gardens

Aldwych

Strand

Surrey St

Portugal St

Carey St

Essex St

Temple

Lancaster Pl

Waterloo Bridge

River Thames

Victoria Embankment

Hungerford Bridge

Jubilee Gardens

Belvedere Rd

York Rd

Waterloo Rd

Lambeth Palace Rd

Westminster Bridge Rd

Lower Marsh

Baylis Rd

Lambeth North

Waterloo

SOUTH BANK

Upper Ground

The Cut

Stamford St

Hatfields St

Blackfriars Rd

Waterloo Rd

Ufford St

Webber St

BOROUGH

Borough Rd

Great Suffolk St

Southwark St

Union St

Union St

Southwark Bridge Rd

Mint St

Great Dover St

Trinity St

Great Suffolk St

Bear La

Sumner St

SOUTHWARK

Tate Boat

Southwark Bridge

London Bridge

Thames Path

Tooley St

Tooley St

St Thomas St

Weston St

Long La

Bermondsey St

Snowsfield's

Guy's Hospital

Borough High St

M Manze (250m)

Abbey St

Tower Bridge Rd

Maltby St

Druid St

Jamaica Rd

George Row

Mill St

Shad Thames

Tower Bridge

Tower of London

St Katharine's

Lower Thames St

Great Tower St

Mark La

Tower Hill

Byward St

Fenchurch St

Eastcheap

Great Tower St

Monument

Cannon St

King William St

Gracechurch St

Cornhill

Bank

Poultry

Cheapside

Queen Victoria St

Upper Thames St

St Paul's

Ludgate Hill

Newgate St

Farringdon St

Little Britain

New Bridge St

Fleet St

Tudor St

New St

City Thameslink

White Lion Hill

Blackfriars

Blackfriars Bridge

Cannon St

Mansion House

Walbrook

THE CITY

Gresham St

Moorgate

Wood St

Bishopsgate

Old Broad St

Wormwood St

Houndsditch

St Mary Axe

Leadenhall St

Lime St

Fenchurch St

Leadenhall St

Minories

Aldgate

Aldgate High St

Whitechapel High St

Middlesex St

Commercial St

Houndsditch

Mansell St

Prescot St

Leman St

Commercial Rd

Whitechapel Rd

Dock St

Royal Mint St

East Smithfield

Commercial Rd

Wattpade St Pl

St Paul's Cathedral

Tate Modern

Borough Market

See Shoreditch & Spitalfields Map (p253)

See West End Map (p248)

1 km
0.5 miles

Numbered markers on map

30, 41, 54, 1, 34, 9, 48, 16, 51, 24, 14, 25, 38, 5, 21, 35, 55, 42, 19, 46, 33, 31, 50, 15, 60, 57, 7, 22, 44, 58, 56, 61, 62, 11, 10, 53, 36, 47, 32, 52, 23, 6, 3, 18, 43, 39, 45, 49, 37, 27, 4, 59, 8, 29, 28, 40, 20, 13, 12, 26, 17

City & South Bank

◎ Sights
1 30 St Mary Axe.. E1
2 All Hallows by the Tower.........................E2
3 Borough Market.. D3
4 City Hall...E3
5 Courtauld Gallery......................................A2
6 Golden Hinde... D3
7 Hayward Gallery...A3
8 HMS Belfast..E3
9 Leadenhall Market....................................E2
10 London Dungeon A4
11 London Eye..A3
12 Millennium Bridge.................................... C2
13 Monument D2
14 Museum of London....................................C1
15 Roupell St..B3
16 Royal Exchange... D2
17 Shakespeare's Globe C3
18 Shard.. D3
19 Sir John Soane's Museum........................ A1
20 Sky Garden...E2
21 Somerset House...A2
22 Southbank Centre A3
23 Southwark Cathedral............................... D3
24 St Mary-le-Bow D2
25 St Paul's Cathedral................................... C2
26 Tate Modern... C3
27 Tower Bridge...F3
28 Tower Bridge Exhibition...........................F3
29 Tower of London...E2
30 Whitechapel Gallery F1

✕ Eating
31 Anchor & Hope...B3
32 Arabica Bar & Kitchen.............................. D3
33 Baltic..B3
34 City Social...E1
35 Counter at the Delaunay..........................A2
   Crypt Cafe...(see 25)
36 Four Corners Cafe A4
37 Maltby Street Market E4
38 Miyama... C2
   Padella... (see 3)
   Sauterelle..(see 16)

   Skylon...(see 22)
   The Delaunay.....................................(see 35)
39 Watch House E4
40 Wine Library..E2
41 Yuu Kitchen F1

🛍 Shopping
42 London Silver Vaults.................................A1
43 Lovely & British E4
44 South Bank Book Market..........................A3
   Southbank Centre Shop..................(see 22)

🍷 Drinking & Nightlife
45 Anspach & Hobday F4
46 City of London Distillery...........................B2
47 Coffee House.. C3
48 Jamaica Wine House D2
49 Jensen..F4
50 King's Arms...B3
   Little Bird Gin....................................(see 37)
51 Madison...C2
   Oblix... (see 18)
   Queen Elizabeth Roof Garden........ (see 58)
52 Rake... D3
53 Scootercaffe...A4
   Sky Pod.. (see 20)
   Skylon.. (see 22)
54 Wine Pantry...E1
55 Ye Olde Cheshire Cheese..........................B1

🎭 Entertainment
56 National Theatre A3
57 Old Vic...B4
58 Queen Elizabeth Hall.................................A3
   Royal Festival Hall...........................(see 22)
   Shakespeare's Globe........................(see 17)
   Southbank Centre.............................(see 22)
59 Unicorn Theatre E3
60 Young Vic B3

🎯 Activities, Courses & Tours
61 London Bicycle Tour...................................B3
62 Thames Rockets A4

West End

⊚ Sights

⊗ Eating

⊚ Shopping

⊚ Drinking & Nightlife

⊗ Entertainment

⊚ Activities, Courses & Tours

West End

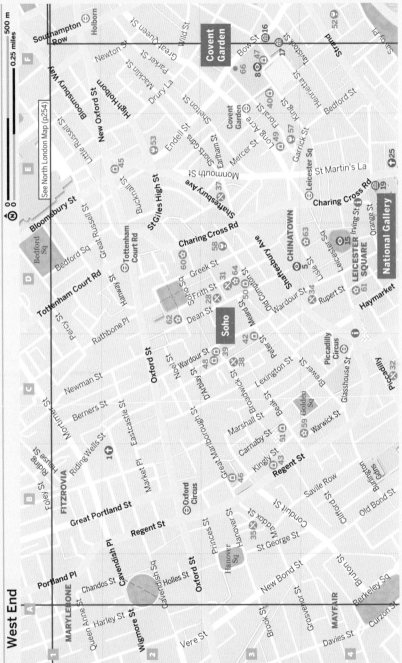

500 m
0.25 miles

See North London Map (p254)

Southampton Row
Holborn

Great Queen St
Newton St
Parker St
Macklin St
Drury La
Wild St
Bow St
Covent Garden
Tavistock St
Strand
52
Wellington St

New Oxford St
High Holborn
Bloomsbury Way
Little Russell St
Shelton St
Endell St
Shorts Gdns
Earlham St
Long Acre
Covent Garden
Floral St
King St
Garrick St
St Martin's La
Bedford St
Henrietta St

66
8 47
17
16
40
49
57
25

Bloomsbury St
Bedford Sq
Great Russell St
Bedford Sq
Bucknall St
St Giles High St
Mercer St
Monmouth St
Shaftesbury Ave
Leicester Sq
Charing Cross Rd

53
45
37
19

Tottenham Court Rd
Bedford Sq
Hanway St
Charing Cross Rd
Greek St
Soho Sq
Frith St
Dean St
Old Compton St
Wardour St
Shaftesbury Ave
CHINATOWN
Lisle St
Gerrard St
Rupert St
Charing Cross Rd
Orange St
Irving St
Leicester St
National Gallery

58
60
31
28
64
34
63
5
15
61
LEICESTER SQUARE

Percy St
Rathbone Pl
Newman St
Berners St
Eastcastle St
Rathbone Pl
Oxford St
Noel St
Wardour St
D'Arblay St
Broadwick St
Peter St
Soho
Meard St
Brewer St
Piccadilly Circus
Glasshouse St
Haymarket
Piccadilly

62
42
48
39
38
32

MARYLEBONE
FITZROVIA
Foley St
Riding House St
Mortimer St
Riding House St
Great Portland St
Market Pl
Great Marlborough St
Lexington St
Berwick St
Marshall St
Carnaby St
Kingly St
Golden Sq
Warwick St
Regent St
Savile Row
Burlington Gdns
Old Bond St

1
59
51
43
46

Portland Pl
Chandos St
Cavendish Pl
Oxford Circus
Regent St
Princes St
Hanover St
Hanover Sq
Maddox St
St George St
Conduit St
New Bond St
Grosvenor St
MAYFAIR
Brook St
Davies St
Curzon St
Berkeley Sq
Bruton St
Clifford St
Old Burlington St

35

Queen Anne St
Harley St
Wigmore St
Cavendish Sq
Holles St
Oxford St
Vere St
Brook St

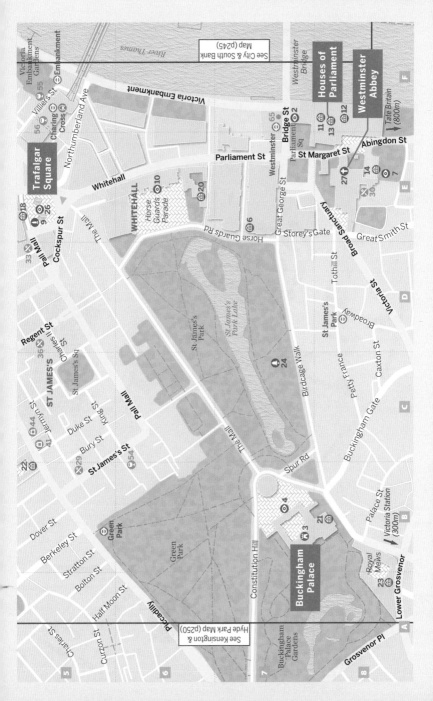

Victoria Embankment Gardens

55 Villiers St

56 Charing Cross

Northumberland Ave

Embankment

River Thames

See City & South Bank
Map (p245)

Victoria Embankment

Westminster Bridge

Houses of Parliament

Westminster Abbey

Tate Britain (800m)

Parliament St

Whitehall

Trafalgar Square

Pall Mall

Cockspur St

33

18
9 26

Whitehall

10

Horse Guards Parade

WHITEHALL

20

9

Horse Guards Rd

Storey's Gate

Great George St

Westminster

Bridge St

65

Parliament Sq

11
13   12

St Margaret St

27

Abingdon St

14
30   7

Broad Sanctuary

Great Smith St

The Mall

Regent St

36

Charles II St

St James's Sq

ST JAMES'S

44 St

Jermyn St

Duke St

King St

Bury St

Pall Mall

St James's St

29

54

22

St James's Park

St James's Park Lake

24

Birdcage Walk

St James's Park

Broadway

Tothill St

Victoria St

Caxton St

Petty France

Buckingham Gate

Spur Rd

The Mall

Green Park

Green Park

Constitution Hill

Dover St

Berkeley St

Stratton St

Bolton St

Half Moon St

Curzon St

Charles St

Piccadilly

See Kensington &
Hyde Park Map (p250)

Buckingham Palace Gardens

Grosvenor Pl

Buckingham Palace

4

3

21

Palace St

Victoria Station (300m)

Royal Mews

23

Lower Grosvenor

5

6

7

8

Kensington & Hyde Park

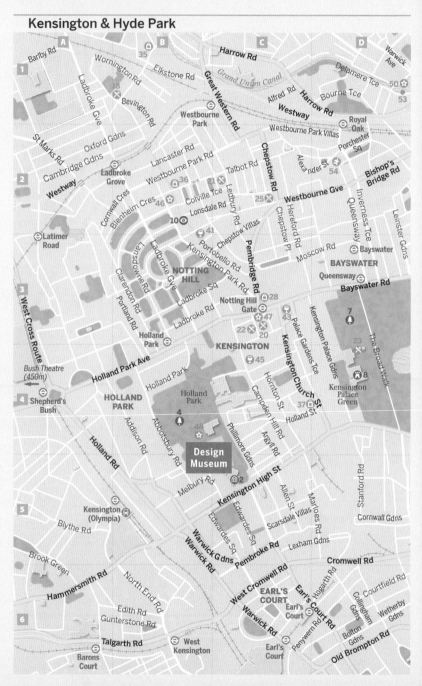

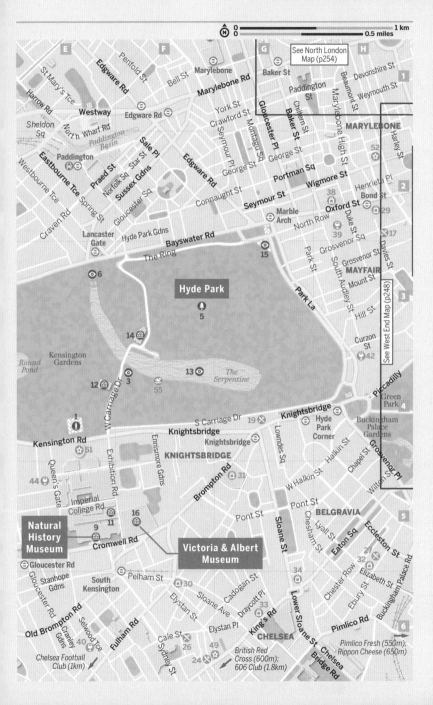

Kensington & Hyde Park

Shoreditch & Spitalfields

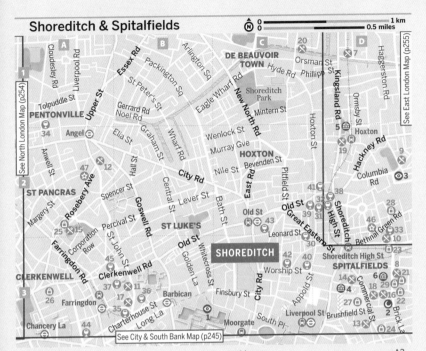

North London

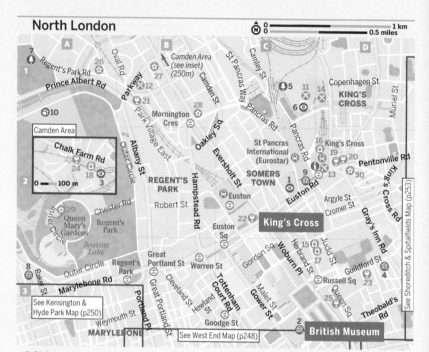

◉ Sights

East London

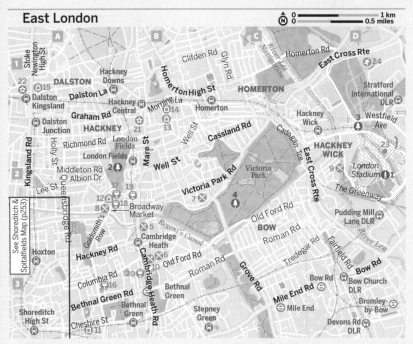

Greenwich

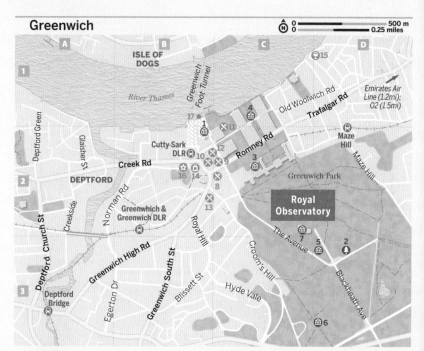